The Case
for Idealism

International Library of Philosophy

Editor: Ted Honderich
A catalogue of books already published in the
International Library of Philosophy
will be found at the end of this volume

The Case for Idealism

John Foster

Fellow of Brasenose College, Oxford

ROUTLEDGE & KEGAN PAUL

London, Boston, Melbourne and Henley

First published in 1982
by Routledge & Kegan Paul Ltd
39 Store Street,
London WC1E 7DD,
9 Park Street,
Boston, Mass. 02108, USA,
296 Beaconsfield Parade,
Middle Park, Melbourne, 3206,
Australia
and Broadway House,
Newtown Road,
Henley-on-Thames
Oxon RG9 1EN
Set in 10/12pt Times by
Saildean Ltd, Surrey
and printed in Great Britain by
T.J. Press (Padstow) Ltd
Padstow, Cornwall

Library of Congress Cataloging in Publication Data
Foster, John, 1941-
The case for idealism.
(International library of philosophy)
Includes bibliographical references and index.
1. Idealism. 2. Realism. I. Title. II. Series.
B823.F67   141   81-21154
ISBN 0-7100-9019-6   AACR2

For Helen

CONTENTS

Contents

PREFACE

The aim of this book is to refute realism about the physical world and to develop, in its place, a version of phenomenalism. The views I defend are, I have to admit, in radical conflict both with our untutored intuitions and with current philosophical fashion. If this makes me uneasy about how the book will be received, I take some comfort from the thought that, whatever its failings, it is unlikely to be considered either platitudinous or unduly derivative.

However idiosyncratic my views, I have greatly benefited from conversations with a number of friends and colleagues. Howard Robinson and Michael Lockwood, in particular, have been very helpful.

J. A. F.
Brasenose College, Oxford

PART I

AN OUTLINE OF THE ISSUES

1

THE OPTIONS

Even among philosophers the term 'idealism' is used in a variety of different senses to denote a variety of different positions. In what follows, I shall be concerned with three kinds of idealism, which can be expressed, summarily, by the following three claims:

(1) Ultimate contingent reality is wholly mental.
(2) Ultimate contingent reality is wholly non-physical.
(3) The physical world is the logical product of facts about human sense-experience.

My defence of idealism will be primarily a defence of claims (2) and (3), though I shall also try to show the plausibility of (1). I shall begin by explaining what the claims mean and how they are related.

Reality is all that exists or obtains, the totality of entities and facts. Thus, if John is heavier than Mary, reality includes the entities John and Mary and the fact that John is heavier than Mary.

I shall not pursue the question of whether facts themselves are entities. Certainly, I do not regard myself as incurring (as philosophers say) an ontological commitment to facts merely by employing the fact-terminology. I do not think I am committed to recognizing facts as entities when I say 'There are several facts we must take into account' anymore than I think I am committed to recognizing *respects* as entities when I say 'There are several respects in which crocodiles and alligators differ'. And certainly it is not *as* entities that I am taking facts to be ingredients of reality when I say that reality is all that exists or obtains, the totality of entities and facts. For a fact to obtain, in this sense, is just for something to be the case, i.e. for it to be the case that ... , for some suitable filling of the blank. The obtaining of the fact that John is heavier than Mary just is its being the case that John is heavier than Mary. Thus I might have said: reality is all that exists or is the case. None of this, of course, precludes our construing facts as entities. But if we do construe them as entities, we must still distinguish the two ways in which facts are ingredients of reality – as elements of what exists and as elements of what obtains. We must still recognize that someone else who rejects this construal is not denying, in the relevant sense, that facts obtain. For, in this sense, he is accepting that facts obtain merely by accepting that John is heavier than Mary or that the earth moves or that $2 + 2 = 4$.

An entity (or fact) is contingent iff its existence (obtaining) is not necessary, in some sense of necessity stronger than merely *natural* necessity. (Here and throughout I use 'iff' as an abbreviation for 'if and only if'.) The number 2, as normally conceived, is non-contingent, since its existence is necessary in the relevantly strong sense:[1] there could not have been a world, however different from the actual world in composition and natural laws, in which 2 failed to exist (though, of course, there could have been a world in which the symbol '2', having a different meaning, failed to denote anything). Likewise, the fact that $2 + 2 = 4$ is non-contingent, since its obtaining is necessary in the relevantly strong sense: there could not have been a world, of whatever composition and natural laws, in which $2 + 2$ failed to be 4 (though, of course, there could have been a world in which the sequence of symbols '$2 + 2 = 4$', having a different meaning, failed to express a truth). In contrast, this chair (if it exists) and the fact there is a chair in this room (if this is a fact) are both contingent: the existence of the one and the obtaining of the other are not necessary in the relevant sense or, indeed, in any sense. Moreover, the fact that unsupported bodies fall is also contingent, since even though its obtaining is or may be the result of *natural* necessity (viz. the law of gravity), it is not necessary in any stronger sense. At least, it is not necessary in a stronger sense unless we define the term 'body' in such a way that it only applies to objects that behave in that way. And even if we do define the term in this way, there could have been a world, with different natural laws, in which objects with the same intrinsic

4

properties as bodies behaved quite differently.

Where a necessity is stronger than natural necessity, I shall, to mark the distinction, call it a *logical* necessity. This is obviously a rather broad use of the term 'logical', since there are many cases where something which is, in that sense, logically necessary cannot be established from (what we ordinarily take to be) the laws of logic alone. Indeed, there are cases where something which is, in that sense, logically necessary cannot be established *a priori* (e.g. it is logically necessary that Hesperus and Phosphorus are numerically identical, though, given the difference in the concepts *Hesperus* and *Phosphorus*, this is not something we can know *a priori*[2]). But this broad use of the term 'logical' seems to me appropriate, because any stronger-than-natural necessity is a necessity of the strongest kind – the kind for which the necessity of logical truth, in the narrow sense, provides the clearest measure.

If reality is the totality of entities and facts, *contingent reality* is, correspondingly, the totality of contingent entities and contingent facts – all that contingently exists or contingently obtains. I might equally have said: contingent reality is the totality of contingent entities and states of affairs. For I shall draw no distinction between contingent facts and states of affairs. I shall draw no distinction between the fact that John is heavier than Mary (i.e. its being the case that John is heavier than Mary) and the state of affairs of John's being heavier than Mary, nor between the fact that there is a chair in this room (i.e. it being the case that there is a chair in this room) and the state of affairs of there being a chair in this room. Maybe, strictly speaking, there is a subtle difference between contingent facts and states of affairs. But if there is, it is not relevant to my purposes.

I will say that a fact or set of facts F is *logically sustained by* a fact or set of facts F' iff F obtains wholly in virtue of F' in the following sense:

(a) F is a logical consequence of F', i.e. it is logically necessary that if F' obtains, then F obtains.
(b) F is mediated by F', i.e. the obtaining of F is achieved through and by means of the obtaining of F'.
(c) F is exhausted by F', i.e. the obtaining of F is wholly constituted by and is nothing over and above the obtaining of F'.

To take a simple and philosophically trivial example, suppose that John weighs 14 stone and Mary weighs 10 stone. Now consider the fact (F_1) that John is more than 2 stone heavier than Mary. In the sense defined by (a), (b) and (c), F_1 obtains wholly in virtue of the fact (F_2) that John is exactly 4 stone heavier than Mary. So F_1 is logically sustained by F_2. And, quite generally, wherever two individuals instantiate some generic relation R, there is a determinate relation R' of R such that their instantiation of R is logically sustained by their instantiation of R'. F_2, in turn, obtains wholly in virtue of, and is thus logically sustained by, the combination of the facts (F_3) that John weighs 14 stone and (F_4) that Mary weighs 10 stone. And, quite generally, wherever two individuals instantiate some determinate weight-relation R, their instantiation of R is logically sustained by the combination of their specific weights. Finally (at least for present purposes), F_3 and F_4 are logically sustained by certain facts (partly general, partly specific to John, Mary and the earth) about mass, distance and gravity.

Since a fact does not mediate itself, the relation of logical sustainment is irreflexive. It is also, for obvious reasons, transitive (if F sustains F' and F' sustains F'', then F sustains F'') and asymmetric (if F sustains F', then F' does not sustain F). It is also asymmetric in a special and stronger sense. Thus let us say that a fact F *contributes* to the sustainment of a fact F' iff there is a set of facts F'' such that F' is sustained by F and F'' together, but is not sustained by either F or F'' on its own. Then the special asymmetry consists in this: that for any facts F and F', if F sustains or contributes to the sustainment of F', F' does not sustain or contribute to the sustainment of F.

I shall say that an entity x is *the logical creation of* (or is *logically created by*) the fact or set of facts F iff the existence of x (i.e. the fact that x exists) is logically sustained by F. For example, and quite trivially, the set {John, Mary} (likewise, the aggregate John + Mary) is the logical creation of, in combination, the existence of John and the existence of Mary. Thus logical creation is a special case of logical sustainment, namely the sustainment of an entity's existence. I shall use the expression ' ... is the logical product of ...' to cover, generically, both cases of sustainment and cases of creation. Thus if F is a fact or set of facts, a fact F' is the logical product of F iff F' is logically sustained by F, and an entity x is the logical product of F iff x is the logical creation of F. Likewise I shall speak of a collection of entities and facts as the logical product of *F* when each element in the collection is the logical product of *F*.

Where a fact is not logically sustained by any fact or set of facts I shall call it *logically basic* (or just *basic*) and where an entity is not the logical creation of any fact or set of facts I shall call it *ontologically primitive* (or just *primitive*). I shall also use the term 'ultimate' to apply generically both to logically basic facts and to ontologically primitive entities. *Ultimate contingent reality* is then the totality of ultimate (i.e. primitive, uncreated) contingent entities and ultimate (i.e. basic, unsustained) contingent facts. It is all that ultimately contingently exists or obtains. For short, I shall refer to it in future as simply *ultimate reality*.

It is true, by definition, that every fact is either basic or sustained. But, in what follows, I shall make the additional assumption that every fact is either basic or sustained by some set of basic facts. In particular, I shall assume that the totality of basic contingent facts, which forms the factual component of ultimate reality, is, in a certain sense, exhaustive: that it encompasses, explicitly or implicitly, all that contingently obtains – that every contingent fact (every state of affairs) is either an element of this totality or sustained by it. This assumption is not one which I require as a basis for my arguments: I could manage perfectly well without it. But without it, the first two idealist claims would have to be re-expressed. For I want these claims to set a restriction on contingent reality as a whole. I want claim (1), that ultimate reality is wholly mental, to imply that every contingent fact is either a mental fact or logically sustained by mental facts, and I want claim (2), that ultimate reality is wholly non-physical, to imply that every contingent fact is either a non-physical fact or logically sustained by non-physical facts. Without the assumption that the totality of basic contingent facts is, in the relevant sense, exhaustive, the claims would not have these implications. (1) would be compatible with the assertion that there are non-mental facts which are not logically sustained by mental facts, and (2) would be compatible with the assertion that there are physical facts which are not logically sustained by non-physical facts. Thus construed, the two claims would be too permissive to carry the philosophical significance which I accord them in my subsequent discussion. To carry this significance, I would have to strengthen them by adding, as extra clauses, the propositions I want them to imply.

7

It is for convenience of exposition that I am adopting the assumption of exhaustiveness: as I have said, I do not require it as a basis for my arguments. But, given the transitivity and asymmetry of sustainment, I also think that the assumption is true. It would only be false if there were some non-basic fact whose sustainment was infinitely regressive, such that every set of facts which sustained it, however directly or remotely, contained at least one fact which was itself sustained. And I can think of no case in which I would acknowledge a regress of this kind. The only case which suggests itself is a regress of physical constitution, whereby each space-occupant is composed of smaller occupants by whose arrangement and organization its existence is sustained. But even if there were such a regress of constitution (and it is far from clear that there is), it would not follow that there were no basic facts by which the existence of each occupant was sustained. For we could still insist that, in the final analysis, all occupants, however large or small, are logically created by facts about the physical properties of points at times. Indeed, such a position is one which I shall defend in chapter 5.

Let us now consider, in more detail, the content of claims (1) and (2). (1) is the claim that ultimate reality is wholly mental. More precisely, it is the claim that:

(a) Apart from purely temporal contingent entities (if there are any), e.g. moments and periods (if these are contingent), the only ultimate (ontologically primitive) contingent entities are mental, i.e. are entities such as minds (or conscious subjects) and mental events.

(b) Apart from purely temporal contingent facts (if there are any), e.g. the fact that time is infinitely extended (if this is a fact and if it is contingent), the only ultimate (logically basic) contingent facts are mind-concerning, i.e. are facts about the existence and intrinsic character of minds, their location and structuring in time, the events and processes that occur in them, and the natural laws to which such events and processes are subject.

In short, (1) is the claim that ultimate reality entirely consists, both ontologically and factually, in a world of time, minds and mind-governing laws. I shall call this claim the *mentalist thesis*, or, for short, *mentalism*. (2) is the claim that ultimate reality is wholly

8

non-physical. More precisely, it is the claim that:

(a) Apart from purely temporal contingent entities (if there are any and if they qualify as physical), no contingent physical entity is ontologically primitive.

(b) Apart from purely temporal contingent facts (if there are any and if they qualify as physical), no contingent physical fact is logically basic.

Thus (2) excludes from the realm of ultimate reality: physical space, bodies, physical colour, elementary particles, electromagnetic fields, physical laws and everything else (apart from time), whether ontological or factual, which either common sense or scientific theory recognizes as an element of the physical world. I shall call this the *physical anti-realist thesis* or, for short, *physical anti-realism*, though often, where the reference to the physical is clear from the context, I shall speak simply of the *anti-realist thesis* and *anti-realism*. Both mentalism and physical anti-realism are theses which confine ultimate reality to entities and facts of a certain sort: mentalism confines it to entities and facts which are (including the temporal) mental, and anti-realism confines it to entities and facts which are not (excluding the temporal) physical. And in both cases, given the assumption of exhaustiveness, the confinements indirectly cover contingent reality as a whole. Mentalism requires that every contingent fact is either mental or logically sustained by mental facts (and therefore, as a special case, that every contingent entity is either mental or the logical creation of mental facts) and anti-realism requires that every contingent fact is either non-physical or logically sustained by non-physical facts (and, therefore, as a special case, that every contingent entity is either non-physical or the logical creation of non-physical facts).

Now it is obvious that these two theses, mentalism and physical anti-realism, are compatible. Indeed, it would be very natural for someone who accepted one to find therein a reason for accepting the other. It would be very natural for a mentalist to conclude, on the basis of his mentalism, that ultimate reality is wholly non-physical and very natural for an anti-realist to conclude, on the basis of his anti-realism, that ultimate reality is wholly mental. None the less, the two positions are, as such, logically independent. Mentalism does not, as such, commit one to anti-realism; nor does anti-realism, as such, commit one to mentalism. Mentalism does not commit one to anti-realism, because mentalism, while claiming that ultimate reality is wholly mental, is compatible with the further claim that some portion of that reality is also physical. A mentalist might reject anti-realism on the grounds that the categories *mental* and *physical* are not mutually exclusive. Conversely, anti-realism does not commit one to mentalism, because anti-realism, while claiming that ultimate reality is wholly non-physical, is compatible with the further claim that some portion of that reality is also non-mental. An anti-realist might reject mentalism on the grounds that, even in the domain of the contingent, the categories *mental* and *physical* are not jointly exhaustive. The logical independence of the two positions can be nicely represented by means of Venn diagrams (Figures 1.1 and 1.2). In both figures,

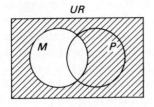

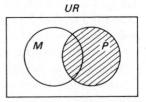

Fig. 1.1   *Fig. 1.2*

the rectangle *UR* represents ultimate reality (the totality of primitive contingent entities and basic contingent facts), while the two intersecting circles, *M* and *P*, represent, respectively, its mental and physical portions. The shading of a region indicates that it is empty (devoid of entities and facts), though the non-shading of a region does not indicate that it is not empty. Thus Figure 1.1, in which only *M* is unshaded, represents the mentalist thesis that ultimate reality is wholly mental, and Figure 1.2, in which *P* is shaded, represents the anti-realist thesis that ultimate reality is wholly non-physical. It can be seen that mentalism is compatible with the denial of anti-realism, since the region common to both circles, which represents that portion of ultimate reality which is both mental and physical, is shaded in Figure 1.2, but unshaded in Figure 1.1. Likewise, it can be seen that anti-realism is compatible with the denial of mentalism, since the region lying outside both circles, which represents that portion of ultimate reality which is neither mental nor physical, is shaded in Figure 1.1, but unshaded

in Figure 1.2. Of course, in claiming that mentalism is compatible
with the denial of anti-realism, I do not preclude there being
philosophical arguments to show that the mental and physical
categories are mutually exclusive, so that, in the final analysis,
mentalism does require anti-realism. Nor, in claiming that anti-
realism is compatible with the denial of mentalism, do I preclude
there being philosophical arguments to show that the mental and
physical categories are jointly exhaustive, so that, in the final
analysis, anti-realism does require mentalism. All I am claiming, at
this stage, is that mentalism without anti-realism and anti-realism
without mentalism are options which we cannot exclude *prior to*
philosophical investigation. These options are initially available,
given the way that mentalism and anti-realism have been defined.
Whether we shall want or be able to make anything of them is
another question.

Whatever their differences, mentalism and anti-realism are
united in their rejection of the common sense view of the status and
character of the physical world. The common sense view is that
ultimate reality includes a portion which is both physical and
non-mental. It accepts the ontological primitiveness of certain
physical entities and the logical basicness of certain physical facts,
and denies that these entities and facts are circumscribed by the
mentalistic framework of time, minds and mind-governing laws. I
shall call this view *standard physical realism* or simply *standard
realism*. It is represented, Venn-diagrammatically, in Figure 1.3.

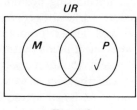

Fig. 1.3

The occurrence of a tick within a region indicates that the region is
not empty. So to represent standard realism (the thesis that some
portion of ultimate reality is both physical and non-mental), we put
a tick in that portion of *P* which lies outside *M*. Obviously, the

11

diagram leaves room for further elaboration, according to what position the standard realist adopts with respect to the status and nature of mind. A dualist, who holds that the mental and physical realms are quite separate, will shade off the common region where *M* and *P* intersect (or, at most, admit to this region only those basic facts, such as the obtaining of certain psychophysical laws, which concern the causal interaction between the two realms). Conversely, a physicalist, who holds that ultimate reality is wholly physical, will shade off that portion of *M* (indeed, that portion of *UR*) which lies outside *P*, thus absorbing the mental realm into the physical. Moreover, if the physicalist is also a mental anti-realist, holding that ultimate reality is wholly non-mental, he will shade off the whole of *M*.

As I have said, mentalism and physical anti-realism are alike in rejecting standard realism. Mentalism claims that ultimate reality is wholly mental and anti-realism claims that it is wholly non-physical. So both are agreed that no portion of ultimate reality is both physical and non-mental. (Again this can be seen from the Venn diagrams, where that portion of *P* which lies outside *M* is ticked in Figure 1.3 but shaded in both Figure 1.1 and Figure 1.2.) But it is worth considering in more detail what options, concerning the status and character of the physical world, are available to someone who rejects standard realism, and how these options are related, on the one hand, to mentalism and, on the other, to anti-realism.

The rejection of standard realism is compatible with three importantly different positions with respect to the physical world. The first and most uncompromising position is that which denies the existence of a physical world altogether – denies the existence of any physical entities and denies the obtaining of any physical state of affairs. At its weakest, it holds that all our physical beliefs, however strongly they seem to be supported by our empirical evidence and however well they serve to systematize our experiences, are uniformly false. At its strongest, it holds that our very concept of the physical embodies some incoherence or contradiction. This outright rejection of the physical realm we may call, appropriately, the *nihilist position* or simply *nihilism*. Now, obviously, nihilism entails anti-realism: if there is no physical world, then ultimate reality, however composed, must be wholly non-physical. But anti-realism does not entail nihilism. For the anti-realist, unlike the nihilist, has the option of saying that there is a physical world, but one which is, in all respects, the logical product of something else. He has the option of saying that there are physical facts, but ones which are logically sustained, and that there are physical entities, but ones which are logically created. It is this option which constitutes the second position, and I shall call it the *reductive position* or simply *reductivism.* Thus the reductivist accepts the existence of a physical world, but as something which is wholly constituted by, and nothing over and above, a non-physical reality which underlies it. The third position accepts the existence of a physical world and, unlike reductivism, accepts that at least some portion of it is ultimate – accepts that at least some physical facts are logically basic and that at least some physical entities are ontologically primitive. Where it differs from standard realism is in holding that this ultimate physical world is, in substance and character, purely mental – that the primitive physical entities are mental entities and the basic physical facts are mental facts. It assigns the same logical and ontological status to the physical world as the standard realist assigns, but gives a non-standard interpretation of its intrinsic nature. This third position, with its distinctive combination of realist and mentalist claims, we may call, appropriately, *mentalistic physical realism* or simply *mentalistic realism.* It should be noted that, despite its title, mentalistic realism, while certainly a version of physical realism, does not entail full-blooded mentalism. For while it asserts that the physical portion of ultimate reality is wholly mental, it leaves open the possibility that some other portion is non-mental. Thus in the appropriate Venn diagram (Figure 1.4), it shades off that portion of *P* which lies outside *M,* but need not shade off the region which lies outside both circles. Mentalistic realism becomes a version of mentalism only on the

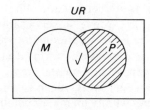

Fig. 1.4

13

additional assumption that, in the domain of the ultimate, the mental and physical categories are jointly exhaustive.

Together with standard realism, which they all reject, these three positions concerning the status and character of the physical world exhaust the range of possibilities (though, of course, there is room for further subdivisions). In the first place, we have an exhaustive opposition between the two generic positions of physical realism and physical anti-realism, where realism asserts that ultimate reality contains a physical portion and anti-realism denies it. Realism, in turn, divides into the exclusive and exhaustive alternatives of standard realism, which takes ultimate physical reality to be (at least in part) non-mental, and mentalistic realism, which takes it to be wholly mental. Likewise, anti-realism divides into the exclusive and exhaustive alternatives of nihilism, which denies the existence of a physical world altogether, and reductivism, which accepts the physical world, but as something logically produced by, and nothing over and above, the ultimate non-physical reality. Thus the taxonomy of positions is as depicted in Figure 1.5.

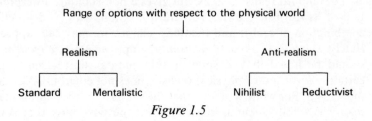

Figure 1.5

Of these options, standard realism, which embodies the common sense view, seems, intuitively, the most plausible. In the first place, the existence of a physical world seems to be amply supported by the testimony of our senses. If there is no physical world, why should the course of sense-experience be so consistently and intricately organized as if there were? Why should our physical beliefs, if uniformly false, prove so serviceable in explaining past experiences and so reliable in predicting new ones? Secondly, assuming that there is a physical world, it is hard to see how it could be entirely composed of mental items or how it could be nothing over and above a reality which is wholly non-physical. If ultimate reality is either wholly mental or wholly non-physical, how could there be room for a genuinely physical world? None the less, despite its initial plausibility, the thrust of my arguments, throughout this work, will be against standard realism in both its aspects. Thus I shall argue that, in the framework of physical realism, the mentalistic version is not only coherent, but, in so far as one can pass judgment here, more acceptable than the standard version it rejects. And, more fundamentally, I shall argue that physical realism itself is incoherent. These two arguments (developed, respectively, in Parts II and III) are not independent. The considerations which, in the framework of realism, establish the coherence and superiority of the mentalistic version, also play a crucial role in establishing the incoherence of realism in any form.

In addition to mentalism and physical anti-realism (claims (1) and (2)), I mentioned, at the beginning, a third idealist thesis (claim (3)), which asserts that the physical world is the logical product of facts about human sense-experience. This thesis is a species of reductivism and, *a fortiori*, of anti-realism. I shall call it *reductive phenomenalism.* By 'facts about human sense-experience' (or, for short, 'sensory facts') I mean not only (a) facts about the actual course of human experience (facts which are recorded by specifying the types of experience which occur in particular minds at particular times), but also (b) facts about the framework of natural necessity in which human experience is controlled (facts about how the course of experience is nomologically constrained, facts about what the laws of experience permit or prohibit). I shall say more about this phenomenalist thesis (in connection with Berkeley) in the next chapter, though the main discussion of it will come in Part IV, where, having already refuted realism, I shall develop and defend a specific version of it. (This development also continues into the final section of the book (Part V), where I consider the nature of time. For although this discussion of time will be largely self-contained, its results have an important bearing on the phenomenalistic enterprise.)

However, there is one point which needs to be stressed at the outset – a point which concerns reductivism in general and the phenomenalist version in particular. I have used the term 'reductivism' to denote the thesis that the physical world is the logical product of an ultimate reality which is wholly non-physical. What needs to be stressed is that reductivism, in this sense, is not, and does not entail, any thesis about the analysis of physical statements. It does not entail that physical statements can be analysed in such a way that all explicit references to physical entities and all explicitly physical concepts disappear. It leaves open the possibility that the physical realm, while ontologically and factually derivative, is conceptually autonomous, so that physical statements cannot, without loss of meaning, be reformulated in non-physical terms. It leaves open the possibility that physical facts, though logically sustained by non-physical facts, cannot be adequately expressed except by means of an explicitly physical vocabulary and an explicitly physical ontology. This point, of course, carries over to the specific case of reductive phenomenalism. The term 'phenomenalism' is normally used to denote an analytical thesis – the thesis that physical statements can be analysed into sensory statements. But reductive phenomenalism, as I have defined it, does not commit one to such a thesis. Reductive phenomenalism commits one to taking physical facts as logically sustained by (as obtaining wholly in virtue of) sensory facts, but not to giving physical statements a sensory analysis. Of course, anyone who holds that physical facts are logically sustained by sensory facts must give some account of the meaning of physical statements which is compatible with this view. He must construe physical statements in such a way that sensory facts can suffice for their truth; and if, as is likely, he holds the view *a priori*, he must construe physical statements in such a way that nothing but sensory facts could suffice for their truth. But none of this commits him to saying that there is even one physical statement which can be re-expressed in sensory terms. It does not even commit him to saying that, for some physical statement, there is a sensory statement which expresses its truth-conditions. For he might want to say that, for each physical statement *S*, there is an infinite set α of possible sensory situations such that (a) each α-situation would, if it obtained, suffice for the truth of *S*, (b) the truth of *S* logically requires that some α-situation obtain and (c) there is no sensory statement, however complex, which expresses the infinite disjunction of all α-situations.

Curiously, reductive phenomenalism does not even entail that the truth of a physical statement could be established merely from an understanding of that statement and a knowledge (if it were available) of the sensory facts by which its truth is sustained. But the reasons for this will only emerge much later (chapter 14), after we have drawn the distinction between *prospective* and *retrospective* sustainment.

2

BERKELEY'S SYSTEM

I have distinguished three forms of idealism, which I have labelled *mentalism, (physical) anti-realism* and *reductive phenomenalism.* Both mentalism and anti-realism are theses about the composition of ultimate reality. The first asserts that ultimate reality is wholly mental – that all that ultimately exists or obtains (all that is ontologically primitive or logically basic) is confined to a framework of time, minds and mind-governing laws. The second asserts that ultimate reality is wholly non-physical – that there are no ontologically primitive physical entities and no logically basic physical facts. As we saw, while these two theses are compatible, neither of them, at least in any straightforward way, entails the other. An anti-realist could reject mentalism by maintaining that the mental and physical categories are not jointly exhaustive. And, more importantly for our purposes, a mentalist could reject anti-realism by maintaining that the two categories are not mutually exclusive. Both theses, however, are united in the rejection of the common sense view – the view we have called *standard realism* – that some portion of ultimate reality is both physical and non-mental. As we also saw, the rejection of standard realism is compatible with three different positions with respect to the physical world. Two of them, namely *nihilism* and *reductivism,* are forms of anti-realism, nihilism denying the existence of a physical world altogether, and reductivism accepting its existence, but as the logical product of (hence nothing over and above) an ultimate reality which is wholly non-physical. The third position, *mentalistic realism,* takes the physical world to be both ultimate but

17

wholly mental. Like standard realism, it accepts the primitiveness of certain physical entities and the basicness of certain physical facts, but offers a non-standard account of their nature. The third idealist thesis, reductive phenomenalism, is a special case of reductivism – the case in which the physical world is taken to be the logical product of facts about human sense-experience.

To deepen our understanding of these positions and the crucial distinctions they involve, I want, in this chapter, to illustrate them by reference to the philosophy of that most celebrated of idealists, George Berkeley. My aim at this stage, in discussing Berkeley, is purely expository: such themes in his work as I want to defend will be developed and defended in subsequent parts. It will suffice, for the time being, if we can use Berkeley as a means of setting the issues which confront us in a clearer perspective.

In trying to provide an exposition of Berkeley, the main problems concern his theory of the physical world. But let me begin by summarizing his account of ultimate reality with a view to seeing, if we can, how his views on the physical world fit into this. This account can be conveniently divided into four parts:

(1) Berkeley recognized only two kinds of ultimate, ontologically primitive entity, namely:

(i) *Conscious subjects* (he calls these *minds* or *spirits*) which, like Descartes, he conceived to be immaterial, unextended substances, and to which he ascribed such states and activities as perceiving, thinking and willing.

(ii) *Ideas*, which are the immediate objects of perception and which have no existence outside the mind.

He restricts ultimate entities to these two kinds because, as he sees it, it is impossible to form a coherent conception of anything else. Any attempt to form such a conception leads, he thinks, either to some definite incoherence (such as the notion of an inert substance with causal power or the notion of an unthinking substance as the subject of mind-dependent qualities) or to something which, so far from being a genuine conception, is no more than an idle gesture towards a know-not-what.

Berkeley speaks of ideas as things whose existence consists in their being perceived – whose *esse* is *percipi* (*Principles* II and III). This might suggest that he thought of ideas, not as ultimate entities, but as logical creations. It might suggest that he thought of an idea either (a) as something whose existence is logically sustained by its being an object of perception, or (b) as something whose existence is logically sustained by the intrinsic character of a certain perceptual experience. But neither of these interpretations of Berkeley would be correct. The (a)-conception is manifestly incoherent, since there cannot be anything whose existence (= being) is mediated by some fact about that thing; nor is there any reason to suppose that Berkeley thought that there was. As for (b), it is clear that in Berkeley's system, it is precisely in the occurrence of an idea that the intrinsic character of a perceptual experience consists: there is no more fundamental way of specifying the character of the experience than in terms of the idea perceived. Thus in asserting that the existence of an idea consists in its being perceived, Berkeley is not denying the ultimacy of ideas. He is only asserting that ideas cannot exist except as objects of perception – that their perception is built into their existence. Likewise, when he asserts (*Principles* CXXXIX) that a spirit is an active being whose existence consists in perceiving ideas and thinking, he is not denying the ultimacy of spirits. He is merely asserting that spirits cannot exist except as subjects of perception and thought – that perceiving and thinking are a spirit's essential attributes.

(2) Within the class of minds or spirits, Berkeley recognized, in particular, (a) an eternal and uncreated spirit, *God,* who is omnipotent and omniscient, and (b) a group of finite and created spirits, *ourselves.* The existence of God and his relation to us is, arguably, the central theme of Berkeley's theory. And certainly it was as a defence of Christian theism that he offered the theory to his readers. His explicit purpose in publishing his *Principles of Human Knowledge* and his *Three Dialogues between Hylas and Philonous* was to expose the errors and confusions latent in atheism and religious scepticism.

(3) Berkeley divided our ideas into two kinds, distinguished by their causal genesis: *ideas of sense (sensations),* which are imprinted on a spirit by some external cause, and *ideas of the imagination (images),* which the percipient frames by his

19

own volition. Berkeley held that all causation is volitional: only spirits have a genuine power of agency, and it is only through acts of will that they can exercise this power. Berkeley concluded that, while images are caused by the volitions of their percipients, our sensations are caused, and directly caused, by the volitions of God.

(4) In this connection, Berkeley noted and stressed that God does not exercise his volition in a random way, but in accordance with certain fixed policies which impose rules on the course of human experience. Berkeley calls these rules the *laws of nature*. These laws of nature ensure a certain coherence, a certain thematic character, in the overall pattern of our sensations – a coherence which characterizes the course of experience, not only in each individual mind, but in the totality of our minds taken collectively. And it is this coherence, this consistent theme in human sense-experience, which explains our physical beliefs. For example, we come to believe that there is an external 3-dimensional arrangement of colours, because such a belief expresses, in its simplest form, the thematic character of visual experience. For our visual sensations are divinely ordered exactly as if they were presentations of such an arrangement, in perspective, to observers (ourselves) who are located in and move continuously through it.

These, then, are the main components of Berkeley's view of ultimate reality. There is one further component, which becomes prominent in the *Three Dialogues* and which I shall mention later.

It is clear from this account that Berkeley is, whatever else, a mentalist. He holds that ultimate reality consists solely of mental entities and mental facts – that, ultimately, there is nothing but time, minds, mental events, ideas and volitional causation. But we have still to discover his theory of the physical world. Obviously, as a mentalist, Berkeley rejects standard realism, since standard realism accepts a physical world which is both ultimate and non-mental. So the options to be considered are nihilism, reductivism and mentalistic realism.

Given his theory of ultimate reality, we might expect Berkeley to be a nihilist. For how can there be a physical world if the only ultimate entities are minds and whatever occurs or exists within them? How can there be room for a 3-dimensional physical space or for the solid and voluminous objects we locate in it, if ultimately, apart from the heavenly world of God and (perhaps) angelic spirits, there is nothing external to our consciousness? True, given the coherence of God's volitional policies, the course of human experience is thematic, and our physical beliefs serve a useful function in recording the theme. But the utility of the beliefs is not enough to make them true. And on Berkeley's account it seems they must be false. On Berkeley's account, it seems that, while our experiences are organized exactly as if there were a physical world, there is not really one.

However, while there are other points where his position is open to different interpretations, it is certain that Berkeley was not a nihilist. Nihilism was a position which he repeatedly and emphatically disowned. It is true that there are certain quasi-nihilistic elements in his thought. Thus he rejects as incoherent the opinion of 'the vulgar' (the ordinary man) that the sensible objects (the collections of sensible qualities) we immediately perceive by sense have an absolute existence outside the mind. Here he sides with 'the philosophers' (paradigmatically, Locke) in holding that the immediate objects of perception are our own ideas – entities whose *esse* is *percipi*. At the same time, he also rejects as incoherent the opinion of the philosophers (again, paradigmatically, Locke) that, beyond the veil of our ideas, there are parcels of unthinking and insensible material substance which (subject to the distinction between primary and secondary qualities) our sense-perceptions represent. Here he sides with the vulgar in holding that the physical world is wholly composed of the sensible items which are immediately perceptible. But in rejecting these opinions, he does not take himself to be rejecting the existence of a physical world, but only to be rejecting certain prevalent but incoherent views about it. He thinks that once the incoherence of these views is exposed, we will see that our ordinary physical beliefs do not require them – see that these beliefs can be retained, without distortion, in his philosophical system. The resulting conception is one which absorbs the physical into the sensible and the sensible into the mental. As he summarizes it himself, at the end of the *Dialogues*:[1]

My endeavours tend only to unite and place in a clearer light
that truth which was before shared between the vulgar and the
philosophers: the former being of the opinion that *those things
they immediately perceive are the real things:* and the latter, that
*the things immediately perceived are ideas which exist only in the
mind.* Which two notions, put together, do in effect constitute the
substance of what I advance.

While this is certainly the substance of what Berkeley advances,
the details are more obscure. Most of the time, he seems content
simply to equate physical entities with ideas or collections of ideas,
thus securing their mind-dependent existence in the most straightforward way. Thus, in a typical passage, he writes:

Some truths there are so near and obvious to the mind, that a
man need only open his eyes to see them. Such I take this
important one to be, to wit, that all the choir of heaven and
furniture of the earth, in a word all those bodies which compose
the mighty frame of the world, have not any subsistence without
a mind, that their being is to be perceived or known.
(*Principles* VI).

This principle of *esse est percipi,* applied to physical entities, I shall
call the *hard-line doctrine.* As I have said, the hard-line doctrine is
what Berkeley seems to accept most of the time. But there are
certain passages which suggest that perhaps his real position was
more flexible. Thus almost at the beginning of the *Principles,* just
before the hard-line doctrine is introduced, he says:

The table I write on, I say, exists, that is, I see and feel it; and if I
were out of my study I should say it existed, meaning thereby
that *if I was in my study I might perceive it,* or that some other
spirit actually does perceive it. (*Principles III,* my italics).

Here he seems to allow that, even when unperceived, a table may
continue to exist in virtue of its potential to be perceived – in virtue
of the fact that if someone *were* in the right place at the right time,
he *would* perceive it. And if he allows this, he cannot consistently
claim that a table is merely an idea, or collection of ideas, whose
esse is *percipi.* Now, taken in isolation, this passage could, perhaps,
be discounted as a momentary aberration. But the same thought
re-emerges in a subsequent and much more elaborate passage.

Thus, addressing himself to the objection that his principles commit him to denying that the earth moves, since its motion is not perceived, he answers:

> That tenet (that the earth moves), if rightly understood, will be found to agree with the principles we have premised: for the question, whether the earth moves or no, amounts in reality to no more than this, to wit, whether we have reason to conclude from what hath been observed by astronomers, that if we were placed in such and such circumstances, and such or such a position and distance, both from the earth and sun, we should perceive the former to move among the choir of the planets, and appearing in all respects like one of them: and this, by the established rules of Nature, which we have no reason to mistrust, is reasonably collected from the phenomena. (*Principles* LVIII).

In the next section, he goes on to elaborate this:

> We may, from the experience we have had of the train and succession of ideas in our minds, often make, I will not say uncertain conjectures, but sure and well-grounded predictions, concerning the ideas we shall be affected with, pursuant to a great train of actions, and be enabled to pass a right judgment of what would have appeared to us, in case we were placed in circumstances very different from those we are in at present. Herein consists the knowledge of Nature, which may preserve its use and certainty very consistently with what hath been said. It will be easy to apply this to whatever objections of the like sort may be drawn from the magnitude of the stars, or any other discoveries in astronomy or Nature.

Obviously, these remarks cannot be discounted as a momentary slip, not only because they are so elaborate, but also, and more importantly, because he explicitly offers them as an answer to someone who takes him to be asserting the hard-line doctrine. And the answer he gives is, in effect, that he is not asserting this doctrine in an unqualified form – that the physical world contains many elements which, while we do not perceive them, exist in virtue of facts about the hypothetical perceptions we would have if our circumstances were different, facts which we can often establish on the basis of the regularities in our past experience. It is not difficult to see why Berkeley should feel the need to modify the hard-line doctrine in this way. In the first place, he wants to do justice to our ordinary physical beliefs, many of which explicitly commit us to accepting the existence of objects and events that are unperceived. Secondly, and more fundamentally, even if the physical world is, in some broader sense, mind-dependent, it cannot be entirely composed of the contents of human experience. For thus composed, it would not have, in relation to us, the publicity and externality required for it to qualify as a physical world in any decent sense. If there is no way in which Berkeley can allow the physical world to extend beyond the scope of our actual perceptions, there is no way in which he can allow for the existence of a physical world at all.

If Berkeley *is* rejecting the hard-line doctrine in its unqualified form, thus allowing for the existence of physical entities that are unperceived, what positive conception of physical existence does he put in its place? How does he suppose the physical world to be constituted, given the purely mental character of his ultimate reality? Perhaps the clue is given in another passage where he tries to refute the charge that his position does, after all, amount to nihilism:

> It will be objected that by the foregoing principles, all that is real and substantial in Nature is banished out of the world: and instead thereof a chimerical scheme of ideas takes place. All things that exist, exist only in the mind, that is, they are purely notional. What therefore becomes of the sun, moon and stars? What must we think of houses, rivers, mountains, trees, stones; nay even of our own bodies? Are all these but so many chimeras and illusions on the fancy? To all which, and whatever else of the same sort may be objected, I answer, that by the principles premised, we are not deprived of any one thing in Nature.... There is a *rerum natura*, and the distinction between realities and chimeras retains its full force....Take here an abstract of what has been said. There are spiritual substances, minds, or human souls, which will or excite ideas in themselves at pleasure: but these are faint, weak, and unsteady in respect of others they perceive by sense, which being impressed upon them according to certain rules or laws of Nature, speak themselves the effects of a mind more powerful and wise than human spirits. These latter are said to have more *reality* in them than the former: by which

is meant that they are more affecting, orderly, and distinct, and that they are not fictions of the mind perceiving them. And in this sense, the sun I see by day is the real sun and that which I imagine by night is the idea of the former. In the sense here given of *reality*, it is evident that every vegetable, star, mineral, and in general each part of the mundane system, is as much a *real being* by our principles as by any other. (*Principles* XXXIV–VI).

Here, Berkeley is saying that, while all ideas exist only in the mind which perceives them, and are, in that respect, equally subjective, ideas of sense are, in another respect, more real, more objective, than ideas of the imagination, since, unlike the latter, they are impressed on our minds by the external volition of God, in accordance with rules over which we have no control and displaying a coherence which is not of our own making. These ideas, while depending for their existence on our minds, are, as it were, the tokens of an objective and independent sensory order constituted by the laws of nature – an order which is manifested by the thematic character of our experience, but which is realized externally in the volitional policies of God. Berkeley sees this as a way of avoiding the charge of nihilism. So perhaps he is claiming that the existence of the physical world, properly conceived, amounts to nothing over and above the obtaining of this sensory order. On such a view, we can retain our belief in the reality of the sun, without abandoning mentalism, because the sensations on which it is founded bear, as it were, the divine *imprimatur*: they are not just the wayward illusions of the human mind, but the controlled output of a divinely ordained system, and, once we have freed ourselves from certain anti-mentalist misconceptions – both those of the vulgar and those of the learned – we recognize that the existence of the sun boils down to that aspect of the divine system manifested by the solar theme in our experience. In effect, our momentary and private solar impressions become, in the framework of the laws of experience, presentational slices of an enduring and public continuant. And, quite generally, physical space and its enduring occupants are constituted by certain persisting possibilities of sensation stemming from the systematic character of God's volitional policies.

Thus interpreted, Berkeley's theory of the physical world would be a version of reductivism. He would be acknowledging the existence of a physical world, but reducing it to an ultimate reality which is wholly non-physical. He would be claiming that physical entities and physical facts are the logical product of the sensory order. He would be denying the ultimacy of the physical world, but claiming that human sense-experience and the nomological system which God imposes on it suffice for the truth of our ordinary physical beliefs. Not only would his theory be reductivist, but it would also be a version of reductive phenomenalism – a version of a distinctively theistic kind, in which the laws of experience are construed as God's fixed policies for causing sensations in us.

There is no denying that this reductivist position accords with much of what Berkeley says in the *Principles*. It fits nicely with the way he draws the distinction between realities and chimeras – between veridical perception and illusion. It does justice to the great stress he lays on the laws of nature and on the way we acquire knowledge of the physical world from the experiential regularities which these laws ensure. It explains how, contrary to the hard-line doctrine, he can accept the existence of unperceived physical objects and events on the basis of mere possibilities of sensation. Moreover, not only does the position accord with much of what Berkeley says, but it also seems to be what he needs. Unlike (apparently) the hard-line doctrine, it goes some way, perhaps the whole way, towards providing what we require of a genuinely physical world. It allows the physical world to extend beyond the scope of our actual perceptions; and, by grounding its existence on the divinely imposed laws of nature – laws which obtain independently of the particular experiences we (in accordance with our circumstances) receive – it accords the physical world something of the publicity and externality which our concept of the physical demands. It provides a Berkeleian mentalist with something which is, or approximates to, an effective defence against the charge of nihilism. On the other hand, we must not underestimate the difficulties involved in attributing this position to Berkeley, given the many passages where the hard-line doctrine is endorsed. The problem is not just that this doctrine and the reductive position conflict, but that the conflict is, on the face of it, so radical. The hard-line doctrine of *esse est percipi* equates physical objects with collections of ideas, and ideas are entities which have, in Berkeley's system, an ultimate existence. In contrast, the reductive position construes physical objects as logical creations, as entities whose existence is logically sustained by the character of and constraints on human experience. Thus the hard-line doctrine is a form of mentalistic realism: it takes ultimate reality to be purely mental, but identifies a portion of that reality with the physical world. But the reductive position, while still mentalist, is a form of anti-realism. It takes ultimate reality to be wholly non-physical and thus leaves the physical world as something whose existence this non-physical reality sustains.

Whether or not Berkeley was, at one time, a reductivist, or close to being one, it is a version of the hard-line doctrine, without qualification, which emerged as his final position. To see how he arrived at this position, we must begin by bringing out an aspect of the doctrine which I have so far suppressed. The hard-line doctrine, as we have said, equates physical objects with collections of ideas – collections of entities whose *esse* is *percipi*. But Berkeley never insists that *all* the ideas which form elements of the physical world exist in our minds or those of other finite created spirits. Indeed, the possibility that at least some of these elements exist in the mind of the infinite and eternal spirit, God, is one which he allows almost as soon as the hard-line doctrine is formulated. Thus the passage from *Principles* VI which we quoted earlier, to illustrate the doctrine, continues:

> Consequently, so long as they (the bodies which compose the mighty frame of the world) are not actually perceived by me, or do not exist in my mind or that of any other created spirit, they must either have no existence at all, or else subsist in the mind of some eternal spirit: it being perfectly unintelligible, and involving all the absurdity of abstraction, to attribute to any single part of them an existence independent of a spirit.

The same thought is picked up later in a famous passage dealing with the problem of physical persistence:

> It will be objected that from the foregoing principles it follows, things are every moment annihilated and created anew. The objects of sense exist only when they are perceived: the trees therefore are in the garden, or the chairs in the parlour, no longer than while there is some body by to perceive them. Upon shutting my eyes all the furniture in the room is reduced to

27

nothing, and barely upon opening them it is again created (*Principles* XLV).

Since this objection is scarcely distinguishable from the one about the motion of the earth, which comes a few pages later, one might expect Berkeley to answer them in the same way. But, in fact, the answers are quite different. In the later passage (LVIII), as we saw, he modifies the hard-line doctrine: he claims that the motion of the earth, which we do not perceive, amounts to no more than the fact that if we were transported to an appropriate viewpoint, we would perceive the earth to move. But in dealing with the question of persistence, raised in the earlier passage, he first reasserts the self-evidence of *esse est percipi*, and then adds, in section XLVIII,

> For though we hold indeed the objects of sense to be nothing else but ideas which cannot exist unperceived; yet we may not hence conclude they have no existence except only while they are perceived by us, since there may be some other spirit that perceives them, though we do not.

It is, presumably, the possibility of God's perceptions that Berkeley has in mind.

Now in the *Principles*, the role of God as a perceiver of physical objects is left as a mere possibility and one to which Berkeley seems to attach little importance. What is asserted and emphasized is the role of God as the author of Nature, the law-giver whose volitional policies control the course of human experience. But in his later work, the *Three Dialogues*, the perceptive role of God takes on a new significance. Thus in the *Second Dialogue*, as a way of rebutting the charge of scepticism (i.e. nihilism), Philonous, who is the mouthpiece for Berkeley himself, says:

> To me it is evident, for the reasons you allow of, that sensible things cannot exist otherwise than in a mind or spirit. Whence I conclude, not that they have no real existence, but that seeing they depend not on my thought, and have an existence distinct from being perceived by me, *there must be some other mind wherein they exist.* As sure therefore as the sensible world really exists, so sure is there an infinite omnipresent spirit who contains and supports it ... Men commonly believe that all things are known or perceived by God, because they believe the being of a God, whereas I on the other side, immediately and necessarily

conclude the being of a God, because all sensible things must be perceived by him. (Luce and Jessop, p. 212).

And in the *Third Dialogue*, when dealing again with the question of persistence, he says:

> Now it is plain that they (sensible things) have an existence exterior to my mind, since I find them by experience to be independent of it. There is therefore some other mind wherein they exist, during the intervals between the times of my perceiving them: as likewise they did before my birth and would do after my supposed annihilation. And as the same is true, with regard to all other finite created spirits; it necessarily follows, there is an *omnipresent eternal Mind*, which knows and comprehends all things, and exhibits them to our view in such a manner, and according to such rules as he himself has ordained, and are by us termed the *Laws of Nature*. (pp. 230-1).

Compared with the *Principles*, these passages enhance the perceptive role of God in three crucial respects. In the first place, Berkeley claims not merely that God *may* perceive physical objects at times when we do not, but that he actually does. Secondly, he claims that God perceives not only those parts of the physical world which we fail to perceive, but also those parts which we do perceive, the whole physical world (according to Berkeley, of course, a purely *sensible* world) being present to and existing in God's mind, independently of our private and fragmentary perceptions. Thirdly, the ideas in God's mind, which compose the physical world as it exists in him, are, in some sense, construed as the originals or archetypes of which our sensory ideas are the secondary impressions or copies. For, as Berkeley puts it, the omnipresent eternal mind, knowing and comprehending all things, '*exhibits them* to our view in such a manner and according to such rules as he himself hath ordained' (my italics). Berkeley exploits this third point later, in answering the objection that the hard-line doctrine does not permit different human subjects to perceive the same physical object. After an initial and unconvincing attempt to dismiss the dispute as merely verbal, Philonous says that the case is exactly the same for the materialist, who also concedes that what we immediately perceive are our own ideas. When Hylas retorts, 'But they suppose an external archetype, to which referring their several ideas, they may truly be said to perceive the same thing', Philonous replies:

> And ... so may you suppose an external archetype on my principles: *external,* I mean, to your own mind; though indeed it must be supposed to exist in that mind which comprehends all things; but then this serves all the ends of identity, as well as if it existed out of a mind. (p. 248).

Now all this puts the hard-line doctrine in an entirely new perspective. It had seemed, at first, that, without some qualification, the doctrine could not accommodate our ordinary physical beliefs nor provide the physical world with that publicity and externality, relative to us, which our concept of the physical requires. But now it seems that Berkeley can and does retain the doctrine without qualification and without these undesirable consequences. By locating the whole physical world in the mind of God, he makes it public and external in relation to us, and sufficiently extensive and complex to accommodate all our ordinary beliefs, so long as those beliefs are exclusively concerned with sensible objects and are not infected by any incoherent views (whether vulgar or philosophic) incompatible with the hard-line doctrine itself. We can think of the situation like this: God has an all-embracing perception of a vast spatiotemporal arrangement of sensible qualities – a perception, of course, of which he is the causal agent, rather than the passive recipient. This arrangement, which is no more than a complex idea in God's mind, forms a kind of blueprint for his volitional policies, the policies being selected with a view to exhibiting the arrangement to human subjects through the sense-experiences they receive: particular experiences exhibit particular fragments of the arrangement, and, from the order and coherence of experiences, taken collectively, we piece the fragments together, interpolating and extrapolating as appropriate, until we achieve some overall picture which approximates to the divine blueprint. As a result, the arrangement, though just an idea in God's mind – an entity whose *esse* is *percipi* – qualifies as *our* physical world. It is something which has, in relation to us, the publicity and externality which our concept of the physical requires. It is something which our sense-experiences represent and with which, reflecting the thematic character of our experiences, our physical beliefs correspond.

This is Berkeley's final solution – a version of mentalistic realism which accepts the hard-line doctrine of *esse est percipi*, but locates the whole physical world in the mind of God. The only problem from Berkeley's standpoint – and it is one which he does not seem to notice – is that, in adopting this position, he is implicitly rejecting that element in the opinion of the vulgar which he is claiming to vindicate, namely that 'those things they immediately perceive are the real things'. By locating the physical world in the mind of God, he locates it beyond the scope of our immediate perception. We can, at best, have a mediated perception of physical objects by perceiving ideas (in our own minds) which represent them. Those who argue for a causal analysis of mediated perception may object, more strongly, that Berkeley puts the physical world beyond the scope of perception altogether. Because it is God's volitions which cause our experiences and because these volitions, even if rationally based on God's perceptions, are not caused by them, physical objects, they may say, do not stand in the right causal relations to our experiences for those experiences to count as genuine, if mediated, perceptions of them. But I think this only serves to show the unacceptability of the causal analysis in its strict form. So long as the aim of the volitional policies is to secure a match between human experience and the physical world, there is a clear sense in which our perceptual ideas not only resemble their physical counterparts, but derive their features from them – a clear sense in which our experiences are as they are because the physical objects are as they are. And this, it seems to me, would be enough to give our experiences the status of representative perceptions. The trouble for Berkeley is only that he wants our perception of physical objects to be immediate and presentative.

In fact, of course, there is no way in which, within the confines of the hard-line doctrine, Berkeley can achieve all that he wants. Certainly, he wants our perception of physical objects to be immediate. But, at the same time, he wants the physical world to have an objective reality – to be public and external in relation to us. He wants the physical world to be both perceptually immanent and, in some way, ontologically transcendent. But, without abandoning the doctrine of *esse est percipi*, there is no way of reconciling these wants – no way of combining the immanence required for immediate perceptibility with the transcendence required for objective reality. The only way of combining them – and even here there is a suspicion of compromise – would be by abandoning

31

physical realism for the reductive position we outlined earlier. For if the physical world is the logical creation of God's nomological system, there is a sense in which we can have it both ways. In that it is created by the system for *human* experience, the physical world is, in one way, directly accessible to human perception: to establish its existence and character we do not have to make inferences to some realm of objects which lies behind the veil of our own ideas. On the other hand, in that the system which creates it comprises the *laws* of nature – laws which are exhibited by, but are not reducible to, the thematic character of human experience – the physical world possesses an objective, external status which transcends the actual course of our experience and gives different human subjects a common empirical framework. But, of course, Berkeley cannot adopt this reductive position and retain the hard-line doctrine.

Admittedly, Berkeley can and does retain one aspect of reductivism in his final position. For while he locates the physical world in the mind of God, as something whose *esse* is *percipi*, he would accept that it only qualifies as a *physical* world in virtue of its being a world *for us*, i.e. in virtue of its functioning as a blueprint for God's volitional control of human experience. This is why he is able, in the end, to speak of the physical world as involving 'a twofold state of things', the one 'archetypal and eternal' (the world as it is exists in itself, as the internal object of God's perception), the other 'ectypal or natural' (the world as God creates it for us, by his volitional control of our experience).[2] It is not that Berkeley accepts two physical worlds, the one (the divine world) to be construed *realistically* (as an ontologically primitive item in God's mind) and the other to be construed *reductively* (as something logically created by the constraints on human experience). Rather, he thinks that there is a unique physical world which *both* is, as something in God's mind, a constituent of ultimate reality *and* acquires its physical status, as a world for us, by being empirically expressed in the constraints on our experience. This is mentalistic realism rather than reductive phenomenalism. None the less, it retains enough of the phenomenalist position to count, in effect, as a reconciliation of the conflicting strands of thought in the *Principles* – to be a way of accommodating the core of theistic phenomenalism to the requirements of the hard-line doctrine. This, I suspect, is (more or less) how Berkeley himself must have seen it.

3

THE NATURE OF ANTI-REALISM

The distinction between physical realism and physical anti-realism is exclusively concerned with the question of what exists or obtains at the level of ultimate reality – with what entities are ontologically primitive (not logically created) and what facts are logically basic (not logically sustained). A realist is one who asserts that ultimate reality is at least partly physical – that it contains primitive physical entities or basic physical facts. An anti-realist is one who asserts that ultimate reality is wholly non-physical – that it contains no primitive physical entities and no basic physical facts. Accordingly, both nihilism and reductivism are forms of anti-realism. The nihilist rejects the existence of a physical world altogether. The reductivist accepts its existence as the logical product of something else. But both are alike in excluding physical entities and physical facts from the realm of the ultimate – the realm of what is un-created and unsustained.

Ultimate reality is the union of two components: an ontological component, comprising all that ultimately exists (the set of ontologically primitive entities), and a factual component, comprising all that ultimately obtains (the set of logically basic facts). So there is the possibility of drawing the distinction between realism and anti-realism more finely, by opposing *ontological* realism, the thesis that some physical entities are ontologically primitive, with *ontological* anti-realism, the thesis that no physical entities are ontologically primitive, and by opposing *factual* realism, the thesis that some physical facts are logically basic, with *factual* anti-realism, the thesis that no physical facts are logically basic. The original distinction between realism and anti-realism could then be drawn by combining these more specific distinctions, the one concerned with the ontological component of ultimate reality, the other concerned with its factual component. Realism would be the disjunction of ontological and factual realism, and anti-realism would be the conjunction of ontological and factual anti-realism.

Now it may seem that these further distinctions, while available, are pointless. If there is to be any point in drawing them, it must be possible to envisage a theory in which the ontological and factual questions are answered in opposite ways. It must be possible to envisage a form of *selective* realism which combines an ontological realism with a factual anti-realism or a factual realism with an ontological anti-realism. But surely no one could seriously entertain such a position. How could one accept the ontological primitiveness of certain physical entities without also accepting the logical basicness of certain physical facts? And how could one accept the basicness of certain physical facts without accepting the primitiveness of certain physical entities?

However, there is a thesis, and one which has been seriously entertained, which threatens to drive such a wedge between the ontological and factual questions. This thesis, which I shall call the *analytical thesis*, asserts that statements about the physical world can be exhaustively analysed into statements which employ no explicitly physical concepts and make no explicit references (whether by designation or by quantification) to physical entities. The most familiar version of such a thesis is analytical phenomenalism, which asserts that physical statements (or some canonical class of them) can be exhaustively analysed into statements about human sense-experience. Now I have already stressed (at the end of chapter 1) that, as I have defined it, reductivism does not commit one to the analytical thesis. Thus to claim that physical facts are logically sustained by sensory facts, does not commit one to claiming that physical statements are analysable into sensory statements. Still, we might have assumed that, at least when combined with the acceptance of a physical world, the analytical thesis commits one to reductivism. We might have assumed, for example, that if all physical statements are analysable into sensory statements, then all physical facts must be logically sustained by sensory facts. But, on closer scrutiny, it becomes apparent that such an assumption is unjustified.

Suppose T is a theory which purports to provide a complete phenomenalistic analysis of all physical statements – a theory which, by some finite and non-question-begging specification, pairs each of the infinitely many physical statements with some phenomenal (i.e. sensory) statement and claims that each such phenomenal statement provides the analysis of the physical statement with which it is paired. Suppose further (though I take this to be already implicit in our concept of *analysis*) that, according to T, all such analyses preserve factual meaning, so that, for each physical statement S, its analysans (i.e. the phenomenal statement which provides its analysis) states exactly what S states, though in a more explicit form. Suppose, moreover, that there are some physical statements whose analysantia express ultimate facts, i.e. facts which are not logically sustained by anything else. How is T to be classified in terms of our distinctions? Well, obviously, in respect of physical ontology, it is anti-realist. For it does not recognize any ontologically primitive physical entities. Indeed, it claims that all our supposed references to physical entities are to be analysed away, that our apparent commitment to a physical ontology disappears when we display, by means of the analyses, what our physical statements really state. It would be too weak to say that T excludes physical entities from the realm of the ultimate. If T is right, the very notion of genuine physical entities involves a misinterpretation of our physical language: once we have a proper understanding of our language and the statements we make in it, we no longer discern a category of entities (the physical) whose ultimacy might be at issue. In respect of physical ontology, T involves the strongest form of nihilism. On the other hand, so long as we accept that physical facts are just what true physical statements express (or, more accurately, that, when true, physical statements express physical facts), T turns out, on our suppositions, to yield a form of factual realism. For if two statements have the same factual meaning, they must, if true, express the same fact. So if, as T claims, the analyses preserve factual meaning and if, as we supposed, there are physical statements whose analysantia express ultimate facts, then there must be physical statements which themselves express ultimate facts, i.e. some physical facts must be ultimate. Thus, on the given suppositions, T answers the ontological and factual questions in opposite ways. It combines ontological anti-realism with factual realism. It excludes the physical from the ontological component of ultimate reality, but includes it in the factual component.

Now, according to my definitions, a theory is realist iff it is either ontologically or factually realist (since realism is the thesis that ultimate reality is at least party physical) and a theory is anti-realist iff it is both ontologically and factually anti-realist (since anti-realism is the thesis that ultimate reality is wholly non-physical). So the hybrid position, which combines ontological anti-realism with factual realism, is nominally a form of realism. But its metaphysical force is anti-realist. It differs from anti-realism not in its theory of ultimate reality, but in its interpretation of physical statements. It denies that ultimate reality is wholly non-physical, but it does so, not by expanding the reality to include facts which the anti-realist rejects, but by construing physical statements as expressing facts which the anti-realist accepts. It accords an ultimacy to physical facts, but only by reducing the commitment of physical statements to meet the anti-realist's restrictions – by showing (or purporting to show) that physical facts are not the kind of facts whose ultimacy the anti-realist intends to deny. Consequently, there is a sense in which the hybrid position allows the anti-realist all that he wants. The issue which divides them is an important one, but it concerns the semantics of our physical language rather than the nature of ultimate reality.

When I first formulated my definition of realism, I did not intend it to cover a position of this hybrid kind. At that stage, I was taking it as uncontroversial that our physical statements involve a genuine commitment to a physical ontology and that, in consequence, to accept the ultimacy of certain physical facts is automatically to accept the ultimacy of certain physical entities. I was ignoring the possibility that someone might want to analyse physical statements in such a way that all physical terms and physical references are eliminated, thereby securing the ultimacy of physical facts within the restrictions of ontological anti-realism. In retrospect, we can see that, to fulfil my intentions, the definitions of realism and anti-realism must be amended (at least if we retain the principle that, whatever their analysis, true physical statements express physical facts). Thus let us say that a physical fact is *merely nominal* if it can be expressed, in fully analysed form, in a language devoid of physical vocabulary and with a universe of discourse (a domain of reference and quantification) devoid of physical entities. Then realism is the thesis that ultimate reality contains a physical portion in addition (if it has one) to its portion of merely nominal physical facts, and anti-realism is the thesis that ultimate reality contains no physical portion apart from (if it has one) its portion of merely nominal physical facts. The effect of this is to strengthen realism so as to entail ontological realism and to weaken anti-realism so as to be entailed by ontological anti-realism. The so-called hybrid position will now count as a case of anti-realism, since the only physical facts whose ultimacy it accepts are merely nominal. This brings things into line with my original intentions, and, I think, puts the boundary between realism and anti-realism in the most appropriate place.

Although, from now on, I want realism and anti-realism to be construed in this way, I shall usually, for simplicity, continue to speak of realism as the thesis that ultimate reality is partly physical and of anti-realism as the thesis that it is wholly non-physical. When I do so, it must be understood that I am treating merely nominal physical facts, if there are any, as irrelevant to the question of whether ultimate reality is partly physical or wholly non-physical in the sense I intend.

We have seen that it is not possible to envisage a genuine form of realism which admits the ultimacy of certain physical facts without admitting the ultimacy of certain physical entities. And, equally, it seems impossible to envisage a genuine form of realism which admits the ultimacy of certain physical entities without admitting the ultimacy of certain physical facts.[1] But it does not follow from this that realism cannot be selective in other ways, that it cannot deny the ultimacy of certain kinds of physical entity or fact that we ordinarily accept or that are ordinarily accepted by the experts in the relevant field of physical inquiry. As we shall see, this point has two aspects – one trivial, the other important. But to appreciate this, we must start by examining the distinction between realism and anti-realism more closely.

As I have been using them, the terms 'realism' and 'anti-realism' are short for *'physical* realism' and *'physical* anti-realism'. But, of course, the distinction between the positions which they signify is a special case of a more general distinction which we can apply to any subject matter. Thus just as, in the case of the physical, we distinguish between those who accept and those who deny that ultimate reality includes a physical portion (discounting as irrelevant merely nominal physical facts), so we can also distinguish, in (say) the case of the mental, between those who accept and those who deny that ultimate reality includes a mental portion, or again, in the case of the moral, between those who accept and those who deny that ultimate reality includes a moral portion. To mark these distinctions, we could speak of *mental realism* and *mental anti-realism,* and of *moral realism* and *moral anti-realism.* Quite generally, for any subject matter ϕ, we can draw a distinction between ϕ-realism and ϕ-anti-realism, according to whether there is an acceptance or a rejection of the claim that there are ultin ite ϕ-entities and ϕ-facts.

Now we might suppose that this general distinction, which is applicable to any subject matter, rests on the principle that, for any category of entities or any category of facts, one is being anti-realist with respect to that category iff one excludes its members from the realm of the ultimate. But such a principle would have some strange consequences. It would mean that whenever someone accepted some fact as logically sustained or some entity as logically created, he would, thereby, be adopting an anti-realist position with respect to it. And in many cases this conclusion would be counter-intuitive. We can see this if we cast our minds back to the original definitions of logical sustainment and logical creation and to the examples by which these definitions were first illustrated. According to these definitions, a fact F is logically sustained by a fact or set of facts F' iff the obtaining of F is a logical consequence of, mediated by, and nothing over and above the obtaining of F'. And an entity x is the logical creation of a fact or set of facts F iff the existence of x (the fact that x exists) is logically sustained by F. Consequently, if John weighs 14 stone and Mary weighs 10 stone, the fact – call it H – that John is 4 stone heavier than Mary is logically sustained by, in combination, the fact that John weighs 14 stone and the fact that Mary weighs 10 stone. Likewise, whatever their weights, the aggregate of John and Mary – call it A – is the logical creation of, in combination, the existence of John (the fact that John exists) and the existence of Mary (the fact that Mary exists). It follows that, however ultimate reality is constituted, its ontological component does not include A and its factual component does not include H. But the recognition of this result hardly constitutes, in any intuitive sense, an anti-realist stance towards the entity and fact whose ultimacy is denied. For to justify the label

38

'anti-realist', a denial of ultimacy must surely, in some way, diminish the ontological or factual status of the items in question: even if not nihilistic, it must surely, in some way, preclude our accepting the reality of these items at face value – impose some qualification on the claim that they exist or obtain. But there is no hint of this, or anything like it, in the case of H and A. This is because the recognition of their sustainment or creation is, and is necessarily, implicit in the way these items are initially conceived. We never, nor could we, think of a weight-relation as obtaining except in virtue of the individual weights of the objects thus related. We never, nor could we, think of an aggregate as existing except in virtue of the existence of its parts. The denial of the ultimacy of such facts and entities does nothing to diminish their status or qualify our acceptance of their reality. We cannot so much as envisage the superior status or full-blooded reality which we might accord such items, but which we deny them by denying their ultimacy in the way we have specified.

But if the mere exclusion of something from the realm of the ultimate does not, as such, constitute an anti-realism towards what is excluded, then in what sense is the position we have called *physical anti-realism* genuinely anti-realist? After all, this position is, as I have repeatedly emphasized, compatible with reductivism. It does not commit us to denying the existence of a physical world altogether. It allows us to retain physical entities and physical facts as the logical product of the ultimate non-physical reality. But if so, in what way does the reductivist exclusion of the physical differ from the exclusion of A and H? In what way does reductivism involve an anti-realist stance towards the entities and facts whose ultimacy it denies, but whose existence and obtaining it accepts? The answer is that reductivism sets these entities and facts in what is, relative to our initial conception of them, a radically different perspective. There is, as it were, a prima facie conflict between the postulated ultimate reality and the retention of a physical world – a conflict which we can only eliminate by uncovering a *flexibility* in our physical concepts which is not apparent in our ordinary understanding of them. The thesis that ultimate reality is wholly non-physical is anti-realist because, set against the background of our initial conception of the physical world, its *prima facie* force is towards nihilism. We may be able both to accept the thesis and avoid the nihilistic consequence; but we can do so only by revising (to suit the new restrictions) our conception of what the existence of physical entities and the obtaining of physical facts involve. In this sense, even a reductivist does not accept the reality of the physical world at face value: he does not accept, in full, the ontological and factual commitments of what forms, and necessarily forms, our initial view of how the physical world is constituted. Thus suppose someone holds that (to put it roughly) ultimate reality is composed of just human minds and the laws of human experience. Such a person may be either a nihilist, who rejects the physical world altogether, or a reductivist, who accepts it as the logical product of the experiential system. But there can be no denying that to accept it in this form, as the product of the experiential system, is to refuse to accept it in the form in which it is (even by the reductivist) ordinarily conceived. This is not to say that reductivism is excluded by our actual physical concepts, but only that, to permit reductivism, these concepts have, on philosophical scrutiny, to reveal an adaptability which our initial grasp of them does not anticipate. The charge of nihilism has at least to be faced, even if it can be successfully answered.

It might be objected, by those familiar with the writings of Michael Dummett, that to classify every form of reductivism as anti-realist is to blur an important distinction. Dummett sees the issue between realism and anti-realism as concerning, not so much the composition of ultimate reality, as the semantic appraisal of statements. To be a realist with respect to some class α of statements is, according to Dummett, to accept the principle that each α-statement is either true or false. Conversely, to be an anti-realist with respect to α is to reject this principle, i.e. to leave open the possibility that some α-statements are neither true nor false. (Rejecting the principle does not involve asserting that there actually is an α-statement which is neither true nor false.) Thus, for Dummett, the distinction between realism and anti-realism turns on the acceptance or rejection of the law of bivalence for some relevant class of statements.[2] Dummett sees the dispute over bivalence as reflecting different conceptions of the kind of meaning possessed by statements in the disputed class. According to the realist's conception,[3]

> we have assigned a meaning to these statements in such a way that we know, for each statement, what has to be the case for it to be true: indeed our understanding of the statement (and therefore its possession of a meaning) just consists in our

knowing what has to be the case for it to be true. The condition for the truth of a statement is not, in general, a condition which we are capable of recognising as obtaining, whenever it obtains, or even one for which we have an effective procedure for determining whether it obtains or not. We have therefore succeeded in ascribing to our statements a meaning of such a kind that their truth or falsity is, in general, independent of whether we know, or have any means of knowing, what truth-value they have.

In contrast, according to the anti-realist's conception,[4]

> the meanings of statements of the class in question are given to us, not in terms of the conditions under which these statements are true or false, conceived as conditions which obtain or do not obtain independently of our knowledge or capacity for knowledge, but in terms of the conditions which we recognize as establishing the truth or falsity of statements of that class.

Such a conception leads to a rejection of the law of bivalence if we can envisage circumstances in which, for a given statement, neither the truth-establishing conditions nor the falsity-establishing conditions obtain. For the assignment of meaning to the statement would not provide any understanding of what it was for the statement to be true, or for it to be false, in such circumstances.

Now if we were to work with Dummett's distinction, we should have to reformulate the dispute between the physical realist and the physical anti-realist as one which concerned the status of the law of bivalence for physical statements (or, more likely, for some canonical class of them). It would then become a mistake to classify all forms of reductivism as anti-realist. For reductivism as such does not entail a rejection of the law of bivalence. There is no contradiction in retaining the principle that each physical statement is either true or false, while claiming that the truth-value of any statement solely depends on what obtains in the ultimate non-physical reality. Rather, we should have to distinguish between realist forms of reductivism, which preserve the law of bivalence, and anti-realist forms, which undermine it. Thus consider the case of the reductive phenomenalist, who holds that physical facts are logically sustained by sensory facts. For each physical statement S, he recognizes a range R_1 of possible total

41

sensory situations each of which suffices for the truth of S and a range R_2 of possible total sensory situations each of which suffices for the falsity of S (i.e. for the truth of its negation). For Dummett, the crucial question is: is it the case that, for each physical statement, these ranges are exhaustive? If it is, then we have a form of realism, since the law of bivalence is preserved (for each statement S, each sensory situation either suffices for the truth of S or suffices for its falsity). If it is not, then we have a form of anti-realism, since the law of bivalence is undermined (for some statement S, there is some sensory situation which neither suffices for the truth of S nor suffices for its falsity). So reductive phenomenalism may be, in Dummett's terms, either realist or anti-realist according to its consequences for the law of bivalence.

I can see the interest of Dummett's distinction (especially in the philosophy of mathematics), but it is not the one which I want to employ. Nor do I think that, in the case of the physical world, it has much to do with the issue of realism and anti-realism as traditionally conceived. Traditionally, reductive phenomenalism counts as a form of anti-realism, irrespective of its consequences for bivalence. And it does so because, irrespective of these consequences, it is incompatible with our ordinary conception of what the existence of a physical world involves – incompatible with accepting physical facts and physical entities *at face value*. Moreover, the discrepancy between Dummett's distinction and the traditional one becomes even more conspicuous when we consider the case of nihilism. Suppose someone takes ultimate reality to be wholly mental (e.g. on the lines of Berkeley) but also sees this as excluding altogether the existence of a physical world. This nihilistic position would count, by traditional standards, as a rejection of physical realism – indeed, as anti-realism in its most uncompromising form. But presumably, by Dummett's standards, it would count as realist. For in denying the existence of a physical world, the nihilist would not be rejecting the law of bivalence for physical statements. His position would be, quite simply, that any statement which asserts the obtaining of some physical state of affairs is false. Admittedly, he might concede that many of our utterances about the physical world, i.e. those which purport to make some singular reference to a physical entity, are neither true nor false, because he might hold that such utterances fail to make genuine statements at all. (This,

presumably, would be the position of a nihilist who accepted
P. F. Strawson's views on reference.[5]) But this would not be a
rejection of the law of bivalence for physical *statements*. Nor would
it be relevant to the issue of realism and anti-realism as Dummett
conceives it.

Naturally, Dummett is aware that his distinction differs from the
traditional one:[6]

> I do not pretend that, in using the term realism in the way
> proposed, we shall be precisely conforming to traditional
> philosophical practice. On the contrary, the point of the
> proposal is to enable us to keep clearly in mind a distinction
> which, under the traditional use of the term, has frequently
> been blurred.

But, of course, considerations of this sort cut both ways. If the
traditional use of the term blurs Dummett's distinction, it is equally
true that Dummett's use blurs the traditional distinction. Thus, in
the case of the physical realm, to classify someone as realist in
Dummett's sense (i.e. as someone who affirms the law of bivalence
for physical statements) does not reveal whether or not he
recognizes certain physical facts and physical entities as ultimate. It
would be pointless to discuss which distinction is the more
important. Depending on their other concerns, some philosophers
will find more interest in the one, and others in the other. All I need
to emphasize is that I am using the terms '(physical) realism' and
'(physical) anti-realism' to mark the distinction as I have drawn it.
And I have no doubt that the issue between the realist and the
anti-realist, in this sense, is, if not the only important issue, one
which it is well worth investigating.

I mentioned some time ago the possibility of a selective version
of physical realism which, despite its realist character, denies the
ultimacy of certain kinds of physical entity and fact that we
ordinarily accept, or that are ordinarily accepted by the experts in
the relevant field of inquiry. And I said that this point has two
aspects – one trivial and the other important. We can now see how
the different aspects arise. Obviously, no realism, however comprehensive, will accept as ultimate all that we ordinarily accept as
genuine. For, as we have seen, there are kinds of logical sustainment and creation whose recognition is already implicit in our
initial conception of the items thus created or sustained. Thus any

realism must acknowledge that the weight-relation between two objects is logically sustained by their individual weights and that an aggregate is logically created by the existence of its parts. This kind of selectivity is purely trivial. It does not carry so much as a hint of anti-realism. Indeed, for this reason, we can hardly speak here of 'selective realism', since the scope of the realism is not reduced by the selectivity. But physical realism can also be selective in a more important way, where the restrictions on the ultimate reality provide, relative to our initial conception of the physical world, a significant change in ontological and factual perspective – where there is a genuine confinement of the physical realm within narrower limits than we ordinarily recognize. In such a case, the realism, by its selectivity, incorporates a degree of anti-realism – not, as in the case of the analytical thesis, by combining factual realism with ontological anti-realism, but by combining a realism (both ontological and factual) about one portion of the physical world with an anti-realism (both ontological and factual) about another. This is a realism which is genuinely selective, and from now on, I shall reserve the title 'selective realism' for a position of this sort.

As we shall see in subsequent chapters, selective realism can take a variety of forms. But most of these forms fall under two main and sharply contrasting themes, which provide, in their quite different ways, a rationale for the selection. One theme is that in which the selection is in favour of those aspects of the physical world which are most accessible to ordinary perception and is, correspondingly, against those aspects which are discernible, if at all, only through scientific experiment and theory. Taken to its extreme, this theme yields a form of realism which confines ultimate physical reality to a spatiotemporal arrangement of sensible qualities (colours, textures, sounds, flavours, etc.) together with the framework of laws which control this arrangement. Such a reality would be devoid, not only of the more rarefied and microscopic entities postulated by modern physics (such as waves and particles), but also of material substance itself: the sensible qualities would inhere in nothing except the regions of space they pervade. This would be a selective realism conforming to Berkeley's position (at least, to his *realist* position), though without, so far, the absorption of the sensible into the mental. The other theme, in contrast, is that which selects those aspects of the physical world which science shows, or claims to show, to be causally fundamental and which discounts, as mere appearance, much of what ordinary perception seems to reveal. Taken to its extreme, this theme yields a form of realism which confines ultimate physical reality to a spatiotemporal arrangement of elementary particles, waves of electromagnetic radiation, and fields of causal potential, together with the laws which control this arrangement. Unless it is wholly physicalistic, such a realism will also recognize as ultimate (though not, strictly as part of the ultimate physical reality) certain psychophysical (strictly physio-psychical) laws, which assign experiential effects to brain states, and which, in conjunction with the physical arrangement and physical laws, explain the sensible appearance of the physical world to human percipients. Thus, on this account, the sensible colours we encounter in visual experience have no ultimate physical realization, although bodies with the appropriate surface structures are, in virtue of the physical and psychophysical laws, disposed to look sensibly coloured when suitably irradiated and observed in appropriate conditions.

Both kinds of selectivity – the one endorsing the perspective of ordinary perception, the other the perspective of scientific theory – involve a genuine anti-realism towards those aspects of the physical world whose ultimacy they deny, each being, in this case, anti-realist towards all or most (apart from the space-time framework) of what the other selects. The sensibly selective realist does not accept, at least at face value, the insensible world of scientific theory; the scientifically selective realist does not accept, at least at face value, the sensible world of ordinary perception. And in each case, as in the case of full-blooded anti-realism, the selection leaves, with respect to the non-selected aspects, a choice between nihilism and reductivism – between rejecting the reality of these aspects altogether and construing them as the logical product of what is selected as ultimate. Thus the exclusively sensible realist can either reject altogether the theories of science, taking them to be, at best, a convenient fiction (useful as a way of recording, in simple terms, the complex regularities in the spatiotemporal distribution of sensible qualities), or interpret these theories as sufficiently flexible, in their ontological commitment and factual import, to be true in virtue of the sensible facts he selects. Likewise, the exclusively scientific realist can either reject altogether the judgments of ordinary perception, conceding, at most, their utility

45

as a route to scientific discovery, or interpret these judgments as sufficiently flexible, in ontological commitment and factual import, to be true in virtue of the underlying reality which science reveals. In both cases, the reductive approach lays great stress on the nomological aspects of the ultimate reality. It appeals to the fact that while the non-selected items cannot be accepted as they are initially conceived – cannot be accepted at face value – their initial conception at least reflects and underlines a genuine aspect of ultimate nomological organization. Thus in accepting, in a logically sustained form, the existence of particles or waves, the sensible reductivist appeals to the fact that the sensible world is organized exactly as if there were an underlying reality of the sort which the particle or wave theories (as initially interpreted) postulate. And in accepting, in a logically sustained form, the physical realization of sensible colour, the scientific reductivist appeals to the fact that the underlying reality is organized, both internally and in relation to human experience, exactly as if there were a spatiotemporal arrangement of colours (as initially conceived) which, in appropriate circumstances, are displayed to human view. In both cases, the reductivist argues that because the non-selected items correspond to certain aspects of the selected organization, it is less misleading to accord them a derivative status as the product of that organization, rather than reject them altogether. Of course, the selective realist does not have to be thus accommodating. He may conclude that the physical concepts whose application is at issue are not sufficiently flexible to allow a reductive account – that we cannot divorce the scientific theories or the perceptual judgments from our initially realist understanding of them without distorting their meaning. If this is what he concludes, then his anti-realism towards the non-selected items will be nihilistic.

Just as the non-selected items may be treated either nihilistically or reductively, so, of course, the selected items may be treated either standardly or mentalistically. Thus with all the new distinctions added (apart from the alternative principles of selection), the taxonomy of positions, concerning the status and character of the physical world, expands from what was earlier depicted in Figure 1.5 (p. 14) to what is now depicted in Figure 3.1.

There is one final point which needs to be emphasized. It is obvious that any move from comprehensive to selective realism is a move in the direction of anti-realism. Indeed, we can envisage

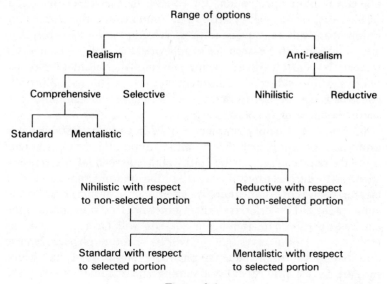

Figure 3.1

arriving at a fully anti-realist position by passing through a series of selective positions in which the realist element gradually diminishes and the anti-realist element correspondingly expands. But what is also true, and perhaps less obvious, is that selective realism may also serve as a route to mentalistic realism. Mentalistic realism is not, on the face of it, a plausible theory. Indeed, it is not clear that it is even coherent – not clear that it makes sense to suppose that, as an ingredient of ultimate reality, the physical world is purely mental. But however intuitively implausible it may be, we must not set the conditions for its truth higher than we need. If we can justify some prior selectivity with respect to the physical items we take as ultimate, it is only these selected items whose nature is at issue: the mentalistic account of the physical world need only be as extensive as the realism with which it combines. We have already seen, in effect, one application of this point in the case of Berkeley – Berkeley, that is, construed as a physical realist. By rejecting material substance and restricting ultimate physical reality to the world of sensible qualities, he is able to achieve a mentalistic realism through the doctrine of *esse est percipi* – a realism which, in its final form, locates the sensible world in the mind of God, as the internal object of divine perception. Of course, in this case, the initial selection is, on the face of it, highly implausible. But it does not follow from this that every form of selection is implausible. And any selection can be seen as simplifying the task of mentalistic realism by narrowing the scope of that (the ultimate physical reality) whose substance and character has to be mentalistically construed. This is not to deny that, even after the simplification, there may be insuperable obstacles.

In these introductory chapters, I have not tried to establish any important philosophical theory, either about the composition of ultimate reality or about the status and character of the physical world. My aim has only been to set the options and issues in a clearer perspective and, thereby, to provide a framework for our subsequent discussion. Given this framework, the main philosophical investigation can now begin. As you will have gathered, my overall aim, in this investigation, will be to refute physical realism and defend a form of reductive phenomenalism. But I shall begin, in Part II, by provisionally assuming the truth of realism and arguing, on this assumption, for the coherence and plausibility of its mentalistic version. The basis of this argument (the topic-neutrality of physical description) will also form a basis for the subsequent argument against realism itself.

PART II

THE TOPIC-NEUTRALITY THESIS

4

THE INSCRUTABILITY
OF MATTER

For practical purposes, mentalistic realism, or, to give it its full title, mentalistic physical realism, is the conjunction of mentalism and (physical) realism – the conjunction of the thesis that ultimate reality is wholly mental and the thesis that it is, at least in part, physical. Strictly speaking, of course, while mentalistic realism is entailed by this conjunction, it does not entail it. For mentalistic realism is compatible with the denial of mentalism. It is compatible with the claim that ultimate reality is partly mental and partly non-mental, though it does entail that the physical world – at least, what remains of it at the level of ultimate reality – is wholly contained in the mental sector. But the possibility of mentalistic realism without mentalism is one which, in practice, we can afford to ignore, not only because our main concern is with the status of the physical world, but also because, if there were any reasons for adopting a mentalist account of physical reality, they would presumably be reasons for adopting a mentalist account of ultimate reality as a whole.

Whether or not it is combined with an unrestricted mentalism, mentalistic realism is not, on the face of it, a plausible position. Part of its implausibility is that, at this stage, we have no conception of how it could be worked out in detail – of how, item by item, the physical portion of ultimate reality could be mentalistically construed. But there is also a more fundamental point. On the face of it, the categories *mental* and *physical* apply to entities and states of affairs of different intrinsic kinds. If we want to specify the intrinsic nature of (say) a material object, we will do so in terms of its figure and extension and its material composition. If we want to specify the intrinsic nature of (say) a propositional attitude, we will do so in terms of the mental character of the attitude (belief, desire, hope, etc.) and the conceptual structure and content of the proposition on to which the attitude is directed. On the face of it, the intrinsic nature of a physical item is to be specified by its physical description and the intrinsic nature of a mental item is to be specified by its mental description. It seems, therefore, that the same portion of ultimate reality cannot be both mental and physical, since, if it were, its mental and physical descriptions would offer conflicting accounts of its intrinsic character.

Before we consider this point in more detail, it will be useful, by way of clarification, to see how the same intuitive problem arises for an analogous, but more familiar, position concerning the status of mind. This analogous position we might call (to mark the analogy) *physicalistic mental realism*. Physicalistic mental realism holds that minds are an ingredient of ultimate reality, but takes them to be, in substance and character, purely physical. So physicalistic (mental) realism, like mentalistic (physical) realism, is, in effect, the conjunction of two theses. It is, in effect, the conjunction of *physicalism*, which holds ultimate reality to be wholly physical, and *mental realism*, which holds it to be, in part, mental. Again, strictly speaking, while physicalistic realism is entailed by this conjunction, it does not entail it. For physicalistic realism is compatible with the denial of physicalism. It is compatible with the claim that ultimate reality is partly physical and partly non-physical, though it does entail that the mental realm – at least, what remains of it at the level of ultimate reality – is wholly contained in the physical sector. But the possibility of physicalistic realism without physicalism in one which, in practice, we can afford to ignore for the same reasons that we can afford to ignore the possibility of mentalistic realism without mentalism.

Applied to the case of human and animal minds, physicalistic realism assumes the familiar form of the mind-brain identity thesis, which identifies minds with brains and identifies mental states and mental processes with brain states and brain processes. Such a thesis does not claim that mental descriptions can be analysed into physical descriptions. It does not claim that when I report that I am in pain or have a belief that colour-additives are carcinogenic, then what I say is logically equivalent to, or even entails, some

physiological description of the relevant event in or state of my
central nervous system. Rather, it concedes that the correlation
between mental and physical descriptions can only be established
empirically, but claims that these descriptions apply to the same
events and states – that what I describe introspectively as a pain is
the very thing which physiological investigation would reveal to be,
for example, an excitation of my C-fibres.

Mentalistic (physical) realism and physicalistic (mental) realism
are, in an obvious sense, diametrically opposite positions: the
former tries to absorb the physical realm into the mental, while the
latter tries to absorb the mental realm into the physical. But
because each position is realist with respect to what it absorbs (give
or take a certain degree of initial selectivity), both positions are in
agreement over one crucial point. Both positions accept that there
is a portion of ultimate reality which is both mental and physical.
We can see this from the appropriate Venn diagrams (see Figures
4.1 and 4.2).

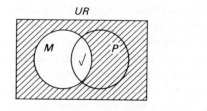

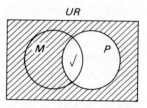

Figure 4.1   *Figure 4.2*

In Figure 4.1, representing mentalistic realism (strictly, mentalism + physical realism), everything is shaded apart from *M*, thus
indicating that ultimate reality is wholly mental. In Figure 4.2,
representing physicalistic realism (strictly, physicalism + mental
realism), everything is shaded apart from *P*, thus indicating that
ultimate reality is wholly physical. But in both figures there is a tick
in the region where *M* and *P* overlap, indicating that some portion
of ultimate reality is both mental and physical.

It is this fact which makes both positions vulnerable to the
intuitive objection that the mental and physical categories are

mutually exclusive, since their items are of different intrinsic kinds. But because the two positions are diametrically opposed, this objection applies to them in subtly different ways. Applied to mentalistic realism, which tries to absorb the physical into the mental, the objection becomes that physical items have, prior to any such absorption, their own distinctively physical intrinsic character, which leaves no room for a more basic mental specification. Physical items, it is objected, cannot be intrinsically mental since their intrinsic character is specified in physical terms. Applied to physicalistic realism, which tries to absorb the mental into the physical, the objection becomes that mental items have, prior to any such absorption, their own distinctively mental character, which leaves no room for a more basic physical specification. Mental items, it is objected, cannot be intrinsically physical since their intrinsic character is specified in mental terms. In effect, then, the original objection divides into two parts, one of which is directed against mentalistic realism and the other directed against physicalistic realism. Although the intuitions behind them may be similar, it is important to keep these two parts distinct. The mentalist is happy to acknowledge that the intrinsic character of mental items cannot be specified in physical terms, just as the physicalist is happy to acknowledge that the intrinsic character of physical items cannot be specified in mental terms.

As I have already said, physicalistic realism is familiar in the form of the mind-brain identity thesis. And since this thesis is not only familiar, but also quite fashionable, we might begin by seeing how its defenders try to meet the inuitive objection or, rather, that part of it which conflicts with their position. There might, after all, be something here which could be re-deployed in the defence of *mentalistic* realism.

What the defenders of the mind-brain identity thesis say, in response to the intuitive objection, is that our mental concepts and mental descriptions are, despite initial appearances to the contrary, *topic-neutral* – neutral, that is to say, with respect to the intrinsic character of the mental items to which they apply. Thus, typically, they claim that when we characterize an item by means of a mental description, e.g. by characterizing it as a pain or as a belief that colour-additives are carcinogenic, what we thereby specify is not the intrinsic nature of the item (what the item is like in itself), but rather its *functional* properties, i.e. the causal contribution made by items of that intrinsic sort (whatever it is) to the production of behaviour, or, more generally, the role of such items in the total causal system which mediates between sensory input and behavioural output. Of course, they do not claim that mental descriptions are *explicitly* functional – if they were, there would be no intuitive objection to be met. Their claim is, rather, that such descriptions, while posing as intrinsic, turn out to be functional on analysis. Thus they might say, as a first approximation, that the mental predicate 'is a pain' is to be analysed (roughly) as 'is an event of a sort apt to cause restless behaviour and to act as a negative reinforcer of response-types that produce it'. Now if these philosophers are right in their claim that mental descriptions are topic-neutral – descriptions which tell us nothing about the intrinsic nature of the items to which they apply – then the intuitive objection to physicalistic realism, in the form of the mind-brain identity thesis, disappears, since we can no longer exclude, *a priori*, the possibility that mental items are intrinsically physical. Moreover, if they are also right in claiming that mental descriptions are implicitly functional, then we can envisage a way of empirically establishing that mental items *are* intrinsically physical and of establishing what intrinsic physical properties they possess. For a physiological and behavioural investigation might reveal that certain types of brain state and brain process have the right functional properties to satisfy certain mental descriptions, and that their occurrence is appropriately correlated with our employment of these descriptions in our introspective reports.

Now it seems to me that this way of defending physicalistic realism against the intuitive objection fails. Indeed, it seems to me that, in a sense, it fails catastrophically, since it manages to get everything exactly the wrong way round. It locates topic-neutrality at the very point where our concepts and descriptions are topic-specific, and it locates topic-specificity at the very point where they are topic-neutral. However, our concern is not with the merits, but with the general form of the defence and whether it might be transferred, *mutatis mutandis*, to the case of mentalistic realism.

The intuitive objection to mentalistic realism is that physical items have their own distinctively physical intrinsic character, a character to be specified in physical terms. Taking as our analogy the defence of physicalistic realism, the counter-claim we have to consider is that our initial intuitions are mistaken and that the physical description of the physical world (strictly, that portion of the world which is included in the sphere of ultimate reality) is in fact topic-neutral – a description which conceals the intrinsic nature of the items it describes. I want to argue that this counter-claim is correct. Just as the defenders of physicalistic realism argue that our introspective reports leave open the question of whether what they characterize is, in intrinsic nature, physical or non-physical, so I shall argue, in defence of mentalistic realism, that physical theories (at least in so far as they are descriptive of ultimate reality) leave open the question of whether what they characterize is, in intrinsic nature, mental or non-mental. Such an argument would not, of course, establish the truth of mentalistic realism, but only defend it against the intuitive objection. Indeed, later on (in Part III), I shall argue that it is false. For I shall argue that any kind of physical realism, whether standard or mentalistic, is false.

As I have conceded, our initial intuition is that physical items have a distinctively physical intrinsic character, a character to be specified in physical terms. There are, I think, two factors which explain the existence of this intuition, without, however, doing anything to ensure its validity. Since my claim will be that the intuition is mistaken, I am going to begin, as a precautionary measure, by isolating these factors, so that we can then consider the issue in a more open-minded way, without the influence of some latent bias. The first factor is that when we consider our information about one sort of physical item, we tend to take for granted the topic-specificity of our information about certain other sorts of physical item to which the first sort is intimately related, and this creates the impression that our knowledge of the intrinsic character of the physical world is more extensive than it really is. The second factor is, to use the words of Hume, that 'the mind has a great propensity to spread itself on external objects, and to conjoin with them any internal impressions which they occasion.'[1] The result is that, without any justification, we come to think of the intrinsic character of these objects as consisting partly in the sensible qualities by which they are represented in experience, and, to that extent, as amenable to physical description.

We can illustrate the operation of both these factors by focusing our attention on what are, on the face of it, the two most fundamental ingredients of the physical world – matter and physical space. The operation of the first factor is seen in the way in which part of our conception of matter concerns its relation to physical space and part of our conception of physical space concerns its relation to matter. We conceive of matter as a substance which is 3-dimensionally extended in physical space and we think of its 3-dimensional extendedness as forming an essential part of its intrinsic nature. Conversely, we conceive of physical space as a 3-dimensional medium in which matter can be located and 3-dimensionally arranged, and even if we accept that it could exist without material occupants (everywhere a vacuum), we think of its capacity to receive such occupants as reflecting its intrinsically physical character. In each case, taken on its own, it may seem that we are setting limits on the intrinsic nature of a certain physical item by specifying its intimate involvement with another item whose intrinsic nature is already known. On the one hand, it may seem that we delimit the intrinsic nature of matter by specifying its essential 3-dimensional extendedness in physical space. On the other hand, it may seem that we delimit the intrinsic nature of physical space by specifying its role as a medium for material objects. But when we take both cases together, it becomes clear that, to a large extent, the two specifications cancel out, leaving us with a combined specification which is, or is more nearly, topic-neutral – a specification which characterizes matter-in-physical-space as a 3-dimensionally extended substance (of whatever intrinsic nature) in a 3-dimensionally extended medium (of whatever intrinsic nature).

The operation of the second factor now serves to add something more specific. It can be seen, in the first instance, in the way in which we ordinarily think of material objects and their spatial arrangement as being, in their intrinsic character, as (in standard conditions) they sensibly appear. Thus we ordinarily think of material objects as pervaded by the sensible colours we experience when we observe them in daylight, and correspondingly, we think of their arrangement in physical space as something whose intrinsic nature is best conceived, *modulo* perspective, in distinctively visual terms. This visual conception of the physical world is, one suspects, largely undermined by the scientific findings. Science reveals that, given some illuminated material object, the only intrinsic properties of the object which affect its colour-appearance are the internal composition and spatial arrangement of its atoms, since it is only these properties which, by affecting the composition of the reflected light, affect the character of our colour-experience. And there seems to be no justification for taking an object to be intrinsically coloured if its being such would contribute nothing to its visual appearance. But even when we try to adjust to these scientific findings, traces of the visual conception may remain. Even when we subtract the subjective layer of colour-appearance and try to reach a more objective view of what the physical world is like in itself, we may find ourselves conceiving of matter-in-space as a greyish stuff suspended in a transparent medium. Indeed, it is hard to eradicate this visual picture until we can find something more acceptable, but equally topic-specific, to put in its place.

The question of whether the physical world has, or might have, a distinctively sensible intrinsic character (whether a character associated with visual experience or some other sense-realm) is, I think, more complicated than most philosophers appreciate. It is a question which I shall consider, in some detail, in chapter 6. But for the time being I am going to adopt what, on the face of it, is the reasonable view, namely that distinctively sensible qualities have no ultimate physical realization. In the case of the so-called secondary qualities, like colour, odour and flavour, what this means is quite clear. It means that these qualities, taken as genuinely sensible qualities (as qualities that can feature in the content of sense-experience), have no place in the ultimate constitution of the physical world. It means that, ultimately, there are no physical colours, odours or flavours except in the form of *powers* to produce certain kinds of visual, olfactory and gustatory experience in us. In the case of the spatial qualities – figure and extension – the point is analogous, but more subtle. Obviously, I am not supposing (not, at least, at this stage) that these qualities have no place in the ultimate constitution of the physical world. (To do so, would be to suppose that, ultimately, there was no physical space and no spatially extended physical objects.) Nor am I supposing that, as physically realized, they should be construed dispositionally. Rather, my supposition is only that these spatial qualities, as qualities in the physical world, do not have whatever is distinctive of their representation in any particular sense-realm. I am supposing that, in its intrinsic nature, physical space is no closer to its representation in one sense-realm than in another, so long as both realms provide an equally adequate representation of its geometrical structure. In particular, I am supposing that physical space is not intrinsically *visual*, though it may have the geometrical structure which, *modulo* perspective, visual experience represents.

Now that we have (provisionally) deprived the physical world, at least at the level of ultimate reality, of any distinctively sensible qualities, and have also noted, in the first factor, a way in which our conception of a physical item may appear to have a topic-specificity which it lacks, the intuition that physical items have a distinctively physical intrinsic character (a character to be specified in physical terms) is already appearing less secure. Our next task must be to examine the issue in more detail. I suggest we continue to focus our attention on matter and physical space and that we begin by considering whether it is possible, within the limits we have imposed, to provide a fuller physical specification of the intrinsic nature of matter – a specification which goes beyond our conception of it as a substance 3-dimensionally extended in physical space.

One obvious suggestion to be considered is that we can enrich this conception by the specification of matter as *solid*. Now the term 'solid' can be used in a variety of different senses. It is used in geometry to signify merely the property of 3-dimensional extendedness, and, of course, its use in this sense is of no interest in the present context. It is used in chemistry and physics to contrast with the term 'fluid', i.e. to distinguish matter in a solid state, such as stone and ice, from matter in a liquid or gaseous state, such as water and air. Again, this is not the relevant sense for present purposes, since, at the moment, we are only concerned with that generic kind of solidity which is characteristic of matter as such – something which is present in all material objects irrespective of their differences. For the same reason, we can ignore the sense in which 'solid' contrasts with 'flimsy' – the sense in which a house of bricks is solid and a house of straw is not. The relevant sense is, presumably, the one which Locke has in mind when he takes solidity to be that intrinsic property of matter which makes material objects mutually impenetrable – that which gives each particle and parcel of matter (in relation to other particles and parcels of matter) exclusive possession of the region of space it occupies, so long as it occupies it.[2] Solidity, in this sense, is a *special kind* of 3-dimensional extendedness: it is the filling of, the taking up of room in, space in such a way as to leave that portion of space no longer available for occupancy by other portions of substance of the same sort. It is what prevents distinct parcels of matter from simultaneously extending through the same 3-dimensional region of space. Locke takes solidity in this sense to be an essential property of matter as such, 'inseparably inherent in body, wherever or however modified'.[3] 'All the bodies in the world, pressing a drop of water on all sides, will never be able to overcome the resistance which it will make, as soft as it is, to their approaching one another, till it be removed out of their way.'[4]

However, it is not clear that, even in this sense, solidity is going to be of any help. For it can be plausibly argued that the very notion of a spatially extended substance requires that, at any time, each portion of substance is individuated by its spatial location, so that it is logically impossible for distinct portions to occupy simultaneously the same 3-dimensional region, simply because, by their principle of individuation, they are numerically distinct only in virtue of being spatially discrete. If this is so, then the mutual impenetrability of material objects is rendered trivial, and if solidity is defined as that in virtue of which such objects are mutually impenetrable – that which gives each portion of matter exclusive possession of the region it occupies – then the concept of solidity is simply the concept of what it is to be a 3-dimensionally extended substance. Obviously, what we were looking for was a form of solidity which would constitute the ground of a causal power – a power to resist penetration, a power which bodies exercise by exerting a mutually obstructive force when they compete for the same spatial position. It is clear, too, that this is what Locke has in mind, although he also endorses, in another context, the spatial principle of individuation.[5] The trouble is that, if we accept the spatial principle, there seems to be nothing left for such a power to do. The mutual impenetrability of bodies is guaranteed by the way in which different portions of material substance (as of any spatially extended substance) are numerically distinguished. To envisage two bodies as overlapping in space is *eo ipso* to envisage them as overlapping in substance and hence to envisage, in the region of overlap, only one parcel of matter – a parcel which is a common part of both.

There are two ways in which we might try to overcome this difficulty, assuming that we want the concept of solidity to be more than just the concept of a 3-dimensionally extended substance. On the one hand, we might reject, in its strict form, the spatial principle of individuation. Thus we might argue that, while location in space provides the general framework of individuation for a spatially extended substance (the occupancy of different positions being the paradigmatic and only clear-cut form of numerical difference at a time), the supposition that two portions of the same substance simultaneously occupy the same region is not incoherent and could, in certain circumstances (where everything, apart from the spatial principle, seemed to indicate its truth), be the best explanation of our empirical data. If we took this line, but continued to regard material objects as *in fact* mutually impenetrable, we could recognize a causal power to prevent penetration and could take solidity to be the intrinsic property of matter on which this power was grounded. On the other hand, even if we retained the spatial principle and construed mutual impenetrability as a trivial consequence of the requirements of individuation, there would remain a further sense in which material objects are mutually obstructive – a sense which is not exhausted by their principle of individuation. After all, the spatial principle is compatible with a case in which, by all empirical tests, two bodies with no internal gaps seem to pass through each other unhindered, each body continuing on its original course completely unaffected by its encounter with the other. The appearance of co-penetration would not *force* us to abandon the spatial principle, since we could always insist on measuring the quantity of matter, at any time, by the extent of materially occupied space. We could say that the quantity of matter steadily diminished as the bodies seemed to merge and that it steadily increased as they seemed to separate. We could say these things, at the cost of certain causal anomalies, even though (as we may suppose) the combined weight of the two bodies remained constant throughout. Now, in actual fact, bodies do not behave in this way. When their paths converge, there is obstructive contact, a contact which deflects at least one of the objects from its original course. So, however matter is individuated, we may suppose that there is something about its intrinsic nature – something which we call *solidity* – which ensures that, in cases of convergence, the quantity of materially occupied space remains the same (the two parcels of matter persisting and competing for spatial position). However individuated, bodies have a power of mutual resistance, whether we construe it as a power to resist penetration (if we reject the spatial principle) or as a power to resist annihilation (if we accept it), and either way we can take solidity to be that intrinsic property of matter on which this power is grounded – that intrinsic property which, in the framework of natural law, ensures that the power obtains.

This suffices to give the concept of solidity some additional content – additional, that is, to what is already found in the concept of a 3-dimensionally extended substance. But it is still not clear that the specification of matter as solid sheds any further light on its intrinsic nature. At least, it is not clear that it does so in a way that is relevant to our present concern. Here, we need to draw a crucial distinction between a mode of specification which is (as I shall say) *transparent* and one which is (as I shall say) *opaque*. Suppose I have a sealed envelope and I know that inside it there is a piece of paper on which someone has drawn a geometrical figure, but I do not know what type. If someone who does know tells me, correctly, that the figure is a triangle, his specification of the type is *transparent*. If he tells me, again correctly, that it is an instance of that type of figure whose geometrical properties are discussed in the fourth chapter of the only leather-bound book in Smith's library, his specification is *opaque*. In both cases, the information he provides is, in a sense, *about* the intrinsic nature of the figure. But there is also a clear sense in which the first specification (the one that is transparent) *reveals* this intrinsic nature and the second (the one which is opaque) does not. Unless I already have further relevant information about the contents of the leather-bound book in Smith's library, the second specification leaves me, in the most obvious sense, none the wiser as to what type of figure the envelope contains.

Now, at first sight, it may seem that the specification of matter as solid is more like the first of these specifications than the second. And certainly, grammatically, it has the same kind of simplicity and directness: it is a specification of matter as *being such and such,* rather than as *having that property which uniquely meets such and such conditions.* But its grammatical form is not what is at issue. After all, without knowing what type of figure the envelope contains, I could coin a term 'envelopoid' to signify it (and to signify it *rigidly*, in Kripke's sense, so that it is a necessary truth, though unknown to me, that envelopoids are triangles[6]). I could then say, quite trivially, that the figure is an envelopoid, without knowing, in any interesting sense what type of figure it is. Clearly, the specification of matter as intrinsically solid is not as trivial as that. But we still need to consider what kind of information it provides.

The point is that, so far, we have only introduced the concept of solidity by reference to the power of resistance which solidity sustains. So there are two possibilities. On the one hand, it may be that we have an independent grasp of what solidity is in itself, and that our specification of matter as solid is *transparent* – one which reveals that aspect of the intrinsic nature of material objects on which their power of mutual resistance is grounded. On the other hand, it may be that our only conception of solidity is as that intrinsic property, whatever it is, on which this power is grounded, and that our specification of matter as solid is *opaque* – one which reveals nothing about what matter is like in itself. Locke himself took the specification to be transparent since he thought that the nature of solidity is revealed in tactual experience. 'If anyone asks me *What this solidity is*', he writes, 'I send him to his senses to inform him. Let him put a flint or a football between his hands and then endeavour to join them, and he will know.'[7] He thought that intrinsic solidity is directly manifested through tactual pressure in the way that sensible colour is directly manifested through sight (though, of course, while he took solidity to be a characteristic of material objects, he confined sensible colour, of the sort visually manifested, to the content of sense-awareness[8]). But in this Locke was clearly mistaken. Tactual pressure only reveals the force of resistance. When I press a football between my hands, I feel it to be solid just in so far as I feel it to be obstructive. I detect its solidity just to the extent that I perceive it as a barrier to the progress of my hands – as a spherical region that I am unable to penetrate. Of course, the total tactual experience contains more than just the feeling of resistance: I feel the shape and size of the football and I feel the texture and temperature of its surface. But these additional components contribute nothing to the experience of solidity. The tactual experience of solidity is no more nor less than the experience of voluminous resistance, and, in so far as our concept of solidity is acquired through tactual experience, the specification of matter as solid is opaque. All it adds to the specification of matter as a voluminous substance is that there is *something* in its intrinsic nature (it does not say *what*) which makes material objects mutually obstructive.

At this point, it might be suggested that the intrinsic nature of matter, including its solidity, would be revealed by scientific analysis. After all, we normally think of scientific analysis as taking us below the level of sensible appearance to a specification of how things really are. But, on reflection, it becomes clear that science cannot help us here. Science is informative, but it does not provide the kind of information we are demanding. Thus suppose we give a scientist (one, we will assume, with a wide-ranging competence in both theory and experimentation) some ordinary material object, like a piece of stone or wood, and ask him to provide a specification of its internal constitution. After making certain tests, he may be able to tell us of what chemical elements (hydrogen, carbon, oxygen, etc.) the object is composed, and how these elements fit together, spatially and in certain kinds of causal bonding, to form the complex item we observe. Suppose we then press our inquiry further and demand a transparent specification of the intrinsic nature of the elements. What is hydrogen or carbon like in itself? If he takes the chemical elements to be physically fundamental, the most he can do, for each element, is to specify the shape and size of its atoms and say what causal powers and sensitivities they possess. Thus he may be able to distinguish hydrogen from carbon by the fact that their atoms differ in size or in weight or in valency. But he will not be able to say what the substances hydrogen and carbon are as such. If he does not regard the elements as physically fundamental, he may go on to specify their sub-atomic constitution. He may tell us that atoms are composed of smaller particles – protons, electrons, neutrons, etc. – and explain how the different chemical elements are formed by the different numbers and types of particles that make up the different types of atom. Still, we can press the same question with respect to these particles. What is the intrinsic nature of a proton or an electron? And here he finds himself in the same position as before. If he takes these particles to be physically fundamental, the most he can specify is their shape and size (if they have any) and their causal powers and sensitivities. Apart from their shape and size, he cannot say what protons and electrons are like in themselves. He cannot specify, transparently, the intrinsic nature of (so to speak) protonic or electronic stuff. Maybe the process of scientific analysis can be taken further. Maybe protons and electrons can be shown to be composed of still more fundamental particles. But however far the process of analysis is taken, it always terminates in entities whose intrinsic nature, apart from shape and size, remains concealed. Scientific analysis uncovers spatiotemporal arrangement and nomological organization, but does not reveal the intrinsic nature of the fundamental space-occupying substance or substances which are thus arranged and organized. It specifies the intrinsic nature of those substances only opaquely, in terms of their causal powers and sensitivities – the powers and sensitivities which, in the framework of natural law, their intrinsic properties sustain.

When you think about it, this limitation on the scope of scientific analysis is hardly surprising. We can expect scientific investigation to reveal, or to go some way towards revealing, the number of distinct types of fundamental particle, their shape and size, their spatiotemporal arrangement, their powers and sensitivities, and, more generally, the laws which control their behaviour. For while these things are not, in the ordinary sense, accessible to observation, competing theories about them are subject to empirical tests. A given theory can be empirically evaluated in terms of how accurately it predicts and how well it explains what the scientist observes. But these tests could not be used to decide between competing theories (if there were any) about the intrinsic nature of particle-substance. Thus suppose, for the sake of argument, we have scientifically established that there is a single type of fundamental particle, have established its shape and size, have established the laws which control its behaviour and have established the way in which other more complex particles, like atoms and molecules, are built out of it. Suppose further that, envisaging two kinds of particle-substance, K_1 and K_2, we formulate two alternative theories, T_1 and T_2, where both theories record all that is already established and differ in only one respect, namely that T_1 takes the substance of the fundamental particles to be of kind K_1, while T_2 takes it to be of kind K_2. It is clear that the respect in which the two theories differ (i.e. over the intrinsic nature of the particle-substance) is not amenable to any empirical test. For within the sphere of what is observable, both theories have the same consequences, and they generate these consequences by ontological and nomological postulates which are exactly isomorphic. Thus in terms of accuracy of testable prediction and structure of explanation they are indistinguishable. And, consequently, there is no scientific way of deciding between them – no empirical tests which would indicate which, if either, of the alternative transparent specifications of particle-substance was correct or more plausible.

Neither ordinary observation nor scientific analysis can provide a transparent specification of the intrinsic nature of matter, in its fundamental form or forms, beyond its specification as a space-occupying substance. Tactual pressure (e.g. pressing a football between one's hands) yields a perception of solidity, but only as an experience of obstructive force – an experience of voluminous resistance, whose intrinsic ground remains concealed. Scientific analysis uncovers the internal structure of material objects, but terminates in fundamental particles whose intrinsic nature, apart from shape and size, it identifies only opaquely – as that which sustains certain causal powers and sensitivities. In short, the most that empirical investigation (whether ordinary or scientific) can reveal are the number of the different fundamental forms of matter, their spatiotemporal distribution and their nomological organization. Beyond this, matter is empirically inscrutable. (The same, of course, is true, and for the same reasons, of any other type of space-occupying or spatially located physical item. Thus, whether we construe light as particles or waves, it is only its spatiotemporal and causal properties that we can empirically detect.) What is even more crucial, for our purposes, is that this limitation on the scope of empirical knowledge is matched by a co-extensive limitation on what we can express or conceive of in physical terms – a co-extensive limitation on the descriptive resources of our physical language and our system of physical concepts. It is not just that we cannot empirically discover the intrinsic nature of matter; we cannot even, in physical terms, formulate or envisage the possibilities – at least, we cannot do so if, as we are assuming, the possibility that its intrinsic nature is distinctively sensible is already excluded. This explains why the limitation on what physical science can reveal is not felt as a genuine limitation from the viewpoint of the scientist. He never finds himself in the position of wanting to adjudicate between alternative physical theories about the nature of particle-substance, since the alternatives do not present themselves in physical perspective. The point where the possibilities fall beyond the scope of empirical tests is the point where the scientist runs out of physical terms with which to express them. Within the framework of his physical vocabulary and physical concepts, the case of T_1 and T_2 cannot arise.

Again, when you think about it, the fact that the limitation on empirical knowledge and the limitation on physical description come at the same point is hardly surprising. The reason for their coincidence is not to be found in a general verificationist theory of meaning – in the claim that we have no way of formulating a possibility that we cannot, in appropriate circumstances, test. Indeed, I shall argue that we *can* formulate some of the untestable possibilities concerning the intrinsic nature of matter, though not in *physical* terms. The reason is more specific. It is that our system of physical concepts and, correspondingly, our physical language, have evolved to meet the needs of empirical theory, and it is as a medium or a vehicle for empirical theory (whether the implicit theorizing of common sense or the explicit theorizing of science) that the system, or the language, acquires its unified physical character. Even if the intrinsic nature of matter can be transparently specified, the fact that it is empirically inscrutable ensures that it cannot be specified in physical terms.

APPENDIX: THE POWERS-THESIS

The only properties of fundamental particles which can be transparently specified in physical terms are (1) spatiotemporal properties, such as shape, size and velocity and (2) causal and dispositional properties, such as mutual obstructiveness, gravitational power and electrical charge. From this, I have concluded that, apart from their shape and size, the intrinsic nature of the particles (the intrinsic nature of, as it were, particle-substance) can, in physical terms, only be specified opaquely, as that on which their behavioural dispositions and causal powers are grounded. But is this conclusion justified? An alternative would be to say that the particles do not have the sort of intrinsic nature which I am supposing – that they are wholly characterized by the spatio-temporal, causal and dispositional properties which our physical language can specify and which empirical investigation can reveal. In particular, it might be claimed that each particle is, in itself, no more than a mobile cluster of causal powers, there being no 'substantial' space-occupant which possesses the powers and on whose categorical nature the powers are grounded. Such a thesis has been endorsed, in different forms, by a number of distinguished scientists and philosophers.[1] If it is coherent, the thesis certainly has some appeal. For there is a natural reluctance to postulate physical properties which are empirically inscrutable and not even transparently specifiable in physical terms.

But is the powers-thesis (PT) coherent? The main problem is that if all the fundamental particles are construed in this way, there seem to be no physical items in terms of whose behaviour the content of the powers could be specified, and consequently, it seems that, in the last analysis, there is nothing which the powers are powers to do. Let us begin with a concrete example. We will assume that atoms are the only fundamental particles and that all atoms are of exactly the same type. Now each atom has a number of causal powers. It has a power of resistance, whereby any two atoms are mutually obstructive. It has a power of gravitational attraction whereby, between any two atoms, there is a force of attraction inversely proportional to the square of their distance. It has a power of repulsion, whereby two atoms which collide, with certain velocities and directions, deflect each other in a certain way. And it has a number of other powers which we need not list. For PT to be true, it is necessary that some subset of these powers constitutes the essential nature of an atom. Let us suppose, for simplicity, that we select the power of resistance as the only (putatively) essential atomic power and leave the other powers to depend on the contingent laws of nature governing the behaviour of atoms. Thus each atom is construed as a mobile sphere of impenetrability, the behaviour and causal interaction of these spheres, apart from their mutual obstructiveness, being governed by additional laws. The problem arises when we ask: 'To what is a sphere of impenetrability impenetrable?' The answer is: 'To other atoms, i.e. to other spheres of impenetrability.' But this means that the specification of the content of the atom-constituting power is viciously regressive: each atom is a sphere of impenetrability to any other sphere of impenetrability to any other sphere of impenetrability ... and so on *ad infinitum*. From which it follows that the notion of such a power is incoherent, since there is nothing which the power is a power to do. To conceive of a sphere of impenetrability, we have to postulate some other type of space-occupant whose passage it is empowered to obstruct.

68

The problem is not avoided if we include further powers in the essential nature of an atom. Thus we might take the atomic nature to combine a power of resistance with a power of attraction, so that each atom is constituted by a mobile sphere of impenetrability surrounded by a more extensive (perhaps infinitely extended) field of gravitational potential (the field being structured, in accordance with the inverse-square-law, around the centre of the sphere). We could then try to specify the content of the power of resistance in terms of the behaviour of gravitational fields or specify the content of the power of attraction in terms of the behaviour of spheres of impenetrability. But neither specification blocks the regress, since it merely specifies the content of one power in terms of another. The only way of avoiding the regress, it seems, is to construe at least one of the powers as a power to affect the behaviour of some type of *substantial* space-occupant – an occupant with an intrinsic nature independent of its causal powers and dispositions. But such occupants are just what PT excludes. Admittedly, the exclusion of such occupants from the actual world is compatible with there being some *type* of substantial occupant in terms of which the content of the powers is to be specified. Thus it would be theoretically possible to construe atoms as spheres of impenetrability and construe impenetrability as the power to obstruct some *uninstantiated* type of voluminous stuff. But such a position would be manifestly perverse. Amongst other things, it would rob PT of all the advantages which were claimed for it, since, in this form, impenetrability itself would cease to be empirically detectable or transparently specifiable in physical terms. If there is to be any reason for postulating a type of substantial occupant which atoms have the power to obstruct, it must be a reason for construing atoms themselves as occupants of that type with the power to obstruct each other.

We have been considering the problem of content in the context of a particular example, in which we assumed that atoms are the only fundamental particles and that all atoms are of exactly the same type. But the problem itself is quite general and arises whatever fundamental particles we select and whatever differences of particle-type we introduce. The problem is simply that, in construing all the fundamental space-occupants as merely power-clusters, PT seems to eliminate the very items which we need as something for the powers to be powers to affect. If we postulate more types of particle, the problem may be temporarily concealed, since there is more room for manoeuvre (specifying the content of one type of particle in terms of the behaviour of another) before the threatened regress becomes apparent. But the threatened regress always becomes apparent if the question of specification is persistently pressed.

It is clear, then, that, if PT is to survive in any acceptable form, the content of the powers must be specifiable in terms of the behaviour of, or events in, things which are neither merely power-clusters nor substantial space-occupants. One possibility would be to try to specify the content of the powers in terms of the experiential responses of human subjects. Some powers (the first level powers) would be specified as powers to affect human experience; others (the second level powers), as powers to affect the spatiotemporal arrangement of first level powers; still others (the third level powers), as powers to affect the spatiotemporal arrangement of second level powers – and so on, as far as we need to go before invoking the framework of contingent law. But the trouble is that it is impossible to make sense of the first level powers without assuming either substantial space-occupants or power-clusters whose content is fixed in some independent way. This is obviously so in the case of our atomistic example (and, indeed, in any example which characterizes the physical world in a scientific way). For although atoms are endowed with powers to affect experience (e.g. each atom has the potential to form an element of experience-causing brain-states, as well as the potential to contribute, in innumerably many ways, to the causation of such brain-states), these powers are ones which the atoms can only possess by already possessing some more basic nature as occupants of space. Indeed, it is clear that these powers are ones which the atoms possess only contingently, through contingent psychophysical laws assigning experiential effects to brain-states. But the point also holds quite generally, however the physical world is conceived. Thus, for the sake of argument, we might conceive of the world as composed of space, time and fields of experience-causing potential (whether static or mobile), such that any subject who is located in such a field is thereby caused to have an experience of a certain type. But even here, we have to postulate some further type of physical occupant (i.e. the subject's body) to make sense of the subject's location in a field. And there is no point in construing these further occupants as mobile fields (or points) of experience-causing potential, since such occupants would merely reintroduce the problem they were designed to solve. As a last resort, we might revise the example in such a way as to make subject-location irrelevant. Thus, in place of the fields of potential we might postulate powers to cause certain types of experience in any subject who is in a certain mental condition – powers whose content can be specified without employing physical concepts at all. But, unless we postulate some additional physical states on which these powers are grounded, the effect of this revision would be to deprive the powers themselves of spatial location and hence deprive them of their physical status. Such powers, indeed, would be equivalent to purely psychological laws whereby a subject's prior mental condition causes him to have a certain type of experience. There could be psychological laws of this sort, but they could not, in the framework of physical realism, provide any ingredients for the physical world.

If the content of the powers is not specifiable in terms of human experience, the only other possibility would be to specify it in terms of the geometry of space (or more precisely, space-time). To see how we might develop this possibility, let us return to our original example which takes atoms as fundamental. Among the powers we have attributed to atoms is a power of gravitational attraction. In the classical (Newtonian) theory, the exercise of this power is thought of in terms of a *direct* causal influence of one atom on the behaviour of another. Two atoms attract each other with a force which is inversely proportional to the square of their distance, and there is no intervening mechanism, bridging the spatial distance, by which the force is mediated. But in the modern (Einsteinian) theory – the General Theory of Relativity – the force of attraction is mediated by the geometrical properties of the intervening space. Put crudely, the location of an atom at a certain point causes a curvature in the surrounding space and this curvature deflects the paths of other atoms towards that point. Thus instead of atoms directly acting on each other across a spatial distance, we have atoms acting on the geometry of space and the geometry of space acting on atoms. Admittedly, we should really speak here of the geometry of *space-time*, rather than of space, but in the present context, the difference need not concern us.[2]

This suggests the following version of PT. We construe each atom as, in itself, a mobile point-centre of space-bending force and then leave all the other properties of atoms to flow from the laws governing the behaviour of such centres in the geometrically changing space. This seems to avoid the problem of content, and in a way which fits the perspective of modern scientific theory.

However, the suggestion is open to a crucial objection. For there is no way of making sense of the claim that the space-bending forces are spatially located. It is true that, for each force, there is a point which is uniquely prominent in specifying its content – a point which forms, as it were, the focus of the geometrical effect. But this does not suffice to give the force itself (that which causes the geometrical effect) any genuine location – to make it point-centred in the suggested way. If we are tempted to think of the force as spatially located, it is only because we began by conceiving of it as something which an atom exerts, the presumption being that the location of the atom is already ensured by some independent aspect (e.g. its substantial character) of its nature. The mistake is then to suppose that location is retained when the whole atomic nature is confined to the exertion of this force. Once the atomic nature is thus confined, atoms are eliminated and the space-bending force becomes merely an unlocated causal constraint on the geometry of space at a certain time.

Of course, it might be suggested that, rather than postulate substantial space-occupants, whose intrinsic nature cannot be transparently specified in physical terms, we should settle for a physical world consisting solely of space, time (or space-time) and geometry-controlling laws. I doubt whether this theory is scientifically plausible: the fact that gravitational fields can be interpreted geometrically does not mean that all physical phenomena can be treated in a similar way. But, in any case, the theory is not a version of PT. It is not a way of construing the fundamental space-occupants as power-clusters, but the denial that there are any occupants at all.

My conclusion, therefore, is that the powers-thesis is incoherent. And consequently, I stand by my previous conclusion that, apart from their shape and size, the intrinsic nature of the fundamental space-occupants (assuming there are occupants at all) cannot be empirically discovered or transparently specified in physical terms.

5

MATTER IN SPACE

Apart from its specification as a substance 3-dimensionally extended in physical space, the intrinsic nature of matter cannot be
transparently specified in physical terms – at least it cannot, if, as
we have provisionally assumed, matter is devoid of the distinctively
sensible intrinsic qualities that feature in the content of sense-
experience. This is not merely a limitation on the scope of empirical
knowledge. It is also a limitation on the descriptive resources of our
physical language and system of physical concepts: beyond our
conception of it as a voluminous substance, we cannot so much as
envisage, in physical terms, what matter might be like in itself. To
this extent, at least, I have found support for the thesis I want to
establish, that, at the level of ultimate reality, the physical
description of the physical world is topic-neutral – neutral with
respect to intrinsic nature. And thus to this extent I have defended
mentalistic realism from the intuitive objection that physical items
have their own distinctively physical intrinsic character – a character to be specified in physical terms.

However, the specification of matter as a voluminous substance – as a substance 3-dimensionally extended in physical space – is
itself, one may suppose, to some degree topic-specific. Moreover,
on the face of it, it seems that the topic-specificity is enough to
exclude a mentalistic interpretation. One is inclined to say, like
Descartes, that the extendedness of material substance suffices to
make it non-mental and that the non-extendedness of mental
substance suffices to make it non-physical (though we would
presumably reject the full Cartesian view that the 3-dimensional

extendedness of matter constitutes its whole essence, with the consequence that matter and physical space are identical). To see whether this inclination is well founded, we obviously need to consider very carefully what can be said about the intrinsic nature of physical space and its role as a medium for material objects. Only then will we be in a position to decide what possibilities are left open by the conception of matter as a voluminous substance, and, in particular, whether they include mentalistic realism.

The most obvious thing we can specify about the intrinsic nature of physical space is its geometrical structure. It used to be thought that, leaving aside the question of whether physical space is bounded, its geometrical structure could be determined *a priori* by the application of Euclid's axioms. It is now generally agreed, and rightly, that this view is incorrect. It has been shown that there are other sets of axioms which are internally consistent but incompatible with Euclid's set at certain points, and it is hard to see how, other than by empirical tests, we could establish the appropriate set for physical space. Thus if our empirical measurements of the metrical properties of space consistently indicated some form of intrinsic curvature (analogous, for example, to the curvature of a spherical surface in plane geometry), and if there was no reason, other than adherence to the Euclidean axioms, for thinking that our measurements were systematically erroneous, there would be a strong case for concluding that physical space was non-Euclidean. Moreover, once we accept the possibility that physical space is non-Euclidean, we must accept the further possibility that its geometrical structure is not, as we intuitively suppose, homogeneous and static, but varies, in detail, from place to place and from time to time. And this, in effect, is what modern physics, in the form of the General Theory of Relativity, holds to be the case. For, in giving a purely geometrical account of gravitational fields, the General Theory postulates a 4-dimensional space-time continuum whose curvature varies from region to region (indeed, from point to point) with the varying density of matter. This theory has still to be reconciled with quantum mechanics, but in the sphere of astrophysics, which is its primary testing ground, it has received significant support.

Even if it goes against current scientific theory, it will be best, for the purposes of our discussion, if we retain the traditional view of physical space as uniformly Euclidean. The points I want to make do not require this view, but they are easier to make within its framework. Without the requisite mathematics, it is hard to come to terms with non-Euclidean geometry, and even harder to come to terms with the rippling curvatures of the space-time manifold. For most of us, the Euclidean view remains the one that is familiar and accessible, and we should try to see what is involved in the geometrical structure of a Euclidean space before we take on anything more complicated and more obscure.

In claiming that physical space is Euclidean, we are claiming that it conforms to the Euclidean axioms. But in the framework of co-ordinate geometry, this claim can be expressed more succinctly in the form of a single rule for determining the distance between any two points, given their co-ordinates. We are already assuming that physical space is a 3-dimensional continuum, and we will also assume, for the sake of argument (though the assumption is also intuitive), that it is unbounded, i.e. infinitely extended in all directions. Now suppose we select three infinitely extended straight lines which intersect at right angles at a certain point. By choosing a unit of measure (e.g. the metre) and taking the point of intersection as the origin, we can use the three lines as an axis-system which assigns to each point in physical space three numbers, in a certain order, each number giving the distance and direction of that point, in the chosen unit, along one of the axes. These three numbers, taken in the relevant order, are known as *co-ordinates*. Every point is uniquely defined by its three co-ordinates and every triple of real numbers (where each number can be either positive or negative) provides the co-ordinates for a unique point. The claim that physical space is Euclidean can now be expressed as the following principle:

> For any co-ordinate system of the kind just described and any points P_1 and P_2, if a, b and c are the co-ordinates for P_1 and a', b' and c' are, in the corresponding order, the co-ordinates for P_2, and if d is the distance between P_1 and P_2 (specified in the relevant unit of measure), then:
> $$d^2 = (a\text{-}a')^2 + (b\text{-}b')^2 + (c\text{-}c')^2$$

We may call this the *Pythagorean* principle, since it is simply the extension of Pythagoras' theorem to three dimensions. The Pythagorean principle assigns a Euclidean metric to every part of physical space and thereby ensures that the space conforms in every respect to the Euclidean axioms.

This account of the geometrical structure of physical space (i.e. its specification as an unbounded, 3-dimensional, Euclidean continuum) has made use of explicitly spatial concepts – concepts such as *point* and *distance*. I want now to provide an alternative and more formal specification which covers the same ground without the use of spatial concepts. We can then ask in what ways, if at all, this (more) formal specification fails to capture all we know about the intrinsic nature of physical space – both what we know *a priori*, from our very concept of such a space, and what we know *a posteriori*, from empirical investigation.

With *P* as a non-descriptive designator of physical space, the formal specification (FS) is as follows:[1]

For some *S*, some *D*, and some *f* and some *g*

(1) *S* is an uncountable set (a set with the same number of members as the set of real numbers).

(2) Each *S*-member is simple (it has no parts or members) and contingent (there is a possible world in which it does not exist).[2]

(3) *D* is an uncountable set of 2-place relations and each of these relations is, and is of logical necessity, irreflexive, symmetric, and non-transitive.

(4) For any pair of distinct *S*-members *x* and *y*, there is one and only one *D*-relation *R* such that *xRy*.

(5) For any *D*-relation *R* and *S*-members *x* and *y*, if *xRy*, then $\Box\, xRy$, and if $\sim xRy$, then $\Box \sim xRy$

(6) *f* is a 1-1 function from *D* to the set of all real numbers greater than 0.

(7) *g* is a 1-1 function from *S* to the set of all ordered triples of real numbers, both positive and negative.

(8) There is, independently of *f* and *g*, some natural way of ordering *D*-relations in a series (with no first or last members) such that, for any *D*-relations R_1 and R_2, R_1 is prior to R_2 iff $f(R_1) < f(R_2)$.

(9) For any *S*-members *x* and *y*, any *D*- relation *R* and any numbers *a, b, c, a', b', c'*, if *xRy* and $g(x) = \langle a, b, c \rangle$ and $g(y) = \langle a', b', c' \rangle$, then $(f(R))^2 = (a\text{-}a')^2 + (b\text{-}b')^2 + (c\text{-}c')^2$.

(10) *P* is the aggregate of all *S*-members.

It will help us to see the point of FS if, in reading through its clauses, we bear in mind the intended spatial interpretation. On this interpretation, S-members are the points of physical space (hence clauses (1), (2) and (10)) and D-relations are distance-relations between physical points (hence clauses (3), (4) and (5)). For any D-relation R, $f(R)$ measures the distance between R-related points (hence clauses (6) and (8), with f reflecting some natural ordering of the D-relations) and the network of f-distances meets the requirements of a 3-dimensional Euclidean geometry (hence clauses (7) and (9), with g assigning co-ordinates to points). Physical space is unbounded (hence, in clause (7), g is a 1-1 function from S to the set of *all* ordered triples of real numbers, both positive and negative).

Given our assumptions (that physical space is unbounded, 3-dimensional and Euclidean), FS seems to provide an adequate specification of the geometrical structure of physical space, though without the use of explicitly spatial concepts. In Part III, when we come to examine the nature of physical geometry more closely we shall see that this is not so and that FS needs to be both revised and supplemented in certain crucial respects. But for the time being, I shall take it as adequate for our purposes, since its deficiencies do not affect the present issue.

FS (or so we shall assume) specifies the geometrical structure of physical space. But it does so in a way which is, in respect of the intrinsic nature of physical points and physical distance, topic-neutral: we are not told what the D-relations are or what S-members are like in themselves. The crucial question is: does this formal specification express all we know about the intrinsic nature of physical space? Does it exhaust our knowledge, both *a priori* and *a posteriori*, of what physical space is like in itself?

Our initial inclination is to say that it does not. For it seems, on the face of it, that FS does not even do justice to our intuitive conception of P as a genuine *space*, let alone our conception of it as a *physical* space. Part of the reason for this may be that we ordinarily conceive of a space in visual terms and attribute to it an intrinsic character distinctively matching our visual conception. In evaluating the adequacy of FS, this is something which we must discount. For we are working on the assumption that, at the level of ultimate reality, the physical world is devoid of any distinctively sensible intrinsic qualities. In particular, we are assuming that, in its intrinsic nature, physical space is no closer to its representation in one sense-realm than in another, so long as both realms provide an equally adequate representation of its geometrical structure. (The assumption, of course, is one which we shall have to justify in due course.) But there is another and, for our purposes, a more important factor. We think of a genuine space as something in which other things can be located – as something whose regions can be occupied and in which events and processes can occur. Yet there is nothing in FS which characterizes P as a space in this sense: there is nothing in the formal specification which indicates the capacity of P to form a medium for other things – its capacity to provide room for occupants and location for events. It would be easy to conclude from this that FS does not express all we know about the intrinsic nature of physical space. For it is natural to assume that our very knowledge that P *is* a genuine space stems from some knowledge of its intrinsic nature.

Such a conclusion, however, would be too hasty. It is true that FS fails to characterize P as a genuine space. But it does not follow from this that we have any further knowledge of its intrinsic nature. After all, the failure to characterize P as a genuine space stems from the failure to characterize P as a potential medium. And even if the role of P as a potential medium is a consequence of its intrinsic nature, there may be a topic-neutral way of specifying that role – a way which, beyond what is expressed in FS, provides no transparent specification of what physical space is like in itself. In any case, if we do have some further knowledge of the intrinsic nature of physical space, in what does that knowledge consist? Nothing seems to be forthcoming here other than the recognition that P is a genuine space. And this does not serve to specify (at least transparently) the intrinsic nature of P, if our only account of what makes something a genuine space is in terms of its role as a medium.

Following this line of thought, we might try to remedy the deficiency in FS by simply adding, as a further clause, the claim that P forms, or has the capacity to form, a medium for material objects – that any continuous 3-dimensional region of P (as defined by the formal specification of geometrical structure) has the capacity to be, at any time, materially occupied. But this just invites the further question as to how, in the context of FS, the notion of occupancy is to be understood. This notion is clear enough if the notion of a genuinely *spatial* region is taken for granted. But the latter is just what we are not taking for granted, but trying to explain in terms of occupancy. There is a danger here of being trapped in a circle of incomprehension – having nothing but an unexplained notion of occupancy to explain our idea of space and nothing but an unexplained notion of space to explain our idea of occupancy.

The solution, it seems, must be to characterize occupancy itself in an equally formal way. Thus just as we have specified the geometrical structure of physical space in terms of certain formal conditions met by an unspecified set of relations (D) in an unspecified domain of entities (S), so we might try to specify the role of physical space as a medium in terms of certain formal conditions met by an unspecified relation (intuitively, occupancy) holding between portions of matter and members of S. To make things relatively simple (with no pretensions to scientific accuracy), let us suppose that any parcel of matter exhaustively divides into spherical particles (atoms), all particles being of the same size, and each having no internal gaps. Let us also adopt the spatial principle of individuation, in its strongest form, whereby each portion of matter is, at any time, individuated by the region it occupies, so that it is logically impossible for distinct portions to occupy the same region at the same time. And let us further adopt a spatial principle of persistence, whereby each portion of matter persists by following a spatiotemporally continuous path. Then, as an attempt to characterize occupancy in formal terms, we might expand FS into FS_1:

For some S, some D, some f, some g, some O, some n

(1) – (10) as in FS.

(11) O is a 3-place relation and it is logically necessary that, for any x, y, and z, if $O(x,y,z)$, then x is an atom, y is an S-member and z is a time.

(12) n is a real number and $n > O$.

(13) It is logically necessary that, for any time t and any atom x, there is an S-member y which is the O-centre of x at t, i.e.
   (a) $O(x, y, t)$;
   (b) for any S-member z and D-relation R, if yRz then: $O(x, z, t)$ iff $f(R) \leq n$.

(14) It is logically necessary that, for any time t, any atoms x and y, any S-members w and z, and any D-relation R, if w is

the O-centre of x at t and z is the O-centre of y at t and wRz, then $f(R) \geq 2n$.

(15) It is logically necessary that, for any atom x, any change in the O-centre of x over time is, relative to g, continuous, i.e. if c is the variable O-centre of x, any change in the value of $g(c)$ over time is numerically continuous.

The additional clauses, (11)-(15), are intented to fix O as the relation of occupancy holding between atoms, physical points and times, so that $O(x, y, z)$ iff x is an atom, y is a point, z is a time and x occupies y at z (i.e. y is a point in or on the region which x occupies at z). The number n measures the radius of an atom in the framework of f and g. It is logically necessary that, at each time, each atom occupies all and only the points of some spherical P-region of radius n (hence clause (13)). Given the principle of individuation, it is also logically necessary that, at each time, distinct atoms occupy the points of *non-overlapping* regions (hence clause (14)). Finally, it is logically necessary that, over time, each atom follows a spatiotemporally continuous path (hence clause (15)).

Unfortunately, however, these additional clauses do not suffice to characterize the relation of occupancy or to express the sense in which physical space forms a medium for material objects. In the first place, even if we interpret S-members as the points of physical space, there are other relations (indeed, infinitely many), in addition to occupancy, which meet the specified conditions. For example, let O be the relation which holds for an atom x, an S-member y and a time t iff there is an S-member z and numbers a, b and c such that $g(z) = \langle a, b, c \rangle$ and $g(y) = \langle a + 1, b + 1, c + 1 \rangle$ and x occupies z at t. O then meets all the specified conditions, its extension being isomorphic with, and geometrically indistinguishable from, the extension of occupancy. But, *ex hypothesi*, O is not the relation of occupancy. The points to which an atom is O-related at a given time are not the points it occupies but the points whose co-ordinates (supplied by g) are related to the co-ordinates of the points it occupies in the specified way. Secondly, apart from the reference we have independently assigned to 'P', the clauses of FS$_1$ do not even force us to interpret S-members as the points of physical space. Thus suppose we (a) take S to be the set of all properties x such that, for some physical point y, x is the property of being identical with *y* and (b) take *O* to be the relation which holds for an atom *x*, an *S*-member *y* and a time *t* iff, for some physical point *z*, *y* is the property of being identical with *z* and *x* occupies *z* at *t*. It is easy enough to fix *D*, *f*, *g*, and *n* correspondingly, so as to make this interpretation meet all the requirements of FS_1 (leaving aside the reference of '*P*')[3]. But, *ex hypothesi*, *S*-members would not, on this interpretation, be the points of physical space. Nor, indeed, would they be the points of any genuine space, and nor, in consequence, would *O* be any form of genuine occupancy.

In both these respects, what is essentially wrong with FS_1 is that it fails to characterize the special intimacy of the occupancy-relation. It allows the deviant interpretations because it fails to express the distinctive way in which, as it were, an object *coincides with* the region it fills – the object drawing its form from the region and the region drawing its state from the object. Noting the failure, however, does not suggest any obvious remedy. For how exactly is the intimacy of occupancy to be expressed? If we invoke explicitly spatial concepts, we shall be going round in circles. If we continue to renounce such concepts, we seem destined to fall short of our target. Until we have solved the problem of occupancy, it is hard to reach any firm conclusion as to whether FS expresses all we know about the intrinsic nature of physical space.

The solution, it seems to me, is to continue with the relatively formal approach, but change our ontological perspective. As we shall see, there may be alternative solutions involving different changes. But before we consider the alternatives, I want to recapitulate a point which came up in an earlier chapter.

In chapter 3, I pointed out that physical realism leaves room for some selectivity in the kind of physical items that are taken as ultimate. The realist is committed to denying that ultimate reality is wholly non-physical; but he is not obliged to accept the ultimacy of every kind of physical entity and fact that we ordinarily recognize or that are ordinarily recognized by the experts in the relevant field of inquiry. As we saw, this point has two aspects – one trivial and the other important. The trivial aspect is that no realism, however comprehensive, can accept as ultimate all that we accept as genuine. For there are kinds of logical sustainment and creation whose recognition is already implicit in our initial conception of the items thus created or sustained. Thus any realism must acknowledge that the weight-relation between two objects is logically sustained by their individual weights and that an aggregate is logically created by the existence of its parts. This kind of selectivity is purely trivial: it does not carry so much as a hint of anti-realism. But physical realism can also be selective in a more important way, where the restrictions on the composition of ultimate reality provide, relative to our initial conception of the physical world, a significant change in ontological and factual perspective – where there is a genuine confinement of the physical realm within narrower limits than we ordinarily recognize. It is for such a case, where the selectivity reduces the scope of the realism, that we have reserved the title 'selective realism'. The exclusion of distinctively sensible qualities from the sphere of ultimate physical reality is an example of selective realism in this sense.

Now it is the possibility of a more radically selective realism which is the key to the solution of our present problem. So far we have been assuming, at least implicitly, that both physical space and its fundamental occupants are ontologically primitive – that both are ingredients of ultimate physical reality. But it seems to me that, to understand the nature of occupancy – in particular, to understand the special intimacy of the connection between the occupiers and the occupied – we must revise that assumption in one of two ways. We must *either* construe physical particles as the logical creation of facts about physical space, in such a way as to be constituted as occupants of that space, *or* we must construe physical space as the logical creation of facts about physical particles, in such a way as to be constituted as a medium for those particles. Following one alternative, we accept space as ontologically primitive, but take the existence of the particles to be logically sustained by properties of points or regions at times, together with laws which ensure that the spatiotemporal distribution of these properties exhibits the kinds of uniformity and continuity characteristic of mobile, space-occupying continuants. Following the other alternative, we accept particles as ontologically primitive, but take the existence of space to be logically sustained by properties of, and relations between, particles at times, together with laws which ensure that the distribution of these properties and relations exhibits the kinds of uniformity and continuity characteristic of a containing, 3-dimensional medium. In the first case, we take the particles to be nothing over and above the distribution and nomological organization of the properties of space at times. In the second case, we take space to be nothing over and above the distribution and nomological organization of properties of particles at times. In either case, the relation of occupancy takes care of itself, since it becomes part and parcel of the way in which either the space or the particles acquire their existence. One way, the particles are ontologically constituted as occupants of the space. The other way, the space is ontologically constituted as a medium for the particles. Either way, we so characterize the ontological status of space and its occupants that there is no further question about the nature of occupancy.

We now have a choice between alternative strategies for explaining occupancy, the one assigning a primitive status to the medium and a derivative status to the occupants, the other assigning a primitive status to the occupants and a derivative status to the medium. Each of these strategies accounts for the special intimacy of occupancy, and each promises to yield a characterization of matter-in-space in a way which both breaks out of the circle and achieves its target. As far as I can see, there is no other strategy with any prospect of success. So how do we decide between them?

Well, on the face of it, the decision is clear. For while both strategies meet the requirements we have so far specified, only the first satisfies our intuitions in three further respects. In the first place, we ordinarily think of material objects as *essentially* spatial: we are prepared to assert not merely (a) that it is logically impossible for something which has no location in physical space to qualify as a material object, but also (b) that, for any material object, it is logically impossible for that object to exist without location in physical space. We think that something only qualifies as a material object if the occupancy of physical space is a logically essential attribute of *that thing*. Secondly, and this is a development of the first point, we think of physical space not merely as containing material objects, but as constituting the very form of their existence. We speak of such objects as *existing in* space; and by this we mean, not merely that they exist and have spatial location, but that they exist *by and through* their spatial location – that location in physical space is, as we may put it, their *mode of being*. Thirdly, and in consequence, we think of physical space as forming, in conjunction with time, the framework of identity for its material occupants. We think of a portion of matter as individuated at a time by the region it occupies, and as persisting through time by the following of a spatiotemporally continuous path. (These are, at least, our *basic* principles of individuation and persistence, even if we may want to refine them to deal with certain abnormal cases.) Now none of these intuitions can be retained if, adopting the second strategy, we take physical space to be the logical creation of pre-spatial facts about particles. For, on such an account, the particles would have the capacity to exist and persist without spatial location, since the existence of space would depend on certain contingent facts about them – facts about the distribution and nomological organization of their properties. Even if the particles would only qualify as *particles* in virtue of having spatial location, location would be a merely contingent attribute – something which the entities which qualify as particles could do without. In contrast, we can retain and, indeed, explain the intuitions if, adopting the first strategy, we take particles to be the logical creation of pre-particle facts about space. For if particles are ontologically constituted as occupants of physical space, it follows automatically that, for them, the occupancy of space is an essential attribute. Moreover, it follows automatically that space will constitute the very form of their existence and, with time, the framework of their identity. It is conceivable, perhaps, that subsequent investigation may lead us to revise our intuitions (I shall take up this point later[4]). But, as things stand, it is clearly right to begin by pursuing the first (space-primitive) strategy before we consider anything else.[5]

How, then, is the space-primitive strategy to be developed? Well, let us continue with the supposition that any parcel of matter exhaustively divides into spherical atoms, all of the same size and with no internal gaps. Let us also, for simplicity (again, with no pretensions to scientific accuracy), add to this the supposition that the intrinsic character of matter is invariant over space and time, so that each atom has the same intrinsic character at all times and all atoms have the same intrinsic character at each time. And taking r as the radius-size of an atom, let us use the expression 'ϕ-region' to signify a spherical region of radius r. Now to construe atoms as the logical creation of pre-atomic facts about space, we must postulate, as underlying material occupancy, an intrinsic property M, applicable to points at times (if you prefer, applicable to point-moments) and a set L of laws, controlling the instantiation of M, such that L ensures, amongst other things, that:

(1) At any time, the total set of M-instantiating points exhaustively divides into non-overlapping ϕ-regions;
(2) All changes over time in M-instantiation are spatiotemporally continuous.

Let us say that a region-moment (i.e. a region-at-a-time) is *M-pervaded* iff all the points in or on that region instantiate M at that time. Then we know, from the partial specification of L, that the total distribution of M over points at times exhaustively divides into a set of series of ϕ-region-moments of M-pervasion, where each series is spatiotemporally continuous and ordered with respect to time, and where ϕ-regions paired with the same moment in different series do not overlap. Moreover, since this aspect of the distribution is guaranteed by law, through the ensuring of (1) and (2), we can infer that in each series the persistence of M-pervasion through the successive region-moments is a causally continuous process, in which, as it were, the deposit of pervasion is passed by each region-moment to its successor.[6] It is not difficult to see how, with this as the underlying reality, atoms (in the form we have supposed) are the logical creation. For we can see in each spatiotemporally and causally continuous series just what is needed to constitute the path of a derivative spherical continuant – a continuant whose existence is logically sustained by, and nothing over and above, the successive instances of M-pervasion, together with the laws which impose on these instances their spherical and (collectively) spatiotemporally continuous form. Atoms are the continuants – the mobile occupants of space – which preserve their identity through the region-moments they successively occupy. And underlying and wholly constituting them are the spatiotemporal distribution of M and the laws which control it.

We can now see how to strengthen FS so as to express the role of P as a medium for material objects and, in consequence, express its character as a genuine space. It is simply a matter of adding to FS (within the scope of the initial quantifiers) (a) a specification of facts about S-members which suffice for the logical creation of P-occupying continuants, in the way just explained, and (b) the claim that material particles are the continuants thus created. Exactly how we do this depends, of course, on our empirical theory of matter. But if we continue with the same simple assumptions (i.e. divisibility into equi-sized spherical atoms and invariance of intrinsic character over space and time), the result will be FS_2:

> For some S, some D, some f, some g, some M, some n, some L
> (1) – (10) as in FS.
> (11) M is an intrinsic property, distributed over S-members at times.
> (12) n is a real number and $n > O$.
> (13) L is a set of laws, controlling the distribution of M, and L ensures (amongst other things) that:[7]
> > (a) For any time t, there is a set α of sets of S-members such that
> > (i)   no two sets in α have more than one S-member in common;
> > (ii) for each set β in α, there is a β-member x such that, for any S-member y and D-relation R, if xRy then: y is a member of β iff $f(R) \leq n$;
> > (iii) for any S-member x, $M(x,t)$ iff x is a member of a member of α.
> > (b) Any change over time in the momentary distribution of M over S-members is, relative to g, continuous, i.e. if we say that M is *assigned* to triple x at time t iff, for some S-member y, $M(y,t)$ and $g(y) = x$, then all changes over time in the assignment of M to triples are numerically continuous.
> (14) Atoms are the logical creation of L plus the S-time distribution of M (M becoming, as it were, in the framework of L, the property of being materially occupied).

Given our ontological strategy (space primitive, matter derivative) and given our assumptions about space (that it is an unbounded, 3-dimensional, Euclidean continuum) and assumptions about matter (its atomistic and invariant character), FS_2 provides an adequate specification of the geometrical structure of physical space and its role as a medium for material objects. (Here, with respect to geometrical structure, I continue to ignore those deficiencies in FS which are to be corrected in Part III.) At the same time, the specification is topic-neutral: it does not reveal the intrinsic nature of, so to speak, the substance of physical space (i.e. the intrinsic nature of S-members) nor does it reveal the intrinsic nature of physical distance (i.e. the identity of the *D*-relations). Indeed, discarding, as it does, all explicitly spatial concepts and any explicit concept of occupancy, FS_2 is *explicitly* topic-neutral: it makes it clear that the intrinsic nature of points and distance is something it does *not* reveal. Obviously, for different assumptions about space and matter, we could construct a different topic-neutral specification along the same general lines.

What conclusions, then, are we to draw with respect to what remains concealed? It seems to me that there are three, the second and third being exactly parallel to the conclusions we have already drawn, in the previous chapter, with respect to the intrinsic nature of matter.

(1) Apart from its contingency and geometrical structure, as specified in FS, we have no knowledge (i.e. transparent knowledge) of the intrinsic nature of physical space. The impression that we do have such knowledge stems either from our conception of space in distinctively sensible (in particular, visual) terms or from our conception of space as a medium for material objects. The first source is to be discounted, given our assumption that physical space does not have a distinctively sensible intrinsic character. The second source too is to be discounted, since the role of space as a medium is adequately specified in a topic-neutral way.

(2) A transparent specification of the intrinsic nature of physical points and physical distance lies outside the scope of empirical discovery. The most we can empirically discover is the geometrical structure of physical space, the role of that structure in providing a framework of spatial arrangement for physical objects and the causal contribution of such arrangement (by, for example, laws of motion and gravity) to the behaviour of the objects thus arranged. The reason for this is the same as the reason for the corresponding restriction on our empirical knowledge of the properties of matter, or, in our new ontological perspective, on our empirical knowledge of those intrinsic states of points and regions which underlie the existence of matter. The point is that if there were alternative theories which differed in their characterization of the intrinsic nature of physical space (i.e. the intrinsic nature of points

and distance), but agreed in their specification of i
geometrical structure, of its role as a spatial medium and
the framework of natural law, there would be no empiric
way of deciding between them. For in terms of accuracy
testable prediction and structure of explanation the tw
theories would be indistinguishable.[8]

(3) This limitation on the scope of empirical knowledge
matched by a co-extensive limitation on what we ca
express or conceive of in *physical* terms. A transpare
specification of the intrinsic nature of physical points a
physical distance is not only beyond the scope of empiric
discovery, but also beyond the resources of our physic
language and our system of physical concepts. Apart fro
its contingency and geometrical structure, as specified
FS, we cannot so much as form a conception, in physic
terms, of what physical space might be like in itself.

As I have said, the last two conclusions are exactly parallel to t
conclusions we have already reached with respect to the intrins
nature of matter. Put together, the two sets of conclusions yield t
general conclusion that, whatever the nature of ultimate physic
reality, its physical description is topic-neutral – a descriptic
which, beyond a specification of formal structure and nomologic
organization, conceals the intrinsic nature of both physical spa
and its fundamental occupants. This is the thesis which I set out
defend.

At this stage, of course, the defence is only provisional. For
rests on the assumption, as yet unjustified, that the physical wor
is devoid of any distinctively sensible intrinsic qualities. It is th
assumption, in a slightly modified form, that I shall try to justify
the next chapter. Once this has been done, we can then go on
consider, in more detail, how the topic-neutrality of physic
description bears on the issue of mentalistic realism.

6

THE CONFINEMENT OF QUALIA

Over the last two chapters, I have argued for the thesis that, whatever the nature of ultimate physical reality, its physical description is, in a certain sense, topic-neutral – a description which, beyond a specification of structure and laws, conceals the intrinsic nature of what it describes. Thus, in chapter 4, I argued that, whatever occupants of physical space we take as fundamental, it is impossible to provide, in physical terms, a transparent specification of their intrinsic properties beyond a specification of their shape and size and other aspects of spatial or spatiotemporal arrangement. Beyond this, we can, in physical terms, only specify their intrinsic properties *opaquely*, as those properties, whatever they are, which, in conjunction with the laws of nature, sustain certain causal powers and sensitivities. Again, in chapter 5, I argued that it is impossible to provide, in physical terms, a transparent specification of the intrinsic nature of physical space beyond a formal specification (as in FS) of its geometrical structure – a specification which does not reveal what physical points and physical distance are like in themselves. Now in arguing for this thesis of topic-neutrality, I have assumed throughout (with respect to both physical space and its occupants) that, at the level of ultimate reality, physical items do not have any distinctively sensible characteristics apart from their dispositions to appear in certain ways to human percipients. I have assumed that, ultimately, physical objects have no colour, odour, flavour or any other of the so-called secondary qualities, except in the form of powers to produce certain kinds of sense-experience in us. And I have assumed that physical space does not resemble its representation in any particular sense-realm (that it is not, in intrinsic nature, distinctively visual or tactual or kinaesthetic or in any other way sense-realm-specific) beyond the extent to which that representation captures its geometrical structure. Someone who rejected these assumptions could reject the topic-neutrality thesis. He could claim that (at least part of) the intrinsic nature of (at least some) physical items can be transparently specified in physical terms by a specification of their intrinsic sensible qualities. He could claim, for example, that even at the level of ultimate reality, material objects have sensible colour and visual shape, and that, to this extent, their intrinsic nature falls within the scope of physical description. It is time to consider whether my assumptions can be justified.

Let me begin by stating more precisely what these assumptions are and what it is that I wish to defend. I shall use the term 'sense-awareness' to signify the 'presentative' component in perceptual awareness, i.e. what is left of perceptual awareness when we subtract elements of recognition and interpretation, and I shall use the term 'sensation' (or sometimes 'sense-experience') to signify an episode of sense-awareness. I shall use the term 'sense-quale', in a somewhat broad sense, to denote those qualitative items (e.g. qualities, relations, modes of arrangement) which satisfy the following two conditions: firstly, each item either is or is capable of being an element or feature (however specific or generic) of the content of a sensation; secondly, for each item, it is logically impossible to have a transparent conception of it – a conception which reveals the item's essential nature – except by knowing what it is or would be like, subjectively, to have a sensation of whose content it forms an element or feature. The point of this second condition is to ensure that sense-qualia are *distinctively* sensible and lie outside the scope of a topic-neutral specification of the physical world. Two examples of sense-qualia, both drawn from the visual realm, are *sensible colours* (the sort of colours which occur in the content of visual sensations) and distinctively visual modes of spatial arrangement (the sort of modes by which sensible colours can be structured in a visual array). Now what I have assumed, in arguing for the topic-neutrality thesis, is that sense-qualia have no ultimate physical realization – that, at the level of ultimate reality, physical items have no distinctively sensible characteristics in virtue of which they resemble, in ways which transcend topic-neutral structure, the content of any sensation. I shall call this the *exclusion-thesis*, and the opposing claim, that some sense-qualia have an ultimate physical realization, I shall call *sensible realism*. Of course, even if some sense-qualia do have an ultimate physical realization, it is not *as* physically realized that they feature in the content of sense-awareness. For (as the case of hallucination shows), given any sensation *S*, it is logically possible for there to be a sensation *S'* (perhaps *S* itself) such that (1) *S* and *S'* have exactly the same intrinsic psychological character and are, therefore, qualitatively identical in content, and (2) there is no physical item which, in having *S'*, the subject of *S'* perceives. So whatever the nature of sense-awareness (and this is something which I shall consider presently), it is never, as such, the awareness of some physical item (i.e. of some sensible portion of the physical world), even if, on occasions, the awareness of a physical item is something which it mediates.

Although the exclusion-thesis is what I have so far assumed, it is a subtly different thesis which I want to defend, namely that sense-qualia have no ultimate *non-mental* realization – more precisely, no ultimate realization *outside the content of sense-awareness*. I shall call this the *confinement-thesis*. The confinement-thesis is, in different ways, both stronger and weaker than the exclusion-thesis. It is stronger in virtue of excluding one possibility which the exclusion-thesis leaves open, namely that, for some sense-qualia, there is a form of ultimate realization which is neither physical nor sensory. It is weaker in virtue of leaving open one possibility which the exclusion-thesis excludes, namely that, for some sense-qualia, there is a form of ultimate realization which is both physical and sensory. The first difference (the respect in which the confinement-thesis is stronger) is of no consequence, since the physical and sensory modes of realization are clearly exhaustive. But the second difference (the respect in which the confinement-thesis is weaker) is crucial. As we have seen, physical realism divides into a *standard* version, which takes the physical world to be non-mental, and a *mentalistic* version, which takes it to be mental. Correspondingly, sensible realism divides into a standard version, which takes the physical realization of qualia to be non-sensory, and a mentalistic version, which takes it to be sensory. Since I do not want to exclude

the possibility of mentalistic realism – indeed, my aim is t
establish its coherence, subject to the coherence of realism itself
it is only the standard version of sensible realism which
am concerned to refute. Moreover, this is all I have to refute fo
the purposes of the topic-neutrality thesis. For if sense-quali
are physically realized, it is only if their realization
non-sensory – outside the content of sense-awareness – that
falls within the scope of physical description in the relevant sens
It is only if their physical realization is non-sensory that it is, a
it were, distinctively physical and thus capable of sustaining th
claim that (at least part of) the intrinsic nature of (at lea
some) physical items can be transparently specified in physica
terms.

Standard sensible realism, the thesis that some sense-qualia hav
an ultimate and distinctively physical (i.e. non-sensory) realizatio
can be developed in two quite different ways, as either (a) a form o
naive realism or (b) a supplement to scientific theory. Taken in th
first way, the thesis is simply an endorsement of the naiv
assumption that, subject to certain corrections for perspective an
other conditions of observation, physical items really are (and a
ultimately and independently of sense-awareness) as they sensib
appear. It asserts, for example, that grass possesses, ultimately an
independently of any visual sensation, the quale of greenne
which it visually presents when observed in daylight, and th
sugar possesses, ultimately and independently of any gustato
sensation, the quale of sweetness which we taste when we eat
Whatever its intuitive appeal, it is hard to reconcile this naive for
of sensible realism with the scientific findings. According to scienc
grass looks green, when observed in daylight, because it is dispos
to reflect certain wavelengths of light, and what disposes it to refle
these wavelengths is not its possession of a colour-quale, but i
atomic structure. Likewise, according to science, sugar tastes swe
when eaten, because it is disposed to cause certain chemic
changes in the taste-receptors on the tongue and palate, and wh
disposes it to cause these changes is not its possession of
flavour-quale, but its chemical composition. In the light of th
scientific findings, naive sensible realism is seen to be bo
unwarranted and gratuitous. If an object's colour is causal
irrelevant to its visual appearance, we might just as well suppo
that only invisible objects, like air, have any colour or that a

objects are uniformly pink. And if an object's flavour is causally irrelevant to its gustatory appearance, we might just as
well suppose that only tasteless (i.e. apparently flavourless) substances have flavour or that all substances are uniformly sour.
Once the scientific facts are known, we have no reason for taking sensible appearance as a basis for the ultimate ascription
of colours or flavours to physical objects in any form – or,
indeed, as a basis for the ultimate ascription of any other sense-
qualia.

What presents a more serious challenge to my position is the case
where standard sensible realism is developed as a supplement to
scientific theory. As we have seen in previous chapters, scientific
explanation, however fundamental, does not reveal the intrinsic
nature of the physical world beyond a specification of its structure
and laws, and, consequently, it leaves a gap in specification to
which some form of sensible realism might be thought a natural
response. Thus given the scientific explanation of colour-
appearance (in terms of an object's atomic structure and the effect
of that structure on the absorption and reflection of light), it would
indeed be wholly gratuitous to ascribe (i.e. ultimately ascribe)
sense-qualia to physical objects *on the basis of how they look,* since
the explanation leaves no gap which *such* ascriptions could fill. But,
at the same time, the explanation does leave a gap, since it does not
reveal the intrinsic nature of the physical entities in terms of which
colour-appearance is explained. It does not reveal, beyond a
specification of their spatiotemporal arrangement, the intrinsic
nature of light and fundamental material particles; nor does
it reveal, beyond a specification of its geometrical structure,
the intrinsic nature of physical space. We have no way of empirically discovering what these intrinsic natures are. But, just
because of this, we cannot dismiss the hypothesis that they are
made up of sense-qualia. Unlike the naive form of sensible
realism, such a hypothesis, while speculative, is not gratuitous. For it fills a gap in the scheme of scientific explanation. It
goes beyond science at the point where scientific progress is
blocked.

To take a simple example (one which makes no claim to scientific
accuracy), suppose science shows the physical world to be composed of the following elements:

(1) time;
(2) an unbounded, 3-dimensional, Euclidean space;
(3) a homogeneous 3-dimensionally extended substance (matter), each portion of matter being a mobile occupant of the space and being individuated, at any time, by its spatial position;
(4) a set L of physical laws which control the spatiotemporal distribution of matter (e.g. Newton's laws of motion and gravity, with quantity of matter as mass).

Following the strategy developed in chapter 5, we will assume that matter is ontologically derivative – that its existence is logically sustained by certain intrinsic states of regions at times, together with a framework of law controlling the way these states are spatiotemporally distributed. In particular, we will suppose that there is a region-pervading quality Q such that ultimate physical reality consists of:

(1) time;
(2) an unbounded, 3-dimensional Euclidean space;
(3) a distribution of Q over regions at times;
(4) a set L' of physical laws which control the distribution of Q, ensuring those distributive uniformities and continuities required for Q-pervasion to amount to material occupancy.

On this supposition, the spatiotemporal distribution of matter and the matter-controlling set of laws L are nothing over and above the spatiotemporal distribution of Q and the Q-controlling set of laws L'. We are now left with the crucial questions: What is Q? And what, beyond geometrical structure, is the intrinsic nature of the physical space? Science does not and cannot provide the answers. So science leaves open the following hypothesis H:

(a) Q is a sense-quality (a quality which is a sense-quale).
(b) Physical space has a distinctively sensible intrinsic character appropriate to its role as a medium for Q.

More specifically, science leaves open the hypothesis H':

(a') Q is a colour.
(b') Physical space has a distinctively visual character.

To make (b') more precise, let V be that 3-place sense-relation

94

(relation which is a sense-quale) such that it is logically necessary that, in the domain of visual field places, V holds for $\langle x,y,z \rangle$ iff x is closer to y than to z. Then H' might be re-formulated as:

(a') Q is a colour.
(b*) It is logically necessary that, for any three points x, y and z of physical space, x is closer to y than to z iff $V(x,y,z)$.

Of course, given the facts of visual perspective, (b*) does not entail that whenever V holds for a triple of visual field places, it also holds for the triple of physical points which these places perceptually represent. (b*) merely requires that whatever is distinctive about relative closeness in a visual field (so as to transcend a purely formal specification of geometrical structure) is also true of relative closeness in physical space, irrespective of how visual fields and physical space are perceptually related.

I have said that the scientific version of standard sensible realism (as exemplified by H and H') presents a more serious challenge to my position than the naive version. And the reason for this is simply that the scientific version, being deliberately fashioned to fit the scientific findings, is protected against any objections to sensible realism which such findings might pose. None the less, since the two versions differ only in scientific plausibility, I need a general argument which refutes standard sensible realism as such and establishes that sense-qualia have no ultimate realization, in whatever form, outside the content awareness. Moreover, it is clear that this argument will have to be of an *a priori* kind. To establish the confinement-thesis, it will have to establish it as a conceptual truth.

In developing this argument, it will be convenient to focus attention on the qualia drawn from a particular sense-realm. And here I choose the visual realm, for two reasons. In the first place, the visual realm provides, in the most conspicuous form, a distinctively sensible mode of spatial arrangement which could be taken as exemplifying the intrinsic nature of physical space. (While it is clear that spatial arrangement features in the *interpretative* content of tactual and kinaesthetic perception, it is harder to detect it – in, as it were, a raw presentative form – as part of the content of tactual and kinaesthetic *sensations*.) Secondly, and at least partly for the first reason, a standard sensible realism developed in terms of *visual* qualia – what I shall call, for short, *visual realism* – is, I think, by far the most plausible version and the hardest for me to meet. If standard sensible realism is coherent at all, it should at least be coherent when applied to the visual realm.

I take visual realism to involve either or both of the following two claims:

(1) Certain colours (colour-qualia) have an ultimate non-sensory realization in physical space.

(2) Physical space has (and has outside the content of visual awareness) a distinctively visual character: it instantiates certain visual space-qualia (i.e. certain spatial relations or modes of spatial arrangement which occur in the content of visual awareness and which, however generic, fall beyond the scope of a formal geometrical specification).

To refute visual realism, I have, therefore, to refute both claims. I have to establish both that colours cannot have an ultimate non-sensory realization and that physical space cannot have, outside the content of visual awareness, a distinctively visual character. However, the first thing to notice is that these two tasks are, in effect, equivalent. If colour-qualia are capable of an ultimate realization in physical space, physical space must have a distinctively visual character. Likewise, if physical space has a distinctively visual character, it must have the capacity to be a medium for the ultimate realization of sensible colour. The reason, in both cases, is that for a space to have a distinctively visual character just is for it to be the sort of space in which colour-qualia can be ultimately realized. Figure and extension are distinctively visual just in case they are the sort of figure and extension which can form elements of a colour-array. The distinctively visual character of a region cannot be divorced from its capacity to be colour-pervaded, and its capacity to be colour-pervaded cannot be divorced from its distinctively visual character. Consequently, any *a priori* refutation of claim (1) is automatically a refutation of claim (2), and any *a priori* refutation of (2) is automatically a refutation of (1). For the time being, I shall focus mainly on claim (1), which concerns the ultimate non-sensory realization of colour.

Is it coherent to suppose that colours (i.e. colour-qualia) have an ultimate non-sensory realization? Our initial response is, I assume, to say that it is. But I want to start by making three points which should make us view this response with some caution.

(1) Whether or not it is coherent, the visual conception of the physical world is one which it is psychologically difficult to relinquish. We may be led by the scientific findings to accept that there are no grounds for the ultimate ascription of colour-qualia to physical objects on the basis of how they look. But, as we noted earlier,[1] even after we have adjusted to these findings, we find it hard to avoid thinking of the underlying physical reality in visual terms. The reason why the visual conception is so persistent, is that, ignoring the possibility of mentalistic realism (a possibility which we would normally discount), we cannot find any other topic-specific conception to put in its place, except, perhaps, a conception in terms of the qualia drawn from some other sense-realm. And if the choice is between conceptions associated with different sense-realms, the visual, given its conspicuously spatial character, is bound to seem (to any but the blind) the most appropriate.

(2) There are some sense-qualities, which we ascribe to physical objects, but where, on reflection, it is clear that, in their physical realization, they are nothing over and above the dispositions of these objects to affect human sense-experience. Thus a piece of food has a certain *flavour* solely in virtue of its disposition to taste a certain way to (cause a gustatory sensation in) someone who samples it in appropriate conditions. We know this, not because of any scientific findings, but because, by our very conception of them, flavours, as physically realized, are qualities of gustatory appearance. We have no grasp of what it is for a physical substance to be sweet or sour except in terms of how it tastes. (Indeed, we use the noun 'taste', with its explicitly phenomenal signification, as a synonym for 'flavour'.) Of course, the same substance may taste sweet to one person and sour to another, or taste sweet to someone on one occasion and sour to him on another. We can handle these variations of gustatory appearance in alternative ways. Thus on the one hand, endorsing the dictum *'De gustibus non disputandum'*, we can simply relativize the physical realization of flavour to a subject and a time, so that a substance is said to be sweet for a subject S at a time t iff it is disposed to taste sweet to S if sampled at t.

Alternatively, we can take as our standard some specific set of circumstances (perhaps the normal subject in normal conditions, or perhaps the discriminating subject in favourable conditions), and equate the absolute flavour of a substance with the way it is disposed to taste when sampled in such circumstances. But whether it is relative or absolute, a substance's flavour consists, one way or another, in its disposition to affect gustatory experience.

Now if the physical realization of a certain sense-quality amounts to no more than a 'phenomenal' disposition – the disposition of some physical object to affect human sense-experience – then, obviously, such a realization is not ultimate: it is the logical product of the disposition, and ultimately, unless the disposition is ungrounded, of those laws and categorical states of affairs by which the disposition is generated. Indeed, it seems inappropriate to count this as a genuine realization at all: it is rather that our ascription of the quality to the physical object is just a convenient shorthand for saying that the object is disposed to cause a sensation of the quality in us. So at least in the case of flavours, the confinement thesis is true: such qualities, as sense-qualities, have no ultimate realization outside the content of gustatory awareness. Now when we consider the case of colours, we do not immediately recognize the dispositional account as correct. It is not obvious that we should take a physical object's possession of colour as constituted by the way it is disposed to look, in the way that it is obvious that we should take its possession of flavour as constituted by the way it is disposed to taste. Indeed, our initial reaction is to take the possession of colour as something ultimate and intrinsic. None the less, it will be hard to resist a dispositional account unless we can show, independently, how colours and flavours are relevantly different. On the face of it, colours and flavours are qualities of the same general type. Both are qualities which feature in the content of sense-awareness and whose essential natures we can only grasp by knowing what it is like to sense them. Both are qualities which are, in themselves (as sense-qualities), non-dispositional. And both are qualities which we ordinarily ascribe to physical objects on the basis of their appearance – of how these objects look or taste. If an object's sweetness can be nothing over and above its disposition to taste sweet when appropriately sampled, how can (say) its whiteness be anything over and above its disposition to look white when appropriately observed?

(3) Although, for colour, our initial reaction is to reject the dispositional account, there is still a point in our ordinary modes of thought where that account gets, as it were, an implicit acknowledgment. For while we do not normally think of an object's possession of colour as wholly constituted by its disposition to look a certain way, we do think of its disposition to look a certain way as logically essential to its possession of colour. Thus, on the one hand, we accept the coherence of the hypothesis that an apparently coloured substance, like paint, is really colourless. (Indeed, in deference to the scientific findings, we may find the hypothesis plausible.) For we think of a substance's possession of colour as more than just its disposition to colour-appearance, and, therefore, as something which could be absent when the disposition obtains. But, on the other hand, we reject the possibility of there being a coloured substance which is totally invisible. For while we think of the possession of colour as something ultimate and intrinsic, we also think of it as something which, of logical necessity, involves a certain mode of visual appearance – as something which is necessarily capable of being visually manifested to an observer in favourable conditions. Admittedly, we would allow, I think, the possibility of there being a coloured substance which is invisible to *us*. We would allow that colours may be physically realized in ways which, owing to the limitations in our sensory equipment, we cannot visually detect. But we still think of the physical realization of colour as entailing the realization of an objective look and, hence, as something which is, of logical necessity, visible to a subject who is suitably equipped.

It is clear how this aspect of our ordinary conception of physical colour involves an implicit acknowledgment of the dispositional account. For unless the physical realization of colour is purely dispositional, a disposition to affect visual experience cannot be essential to it. Thus suppose that a certain physical substance S possesses a certain colour-quale C and that S's possession of C is ultimate and intrinsic. Now even if, in the actual world, S's possession of C is connected with a disposition of S to look C-coloured, when observed by an appropriately equipped subject in appropriate conditions, this connection is only contingent. There is a logically possible world in which S possesses C, but in which, with different physical or psychophysical laws, it does not have this disposition. Indeed, there is a logically possible world in which S possesses C, but in which, with different physical laws, this possession neither has nor is correlated with any causal power at all – hence, a world in which the possession of C is wholly irrelevant to any way in which S might be disposed to appear (whether visually or in some other sense-realm) to an actual or hypothetical subject in any conditions. The only way of securing an essential connection between the possession of C and a phenomenal disposition is by construing the physical realization of colour in purely dispositional terms. And this, of course, involves denying that colour-qualia can have any ultimate realization outside the content of visual awareness.

Taken together, these points provide some case for denying the coherence of visual realism. But, obviously, the case is not conclusive. The first point merely shows how, even if visual realism is incoherent, we may be misled into accepting it. And this, of course, does not establish that visual realism is incoherent – any more than Hume's psychological explanation of how we could come to think we have a coherent idea of natural necessity shows that we do not. The second point challenges the visual realist to find a relevant difference between colours and flavours, but it does not establish that there is none. The third point picks out one component of our ordinary conception of colour which is incompatible with visual realism. But we have yet to show that this component has any objective justification. All in all, visual realism is under pressure, but is not yet refuted.

We have agreed that a physical object's possession of flavour is purely dispositional – the disposition of the object to taste a certain way when appropriately sampled. But we have yet to see *why* this dispositional account is correct. We have yet to see why it is impossible for flavour-qualia (which are, in themselves, non-dispositional) to have an ultimate realization outside the content of gustatory awareness. Perhaps if we could identify the reason, we would be in a better position to see how, if at all, the analogy with colour is to be developed.

The reason emerges when we consider a further class of sense-qualia which we are never even tempted to think of as having the capacity for an ultimate non-sensory realization. The class in question comprises what I shall call *somatic* qualia, where a quale is somatic iff it forms, or has the capacity for forming, the content of a bodily sensation – a sensation such as an itch or a tickle. Now the reason why these somatic qualia have no ultimate non-sensory realization is obvious. Such qualia are simply the determinate sensation-types of which bodily sensations are the tokens. If I have an itch on my back, the itch-quale is nothing less than the sensory universal of which the itch-sensation is a particular instance and the itch-sensation is nothing more than a sensory particular of which the itch-quale is the determinate type. It is impossible for a somatic quale to have any ultimate non-sensory realization simply because, since the quale is a sensation-type, any genuine instance of it is a sensation. This is not to deny that, when realized, a somatic quale forms an object of sensual awareness. It forms an object of sensual awareness simply because the sensation which instantiates it is, like any other conscious experience, self-revealing. The quale is just a sensation-type and the sensation is just a quale-token, but the sensation displays its quale, as an object of awareness, by displaying its own intrinsic character; and it displays its own intrinsic character because it is in the nature of any episode of consciousness to be self-revealing.

It is clear that a similar account holds for the case of flavour. As intrinsic qualia, which form the content of gustatory awareness, flavours are simply the determinate sensation-types (or sensory universals) of which gustatory sensations are the tokens (or instances). And the qualia are displayed by the sensations which instantiate them, simply because, as episodes of consciousness, these sensations display their own intrinsic character. This is why flavour-qualia cannot have an ultimate non-sensory realization. And it is why we can only ascribe them to physical objects as

101

qualities of gustatory appearance – as the ways in which such objects are disposed to taste. To say that a physical substance is sweet is just to say that it is disposed to cause a sensory realization of the quale of sweetness when orally sampled, in the same way that to say that it is itchy is just to say that it is disposed to cause a sensory realization of the quale of itchiness when placed on the skin.

Can we extend this account to the case of colour? I think we can, but, to do so, we need to prepare the ground more carefully. To begin with, we need to recognize, as a universal principle, that, whether or not it has the capacity for an ultimate *non-sensory* realization, every sense-quale has the capacity for an ultimate *sensory* realization. For every quale achieves an ultimate realization whenever it occurs as or in the content of a sensation. That this is so for somatic and gustatory qualia is, of course, implicit in what we have just been saying, namely that such qualia are the universals of which bodily and gustatory sensations are the instances. But I want to put this point temporarily on one side (I shall return to it later) and argue for the principle in a purely general way.

I take it to be uncontroversial that any qualitative item which can form the content of a sensation can also, in principle, form the content of a mental image. I also take it to be clear that, when they share the same content, sensations and mental images differ in their intrinsic character. Admittedly, they also, typically, differ in their mental context – in particular, in the character of their mental causes and effects. Typically, imaging, unlike sensing, is the result of the subject's volition: it is something of which he is the agent rather than the passive recipient. Again, typically, sensing, unlike imaging, inclines the subject to form a corresponding belief about the current state of his physical environment: it inclines him to believe that things are physically as the sensation represents them. But these differences are not essential, nor even universal. A mental image may occur unsummoned, as in the case of a dream or a memory that haunts one; and it is at least logically possible that someone should be able to initiate a hallucinatory sensation, as he can a mental image, by an act of volition. Likewise, someone may have a sensation, but, because he knows it is hallucinatory, feel no inclination to form, on its basis, any belief about the physical world; and conversely, someone who is deranged may take his own mental imagings to be veridical perceptions of physical objects.

Sensations and images differ in their intrinsic character. But in what does their difference consist? Suppose, for example, Q is a visual colour-pattern (e.g. a circular patch of navy blue) and on one occasion I have a visual sensation of Q (e.g. when looking at some physical object) and on a later occasion I form (in, as we say, my mind's eye) a mental image of Q (e.g. in the context of recollecting my earlier sensation). On both occasions, Q occurs as an immediate and internal object of awareness: *immediate*, in that the awareness of it is not mediated by the awareness of something else; *internal*, in that it is part of the intrinsic character of each of the episodes of awareness that it is an awareness of *that* qualitative item. And on neither occasion is the awareness of Q, as such, an awareness of a Q-instantiating physical item, even if (as visual realism would allow) it is the means by which such an item is perceived or recollected. How then do the sensation and image qualitatively differ? Our first response is to say, with Hume, that the sensation has greater force and vivacity (Hume speaks of 'impressions' and 'ideas' where I speak of 'sensations' and 'images').[2] But what does this mean? It is no use construing vivacity as a feature of the presented pattern (e.g. bright colours and sharp contrasts) since, *ex hypothesi*, it is the same pattern, Q, which forms the object of awareness on both occasions. Nor is it any use construing force in causal or dispositional terms (e.g. as an influence, or a power to exert an influence, on belief about the physical world) since this would not be relevant to finding an *intrinsic* difference.

How then is the intrinsic difference between sensations and images to be characterized, given that they can be qualitatively identical in content? The only possible answer is that while, in imaging, qualia are merely (albeit transparently) *conceived*, in sensing they are, in some way or other, *realized*. By occurring in the content of a sensation, a quale achieves, in some way, a concrete realization; by occurring in the content of a mental image, its realization is only (though with a peculiar vividness) represented.

We are forced to this conclusion to account for the difference between sensations and images. At the same time, we have to consider how it can be coherently developed. How is it possible for qualia to achieve a sensory realization? And what form does such realization take? One suggestion would be that qualia achieve their sensory realization by being objects of a certain kind of awareness. This suggestion is not compatible with our earlier account of the realization of somatic and gustatory qualia. But there is some initial temptation to apply it to the visual and auditory realms, where the presentative character of the sensations is more conspicuous. Thus it is tempting to say that a colour-pattern is visually realized by being visually presented (by being an object of visual sense-awareness) and that a sound-quale is auditorily realized by being auditorily presented (by being an object of auditory sense-awareness). For our primary conception of a visual or auditory sensation is as an awareness of some qualitative item, and, in the framework of this conception, it is hard to see in what the sensory realization of the item could consist except its occurrence as an object of the awareness. Of course, if we say that visual and auditory qualia are realized by being objects of sense-awareness, we shall have to recognize, in addition to the qualia, a class of awareness-dependent particulars to serve as qualia-tokens (or qualia-instances). We shall have to recognize visual qualia-tokens whose *esse* is *videri* and auditory qualia-tokens whose *esse* is *audiri*. In this way, the position comes to assume the familiar form of the traditional sense-datum theory.

As I have said, there is some initial temptation to adopt this position for the visual and auditory realms – to say that visual and auditory qualia achieve their sensory realization by being objects of a certain kind of awareness. But if we are to say this, we need to give some account of how the relevant kind of awareness has this realization-conferring character. Obviously, it will not help to point out that, in sensation, visual and auditory qualia are the immediate and internal objects of awareness, since this is also true of them in imaging. Nor will it suffice to say, negatively, that sense-awareness is not a species of conceiving. For while it is true that a quale cannot achieve a genuine realization by being conceived (what could?), what we need is a positive account of the nature of sense-awareness which reveals how a quale can and does achieve a genuine realization by being sensed. The trouble is that no such account is forthcoming. There is simply no way of understanding how any form of awareness could have this realization-conferring character. Moreover, so long as we continue to think of visual and auditory sensations in terms of an act-object distinction of the traditional kind – sensations as acts of awareness, qualia as their

bjects – there is no way of understanding how they could turn out
o be anything other than an especially vivid species of conceiving.
Iow, if not by some form of conception, could a subject be aware
f anything except his own conscious states?

Qualia are realized in sensation. But we shall never obtain a
oherent account of this, for any sense-realm, if we suppose their
ensory realization to consist in or stem from their occurrence as
bjects of awareness. To get a coherent account, we must think of
he dependence as running in the other direction. We must take the
ensory realization of qualia as fundamental, and see their
ccurrence as objects of awareness as something to be explained in
erms of it. We must say, not that qualia are realized by being
ensed, but that they are sensed by being realized. This, of course,
s just the position we have already and independently accepted for
he case of somatic and gustatory qualia. Such qualia, we have
lready agreed, are the very sensation-types (or sensory universals)
f which somatic and gustatory sensations are but the tokens (or
nstances). And when realized, these qualia are displayed, as
bjects of awareness, simply because the sensations which instan-
iate them, being episodes of consciousness, are self-revealing: the
ensations display their own intrinsic character and, thereby,
lisplay the sense-qualia they entoken. All we now need to do is to
pply the same model to all sense-realms. We must say that any
ensation, in whatever sense-realm, is just a token or instance of a
ertain sense-quale, and that it constitutes an awareness of that
uale simply by being, as an episode of consciousness, self-
evealing. Thus we must say that colour-patterns are visually
ealized because they are the very sensation-types (sensory univer-
als) of which visual sensations are the tokens (instances), and that
ound-qualia are auditorily realized because they are the very
ensation-types (sensory universals) of which auditory sensations
re the tokens (instances). And we must say that these sensations
lisplay the qualia they entoken, as objects of awareness, by
lisplaying their own intrinsic character. Finally, to mark the
lifference between sensing and imaging, we must say that a mental
mage of a quale is just a transparent conception, of an especially
imple and vivid kind, of its realization.

Let us now consider how these conclusions bear on the status of
isual realism. We know that no quale which is capable of forming
he complete content of a sensation can have any ultimate

non-sensory realization. For such qualia – *complete* qualia we may call them – are the determinate sensation-types (determinate universals) of which sensations are the tokens (instances). A complete quale cannot have an ultimate non-sensory realization, simply because, for the existence of a sensation, nothing more is required than an ultimate realization of the quale. So, in particular, we know that no complete visual quale (i.e. a visual colour-expanse or colour-pattern) can have an ultimate non-visual realization. Now the fact that the confinement-thesis holds for *complete* qualia does not, of course, entail that it holds for *all* qualia. It leaves open the possibility that certain non-complete qualia are detachable from all the sensation-types in which they feature and are capable of ultimate realization outside the content of awareness. Thus, in the case of the visual realm, it leaves open the possibility that colours have an ultimate non-sensory realization, though detached from visual extension, and the possibility that visual extension has an ultimate non-sensory realization, though without the capacity to combine with colour.[3] However, these are possibilities which, for independent reasons, we are forced to reject. For, as we have already said, the distinctively visual character of a region cannot be divorced from its capacity to be colour-pervaded, and its capacity to be colour-pervaded cannot be divorced from its distinctively visual character. If a visual colour-expanse cannot have an ultimate non-sensory realization, nor can the colour and spatial elements it contains. Consequently, we must accept the confinement-thesis for *all* visual qualia and reject visual realism as incoherent. It is also clear that similar considerations would establish a similar conclusion for each sense-realm.

There is something else which now falls into place. Sense-qualia are distinguished from other qualitative items by the fact that we can have a transparent (essence-revealing) conception of them only by knowing what it is like to sense them. Thus a transparent conception of a colour has to be a conception in visual perspective (in terms of what it is like for the colour to feature in the content of visual experience) and a transparent conception of a sound-quale has to be a conception in auditory perspective (in terms of what it is like for the quale to feature in the content of auditory experience). The confinement-thesis explains, in the simplest possible terms, why this should be so. Obviously a transparent conception of any qualitative item involves a grasp of what it is for that item to be realized. And if the item is capable of an ultimate realization, it involves a grasp of what it is for that item to be ultimately realized. Thus it is precisely because the ultimate realization of a sense-quale has to be sensory, that a transparent conception of it has to be in sensory terms – a conception which involves the knowledge of what it is like for the quale to be sensed.

7

MENTALISTIC REALISM

Mentalistic realism is the thesis that ultimate reality includes a physical world, but one which is, in its intrinsic nature, purely mental – a world wholly confined by the framework of time, minds and mind-governing laws. The original objection to this thesis was that it ran counter to a certain apparently fundamental intuition, namely that physical items have their own distinctively physical intrinsic character – a character to be specified in physical terms. Our arguments have shown that this intuition is mistaken. They have shown that the physical description of the physical world (at least, that portion of the world which lies within the sphere of ultimate reality) is topic-neutral – a description which, beyond a specification of structure and laws, conceals the intrinsic nature of what it describes.

If its physical description is topic-neutral, we cannot just dismiss the suggestion that the physical world is intrinsically mental. At the same time, it is not clear how seriously this suggestion should be taken. We have yet to see what, in detail, a mentalistic interpretation of the physical world involves, and, at present, we do not even know whether one can be provided. Moreover, and more fundamentally, even if physical descriptions are topic-neutral, it might still be a conceptual truth that, whatever its intrinsic nature, the physical world is non-mental and capable of existing without the existence of minds. It might be essential to our concept of the physical that it is only when the topic-neutral conditions are satisfied by *non*-mental items that a resulting reality qualifies as a *physical* world. The fact that a physical description does not reveal ɪe intrinsic nature of the physical world does not ensure that ɪentalistic realism is a genuine possibility.

To see the issues more clearly, it will be best if we focus our ttention on a concrete example of a mentalistic realist theory. The xample I have chosen is a particularly simple one. Indeed, from a cientific viewpoint it is clearly too simple, since it does not allow ɔr enough diversity of ultimate physical ingredients. But the implicity will serve to clarify the philosophical issues and, at the ame time, to indicate a general strategy which could be adapted to ther and richer scientific theories.

Let us assume that, apart from the ontological basis of matter :self, all physical entities and physical facts are either part of or the ɔgical product of a reality consisting of:

(1) time;
(2) an unbounded, 3-dimensional, Euclidean physical space (*P*);
(3) a homogeneous 3-dimensionally extended physical substance (matter), each portion of matter being a mobile occupant of *P* and being individuated, at any time, by its spatial position;
(4) a set α of physical laws which control the spatiotemporal distribution of matter (e.g. Newton's laws of motion and gravity, with quantity of matter as mass);
(5) human minds;
(6) A set β of psychophysical (strictly, physio-psychical) laws whereby certain types of spatial configuration of matter (intuitively, certain types of brain-state) and certain types of change in the spatial configuration of matter (intuitively, certain types of brain-process) are causally sufficient for the immediate occurrence of certain types of experience in human minds.

n assuming the physical reality to be thus constituted, we are, in onformity with the confinement thesis, excluding any ultimate ɪon-sensory realization of sense-qualia. At the same time, we are to uppose that, in virtue of the distribution of matter and the ɔhysical and psychophysical laws, physical items retain their ɪormal sensible appearance to human percipients. Thus we are to uppose that (via their dispositions to produce β-relevant configura-ions) grass is disposed to look green when observed and sugar is disposed to taste sweet when sampled. Of course, the scientific explanation of these dispositions (or, more precisely, of the dispositions to produce β-relevant configurations) would have to be adapted to the simplifying assumption that, apart from space and time, matter is the only ingredient of the physical world and that (matter being homogeneous) one portion of matter is just like any other portion except, at most, in quantity and spatial arrangement.

Following the strategy developed in chapter 5, let us next assume that matter is ontologically derivative – that its existence is the logical product of certain intrinsic properties of points or regions at times, together with a framework of law controlling the way these properties are spatiotemporally distributed. More specifically, and to prepare the way for the mentalistic interpretation, let us assume that there are two region-pervading qualities Q_1 and Q_2, where, at any time, Q_1 pervades those regions which are materially occupied and Q_2 pervades those regions which are materially empty, such that the ultimate reality consists of:

(1) time;
(2) P;
(3) the spatiotemporal distribution of Q_1 and Q_2 (i.e. their distribution over P-regions at times);
(4) a set α′ of physical laws which control the distribution of Q_1 and Q_2 and ensure those distributive uniformities and continuities required for Q_1-pervasion to amount to material occupancy and Q_2-pervasion to amount to material emptiness;
(5) human minds;
(6) A set β′ of psychophysical laws whereby certain types of spatial configuration of Q_1 and certain types of change in the spatial configuration of Q_1 are causally sufficient for the immediate occurrence of certain types of experience in human minds.

On this assumption, the spatiotemporal distribution of matter and the matter-relevant sets of laws α and β are nothing over and above the spatiotemporal distribution of the qualities Q_1 and Q_2 and the quality-relevant sets of laws α′ and β′.

Given these assumptions, the mentalistic theory I want us to consider makes the following claims:

110

(1) There is a non-human mind M whose mental life includes or consists in a continuous stream S of sensations, all within a single sense-realm R.

(2) R comprises an unbounded and continuous sense-field F and two sense-qualities C_1 and C_2.

(3) The internal field-relations between different positions in F give F the geometrical structure of a 3-dimensional, Euclidean continuum (as specified, in chapter 5, by FS).

(4) For any time t, the total S-sensation at t consists in a certain distribution of C_1 and C_2 over F, in such a way that F exhaustively divides into non-overlapping 3-dimensional regions each of which is either pervaded by C_1 or pervaded by C_2.

(5) $F = P$, $C_1 = Q_1$ and $C_2 = Q_2$, so that

(6) α' (the set of *physical* laws) turns out to be a set of *psychical* laws which control the distribution of C_1 and C_2 in F and time, and β' (the set of psycho*physical* laws) turns out to be a set of psycho*psychical* laws which causally link R-states in M with experiences in human minds.

Let us call this the *sense-field theory* (SFT). Notice that SFT, as well as being a version of mentalistic realism, is also a version of what I called in the previous chapter 'mentalistic *sensible* realism'. For it postulates, for certain sense-qualia (i.e. for C_1 and C_2 and for modes of arrangement in F) a form of ultimate realization which is both physical and sensory. It is also, of course, reminiscent of Berkeley's final position, in which the physical world is taken to be an idea in the mind of God – a spatiotemporal arrangement of sensible qualities which exists as the object of divine perception. But the similarities with Berkeley must not be allowed to mask the crucial differences. On Berkeley's account, the physical world is a single complex idea, whose *esse* is *percipi*, while, in SFT, it is a stream of sensations. On Berkeley's account, the physical world is, in its intrinsic sensible character, as (though in a fragmented and perspectival way) our perceptions represent it, while, in SFT, its sensible character is adapted to the requirements of scientific theory. On Berkeley's account, the physical world is causally inert (though it serves as a blueprint for divine volition), while, in SFT, it is causally active – both internally, in the way in which one physical event causes another, and externally, in its causal influence on human experience. Apart from its mentalistic realism, there is no much in the sense-field theory which Berkeley would have foun congenial.

Granted our assumptions, is SFT a possible option? Migh physical reality be as the theory claims? We must begin b distinguishing three quite different kinds of objection. Firstly, might be objected that, whether or not it includes a physica portion, ultimate reality cannot be purely mental, since (th objector claims) the existence of minds logically depends on ther being some more fundamental framework of non-mental realit There is, of course, a variety of ways in which someone might try sustain this objection, ranging from arguments in support behaviourism (the thesis that mental states are dispositions t behave) to arguments that the identity of minds is parasitic on th identity of bodies. Secondly, it might be objected that, even ultimate reality could be purely mental, there could not be a strea of experience of the kind which the theory postulates. In particula it might be said, there could not be a sense-field with th geometrical properties ascribed to F. Thirdly, it might be objecte that, even if ultimate reality could be purely mental and could tak the particular form which the theory specifies, it would not suffic for the ultimate existence of a physical world: F would not quali as a physical space, and C_1 and C_2 would not qualify as physic qualities. These three objections concern different aspects of SF The first is an objection to the coherence of mentalism as such, th second an objection to the specific version of mentalism which th theory adopts, and the third an objection to the combining of th mentalism with physical realism.

The first objection is one which I shall not directly consider. Fo it raises a number of very large issues about the nature of min which I do not have the space to discuss. Instead, I shall, for prese purposes, work on the assumption that mentalism is coheren whether or not it can combine with physical realism, and wheth or not it leaves room for the existence of a physical world at al The qualifying phrase 'for present purposes' needs to be stresse For the assumption that mentalism is coherent is not require either by my subsequent argument against physical realism (de veloped in Part III) or by my subsequent argument for reductiv phenomenalism (developed in Part IV), though, in expoundin these arguments, I shall make use of mentalistic examples. Indee these subsequent arguments serve, indirectly, to support the assumption. For in all its standard versions, the anti-mentalist objection accords the physical world a status which the arguments exclude. Even in the framework of physical realism, the anti-mentalist objection does not, in my view, have much plausibility. But once it has been established that physical realism is incoherent and that the physical world, if it exists at all, is nothing over and above the constraints on human experience, it is hard to see how the objection could even get started.

Setting the anti-mentalist objection aside, there are two objections to SFT to be considered. One of them (originally, the second objection) attacks the specific version of mentalism which the theory adopts. The other (originally the third objection) attacks the combining of this mentalism with physical realism. Of these two objections, the second is the more crucial, since, in its most general form, it concerns the coherence of mentalistic realism as such. But I shall start by saying something about the first. In particular, I shall consider two possible objections to the geometrical characterization of F – objections which concern, in different ways, the *non-finite* character of the sense-field as specified in the theory.

In the first place, it might be objected that it is incoherent to postulate a sense-field which is unbounded, i.e. one which is infinitely extended in all directions. It is very difficult to evaluate this objection. How exactly are we to distinguish between the postulation of something which is, by the standards of human experience, very peculiar, and the postulation of something which is, by all standards, impossible? How do we tell whether we are dealing with something which is genuinely contrary to reason, or something which merely defies imagination? My own inclination in this, as in similar cases, is to put the onus of proof on those who deny that something is possible – to hold hypotheses innocent of incoherence until proved guilty. Accordingly, I am inclined to take the postulation of an unbounded sense-field as coherent, since I know of no way of demonstrating its incoherence. But even if we take it to be incoherent and thus accept the objection, the sense-field theorist has a simple remedy, namely to modify his initial account of physical space so as to accommodate the new restriction on its mentalistic interpretation. After all, we do not have any *empirical* evidence that physical space is unbounded. The assumption of its boundlessness reflects, rather, the difficulty we have, prior to any mentalistic interpretation, in understanding what form the boundaries, if there were any, would take – in understanding how physical space could be bounded without there being some further space which encloses it. If we construe physical space as a sense-field, this difficulty disappears. We are already familiar, in the visual realm, with a sense-field which is bounded but not enclosed. Indeed, if there is a difficulty, it is that of understanding how anything like a visual field could fail to be bounded. So, if we think that an unbounded sense-field is impossible, we can meet the objection merely by assuming that physical space is bounded and by altering the specification of F accordingly.

The second objection to the geometrical characterization of F is that it is incoherent to postulate a sense-field which is continuous. This objection, like the first, is concerned with a distinction between the finite and the infinite. While the first objection claimed that no sense-field can be infinitely extended, the second claims that no finitely extended portion of a sense-field can be infinitely divisible. The claim rests on the following argument:

(1) If a finitely extended portion of a sense-field is infinitely divisible, then there is no limit on the fineness of the texture of quality-patterns that can occur within it. Thus suppose A is a finitely extended 3-dimensional portion of F. We can envisage A being covered by a chequer-pattern of equal-sized cubes, alternately pervaded by Q_1 and Q_2, so that each Q_1-pervaded cube is flanked on each side by a Q_2-pervaded cube, and each Q_2-pervaded cube is flanked on each side by a Q_1-pervaded cube. If A is continuous and thus infinitely divisible, there is no lower limit on the size of the cubes that can occur in such a pattern – no upper limit on the number of cubes such a pattern can contain.

Hence:

(2) If a subject has a continuous sense-field (whether bounded or non-bounded), he has, in respect of that field, unlimited powers of sensory differentiation. Provided there are at least two region-pervading qualities to be arranged within the field, there is no limit on the internal complexity of the sensations he is capable of having – no limit on the fineness of differentiation he can achieve.

But:

(3)   There must be such a limit.
 Hence:
(4)   No sense-field is continuous.

What are we to make of this argument? Well, there are two
initial points analogous to those we made in the case of the earlier
objection. In the first place, the objector has yet to establish the
truth of premise (3), and I know of no way in which this can be
done. An unlimited capacity for sensory differentiation may be, by
human standards, abnormal, but I see no reason to assert its
impossibility. Secondly, even if the conclusion of the argument
were accepted, we could still salvage the essentials of SFT by
altering our assumptions about the nature of physical space. Thus
we could say that space is finitely grained, but grained so finely in
relation to the processes that take place within it, that, within the
limits of accuracy of our measurements, it passes all the empirical
tests for continuity. However, there is a further and equally crucial
point. When we speak of a *limit* on the possible fineness of sensory
differentiation – of a limit on the possible complexity of a quality-
pattern within a finite portion of a field – we must be careful to
distinguish between a *logical* and a *causal* limit – between a limit
on what is *logically* possible and a limit on what is *causally* possible.
Thus if the portion is infinitely divisible, there is no logical limit on
the possible complexity of a quality-pattern within it, since there is
enough room for any number of distinct quality-patches. But there
could still be a causal limit – a causally minimum unit of quality-
pervasion: if the field is 3-dimensional, there may be a distance d
such that it is causally necessary that, for any quality Q and any
Q-pervaded region R, R either is or contains or is contained in a
spherical Q-pervaded region of diameter d. Now, in effect, the
argument we are considering trades on a confusion between these
two kinds of limit. Thus, for premise (3) to have any plausibility, we
must construe it as asserting the logical necessity of a *causal* limit,
while, for premise (1) to be acceptable, we must construe it as
denying, for a continuous field, the existence of a *logical* limit. So if
(2) is concerned with the question of a *causal* limit, it does not
follow from (1), and if it is concerned with the question of a *logical*
limit, it has no relevance to (3). Either way, conclusion (4) is not
derivable. Thus, once the distinction between a logical and causal
limit is clearly drawn, the argument collapses.

It is worth noting, *en passant,* that as well as undermining th
argument, this point also has an important bearing on the accour
we should give of our own visual experience. It is often argued tha
the visual field must be finitely grained (perhaps more finely i
some subjects than in others) since even those of us with superic
vision find, empirically, a limit on the minuteness of a differentia
ed colour-spot (i.e. a spot whose colour is different from the colou
of its background) that can occur in any portion of the field. Thu
Hume says: [1]

> Put a spot of ink upon paper, fix your eye upon that spot, and
> retire to such a distance that at last you lose sight of it; it is plain
> that the moment before it vanished the image, or impression,
> was perfectly indivisible. It is not for want of rays of light
> striking on our eyes that the minute parts of distant bodies
> convey not any sensible impression; but because they are
> removed beyond that distance at which their impressions were
> reduced to a *minimum* and were incapable of any further
> diminution.

But the most we are entitled to infer from the empirical evidence
that minuteness is subject to a *causal* limit. We cannot concluc
that the causally minimum unit of colour pervasion is logicall
indivisible. Indeed, it is hard to see how it could be. It is hard to se
how a colour could be spatially realized except by pervading a
extended region – a region divisible into further parts. And cons
quently, it is hard to avoid the conclusion that the visual field
continuous. If this conclusion is correct, then the continuity of F, a
postulated in SFT, is not even abnormal by the standards
human experience.[2]

I shall take it, therefore, that, with or without some modificatic
of the geometrical properties of F (at most, I think, with respect
unboundedness), there could be a stream of experience of the so
which the theory postulates. So let us now move on to the centr
issue. Could such a stream, together with the laws which control i
internal development and its effects on human experience, const
tute a physical world? Could a sense-field with the appropria
geometrical structure constitute a physical space? Could sens
qualities with the appropriate distribution and nomological orgar
zation constitute the physical qualities which underlie materi
occupancy and emptiness? It is arguable that they could not. It

arguable that, while our physical theories provide no positive information about the intrinsic nature of the physical world, our very concept of the *physical* excludes the possibility envisaged in SFT. For it is arguable that our concept of the physical excludes *any* form of mentalistic realism – that it requires that, however intrinsically constituted, the physical world be non-mental and mind-independent. Let us call this alleged requirement the *non-mental-requirement* (NMR).

Should NMR be accepted? Well, certainly it has some intuitive plausibility. If we were asked, outside the context of our previous arguments, 'Given an ultimate reality consisting solely of time, minds and mind-governing laws, is there room for the ultimate existence of a physical world?' the intuitive answer would be 'No'. But, at the same time, we give this answer in the conviction that NMR has a rationale. We assume that the requirement cannot be eliminated and leave what remains in our concept of a physical world coherent and serviceable. The trouble is that, set in the context of the topic-neutrality of physical description, NMR looks gratuitous. If all the other requirements for the existence of a physical world are neutral with respect to the intrinsic nature of physical items, and thus compatible with mentalistic realism, we can subtract the non-mental-requirement without affecting the coherence or utility of our physical concepts. And if the requirement turns out to be gratuitous, the mentalist can afford to ignore it. He can claim that if his position is in conflict with our ordinary concept of the physical, then the fault lies in the arbitrariness of our concept rather than in the inadequacies of his position. If mentalistic realism is to be excluded, we need to give NMR itself a firmer foundation. We need to show that our concept of the physical cannot survive in an acceptable form without it.

One suggestion might be that NMR is a consequence of the deeper requirement that the physical world should be public and external – something which is perceptually accessible to different subjects and whose existence is logically independent of their conscious states. But how would this deeper requirement help to exclude mentalistic realism? Consider the case of the sense-field theory. The postulated stream of sensations S is private and internal to M, but public and external for the human minds whose experiences, through the operation of β', it causally controls. In whatever way, on our original assumptions, human subjects are the percipients of public and external items in physical space, they are, in SFT, percipients of public and external items in F. How could it be otherwise? For SFT retains all the original assumptions, and merely adds a specification of what the physical world, as we assumed it to be, is like in itself. This additional specification cannot make any difference to the relationship between the physical world, thus specified, and the subjects whose experiences it causally controls. The fact that the world turns out to be private and internal to M cannot affect its publicity and externality for us.

Again, it might be suggested that NMR is grounded on the requirement that physical space be something in which, via our bodies, we are located. For how could we be located in something purely mental, like a sense-field? But the same answer applies. Let the defender of NMR tell us in what way we are located in physical space, and we will find that we are located, in the same way, in F. Or let him show the impossibility of our location in F, and he will thereby show the impossibility of our location in physical space. For whatever relationship obtains between us and physical space on the original assumptions, is preserved between us and F in SFT. As we have already said, SFT denies nothing in the original topic-neutral specification of the physical world. It simply adds a specification of intrinsic content.

It is clear, I think, that once we have accepted the topic-neutrality thesis – once we have accepted that (beyond a specification of structure and laws) the intrinsic nature of the physical world cannot be specified in physical terms – we can find no justification for NMR. If the requirement holds, it holds gratuitously, and can be eliminated without disturbing what matters in our concept of the physical. And this means, as I have said, that it is something which the defender of mentalistic realism can afford to ignore.

But as well as being gratuitous, the non-mental-requirement has another and more serious drawback. For not only does it cost us nothing to eliminate it, but it also costs us a great deal to retain it. The cost is not the exclusion of mentalistic realism, but the forfeiture of any grounds for accepting the existence of a physical world at all. As an anti-realist (in the making), I think I could bear such a loss with equanimity. But it would be unfair of me to put the realist unnecessarily in such an uncomfortable position. Let me now explain how this loss is incurred.

Let us use the description 'fully neutral' to apply to a physical theory iff that theory not only fails to provide an intrinsic specification of the physical entities and states of affairs it postulates, but also leaves open the question of whether these physical items are mental or non-mental. Now suppose T is a fully neutral theory which accords with our initial assumptions about the nature of ultimate reality. Thus T is a theory which, on the one hand, specifies the geometrical structure of space, the number of primitive region-pervading qualities, the physical laws which control the spatiotemporal distribution of these qualities and the psychophysical laws which control the effects of this distribution on human experience; but which, on the other hand, does not reveal the intrinsic nature of the 'substance' of space or the identity of the region-pervading qualities, and does not even indicate, explicitly or implicitly, whether or not this space and these qualities are intrinsically mental. Suppose further that, in deference to NMR, we introduce a stronger theory T' which is the conjunction of T and the claim that the space and qualities are non-mental – a claim which excludes SFT and any other form of mentalistic realism. Now whatever empirical evidence there may be for or against the acceptance of T, it is clear that the additional claim in T' is not subject to any empirical tests. It is not subject to any empirical tests, since it affects neither the prediction nor the explanation of empirical data: it contributes nothing to the observable consequences or explanatory power of the resulting theory. But if this additional claim is empirically untestable, then, short of divine revelation, we have no grounds for accepting it, and, therefore, to the extent that T' goes beyond T, no grounds for accepting T'. When these considerations are generalized (as they can be), we are forced to conclude that if our concept of the physical does include the non-mental-requirement, then we have no grounds for believing that there is a physical world. For given any physical theory, we have no grounds for believing that such a theory, with its anti-mentalist commitment, is true.

It might be objected that this line of argument assumes a false account of how physical theories are empirically tested. It seems to assume that, for each theory, the evidence relevant to its evaluation is of a raw experiential kind and does not include any prior knowledge of how things stand in the physical world. It seems to assume that each theory is to be evaluated solely in terms of how accurately it predicts and how well it explains the course of human experience, and that, for this purpose, we have an adequate, if partial, record of the course of experience independently of our physical beliefs. If this assumption were true, then the non-mental-requirement would indeed deprive us of any grounds for accepting a physical theory, in so far as the theory (permeated by that requirement) exceeded the conditions of full neutrality. But, it will be objected, the assumption is false. For, in evaluating a physical theory, part of the available evidence consists in physical information we already possess. Moreover, it will be claimed, such information is indispensable. For if we were to start by renouncing all our physical beliefs, and confine ourselves to information of a raw experiential kind, we would have no grounds for accepting any physical theory at all, *even if NMR were rejected.* This is so, not only because, once confined to the realm of experience, it would be hard to justify taking any step beyond it, but also because, in practice, it is only through our knowledge of the physical world that we have any significant information about the course of experience. Without such knowledge, the information available to each subject, at any time, would be confined to what he could gain from introspection and direct recall, and such information would be too thin and too selective to justify the acceptance of even a fully neutral theory of how things are externally. But if we reject the assumption and admit certain items of physical knowledge as part of our empirical evidence, then the acceptance of NMR is apparently innocuous. For if the requirement obtains, it permeates the physical theories and the evidence alike: the commitment to a non-mental physical world becomes part of the very framework in which even neutral theories are assessed. Thus, however you look at it, it seems that NMR does not deprive us of our grounds for accepting the existence of a physical world. For either we are already deprived by a prior confinement of the empirical eviden-ce – a confinement which puts even neutral theories beyond the scope of empirical tests – or else, as part of the evidence itself, we possess knowledge of the physical world – knowledge which, if the requirement obtains, excludes mentalistic realism.

This objection would have some force if the non-mental-requirement had a rationale – if we could not eliminate it and leave our concept of the physical as coherent and serviceable as before. Let us, for the sake of argument, grant the claim that a crucial part of the evidence available for evaluating a physical theory consists in physical information we already possess. Then if NMR were so deeply entrenched in our concept of the physical that this evidence would not survive reformulation in neutral terms, it would be true that, in so far as we have grounds for accepting a fully neutral theory, we have the same grounds for accepting one which is explicitly anti-mentalist – e.g. our grounds for accepting T would be grounds for accepting T'. But, in fact, NMR is not entrenched in this way. Even if it obtains, it can be systematically subtracted from our physical concepts without affecting their coherence or utility. And this means that, when comparing neutral and anti-mentalist theories, it is simply begging the question to lay claim to evidence which is already infected by the gratuitous requirement – to formulate the evidence in terms which, because they are governed by that requirement, automatically exclude a mentalistic account. For if the requirement is gratuitous, it should be subtracted from the evidence before we evaluate the theories. We cannot claim that the commitment to a non-mental world is essential to the framework in which physical theories are empirically assessed, since NMR can be detached from the framework as readily as it can be detached from the theories. We cannot justify a formulation of the evidence in anything but a neutral form, just as we cannot, on the basis of the neutral evidence, justify the acceptance of anything but a neutral theory. This is not to advocate a confinement of the evidence to that of a raw experiential kind, which might well prove insufficient to sustain even a neutral theory. It is simply to insist that we do not pervert whatever additional evidence we admit by needlessly describing it in terms which beg the question – terms which already exclude the possibility of a mentalistic theory.

Consequently, I stand by the claim that NMR deprives us of any grounds for accepting the existence of a physical world, since it deprives us of any grounds for believing that our physical concepts, thus restricted, are ever satisfied. This means that the requirement is not only gratuitous, but positively embarrassing. For even if it does not undermine the coherence of our physical concepts (and so far we have found no reason why it should), it does, in a crucial respect, undermine their utility, by eliminating the grounds for their application. None of this, of course, proves that NMR does not obtain. To prove *that*, one would have to show, I suppose by a survey of opinion, that when all the relevant considerations are known and fully appreciated, there is a consensus of intuition in favour of rejecting it – a consensus in favour of saying that our concept of the physical is fully neutral. My own intuition is that this is so, but others may differ. Others may hold that, although gratuitous and embarrassing, the non-mentality of the physical world is a conceptual requirement. But what the discussion does establish is that if there is such a requirement, then, to that extent, our concept of the physical defeats its own purposes and needs to be replaced by one which, with the requirement removed, serves these purposes better. Moreover, in evaluating the possibility of mentalistic realism, it is this, rather than the analysis of our actual concept, which matters. What matters is how mentalistic realism stands with respect to that concept of the physical which we have reason to adopt. And that concept, whether or not it is our actual concept, is one to which the non-mental-requirement is not attached.

Granted the coherence of mentalistic realism, are there any reasons for adopting it? Well, yes and no. On the negative side, we cannot claim that there are any empirical grounds which support it, just as we cannot claim that there are empirical grounds for rejecting it. Our empirical evidence only supports a neutral theory, which leaves open the question of whether the physical items it postulates are mental or non-mental. We cannot claim that by construing the physical world as mental we help to explain its observable features, in the way we can legitimately claim that by crediting human beings with minds we help to explain their behaviour. For a mentalistic interpretation is something we add to a physical theory only after all its explanatory work has been accomplished. On the other hand, there is, it seems to me, a philosophical reason for preferring mentalistic realism to standard realism. For we can form no positive conception of what the intrinsic nature of a non-mental world might be. The only positive conception we can have of a non-mental world is a conception in physical terms, and such a conception has been shown to be topic-neutral – one which does not reveal intrinsic nature. Consequently, to construe the physical world as non-mental is to put its intrinsic nature beyond the scope of positive transparent specification of even the most generic kind. We do not and cannot have the faintest idea of what a non-mental space and its non-mental occupants might be like. To claim that there could be such a world, is to make a claim which we cannot substantiate by even the sketchiest of examples. This does not establish that standard realism is incoherent. But it does show that, if we are to be realists at all, anything other than mentalistic realism is the merest of fancies: it is something which we would never have entertained but for our faulty intuition that the intrinsic nature of the physical world can be specified in physical terms.

PART III

THE REFUTATION OF REALISM

8

NOMOLOGICAL DEVIANCE

Throughout Part II, I have been concerned with issues which arise within the framework of physical realism. I have argued that, at the level of ultimate reality, the intrinsic nature of the physical world cannot (beyond a specification of structure and laws) be transparently specified in physical terms. And, on this basis, I have argued for the coherence and plausibility of mentalistic realism, which claims that ultimate physical reality is intrinsically mental. In all this I have assumed a realist position: I have assumed that the physical world, or some selected portion of it, is a component of ultimate reality. In this third part, however, I shall be concerned with the issue of realism itself. I shall argue that realism is incoherent – that we can establish *a priori* that ultimate reality is wholly non-physical. The conclusions we have already reached on the assumption of realism – in particular, the topic-neutrality thesis – will continue to play a role in the development of this argument.

My anti-realist argument will be long and complex. With so much detail, there is a danger of losing our bearings at some point – of failing to see, so to speak, the strategic wood for the tactical trees. For this reason, I want to begin by providing a rough sketch of the overall strategy, so that, as the full argument unfolds, we may retain our sense of direction and have some idea of the relevance of each point to the final conclusion.

Taking *P* as physical space, the core of the argument consists, roughly, in the establishing of three propositions, namely:

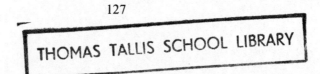

(1)   The geometrical structure of *P* is essentially linked with the nomological organization of *P*, i.e. with the laws which govern what takes place within it. More precisely, if *G* is the geometrical structure of *P*, there are certain aspects of the nomological organization of *P* such that *P*'s having an organization with those aspects is logically essential to *P*'s possession of *G*.

(2)   *P* possesses its geometrical structure *essentially*. That is, if *G* is the geometrical structure of *P*, it is logically impossible for *P* to exist without possessing *G*.

(3)   No component of the physical world is ultimate unless *P* is (strictly, unless *P*-points are) ultimate.

When, in (1), I speak of the nomological organization of *P*, or of the laws which govern what takes place within it, I do not intend this to include anything which is deducible merely from a geometrical description of *P*, or from such a description together with the most basic categorization of the objects whose behaviour in *P*, or the qualities whose realization in *P*, the laws control. I am not counting as a genuine law – as an aspect of the nomological organization – any restriction on behaviour or quality-realization in *P*, if, *a priori*, we can recognize that the same restriction holds for *any* space with the same geometrical structure in respect of occupants or qualities of (relevantly) the same basic type. Thus if *P* is Euclidean, I do not count it as a law that, by following a straight path in a single direction, no *P*-occupant can return to the point from which it started. For we know *a priori* that this behavioural restriction holds for the occupants of any Euclidean space. Likewise, if *P*-occupants are chunks of some homogeneous stuff, each portion of stuff being individuated, at a time, by the region of *P* it occupies, I do not count it as a law that *P*-occupants are mutually impenetrable (though I would count it as a law that, where there is competition for spatial position, the quantity of stuff is conserved[1]). For we know *a priori* that this behavioural restriction holds for any space whose occupants are individuated in that way. All this was, I suppose, fairly obvious, given the way I have used the term 'law' (= 'law of nature') hitherto. But the reason I stress it is that I want it to be clearly understood that (1) is making a significant and, on the face of it, highly contentious claim about the nature of *P*. I want (1) to be understood as claiming that, if *G* is the geometrical structure of *P*, there are certain aspects of the nomological organization of *P* such that, while it is conceivable that there should be a space which has the same geometrical structure but lacks an organization (in respect of the relevant type of occupant or quality) with those aspects, *P*'s having an organization with those aspects is logically essential to *P*'s possession of *G*. This claim is certainly significant. Indeed, our initial inclination is to reject it as clearly false. That is why I saw the danger that, following the principle of charity, someone might misinterpret (1) in a way which renders it uncontroversial, but useless for my purposes.

From (1) and (2) we can immediately deduce that certain aspects of the nomological organization of *P* are logically essential to *P*, so that it is logically impossible for *P* to exist without having an organization with those aspects. It is this which, given an acceptance of (1) and (2), necessitates the first step towards anti-realism. For we have to ask how it is possible for such a consequence to obtain. How can any aspects of *P*'s nomological organization (in the relevant sense) be essential to *P*? Why is there no possible world in which *P* exists, and retains its essential geometrical structure, but is conjoined with quite different laws or with no laws at all? The answer we are forced to accept (given our acceptance of (1) and (2)) is that *P* is ontologically derivative. More precisely, we are forced to say that:

(a) *P* is logically created by the nomological organization of something else.

(b) Certain aspects of this underlying organization are *both* essential to the creation of *P and* logically determine certain aspects of *P*'s nomological organization. And consequently, since anything which is ontologically derivative is so essentially,

(c) certain aspects of the nomological organization of *P* are essential to *P*.

But given the non-primitiveness (i.e. non-ultimacy) of *P*, we can infer, from (3), that no component of the physical world is ultimate, i.e. that ultimate reality is wholly non-physical. In other words, given (1), (2) and (3), anti-realism is established by the following steps:

(4) If *P* is ultimate, no aspect of its nomological organization is essential to it.

Hence, from (1) and (4)

    (5)   If *P* is ultimate, it is logically possible for *P* to exist with a different geometrical structure.

Hence, from (2) and (5)

    (6)   *P* is not ultimate.

Hence, from (3) and (6)

    (7)   Ultimate reality is wholly non-physical.

This, then, is the preliminary sketch of the anti-realist argument I shall develop. Of the three initial propositions, (1) is, I think, the most contentious and I shall devote the rest of this chapter, chapter 9 and part of chapter 10 to defending it. (2) seems uncontroversial, but there are a couple of objections which I shall deal with in chapter 10. (3), which is plausible, but not uncontroversial, will be established in chapter 11.

There is one further preliminary point. The anti-realism which I defend in this part will be developed in a particular direction (reductive and phenomenalistic) in Part IV. This development, of course, will take for granted the anti-realist conclusion already established. But there is also a sense in which the *basis* of the principles which underlie the anti-realist argument is only fully discernible in the context of the subsequent development. This does not mean that, without the subsequent development, the argument is less than conclusive. It means only that, through the subsequent development, the argument can be seen in a new perspective – a perspective which brings to light factors that had been operative, but hitherto concealed.

As will be evident from the sketch, the argument focuses on the relationship between physical geometry and natural law. In particular, it will focus on a property which I call 'nomological deviance'. I want to begin by explaining what this property is.

Putting it intuitively, a space *S* (whether physical or non-physical) is nomologically deviant iff, if *G* is its geometrical structure, there is a different geometrical structure *G'* such that the laws which govern what takes place within *S* ensure that everything behaves exactly as if *S* has the structure *G'* rather than *G*. I have chosen the term 'nomological deviance' because, when a space is of this sort, the laws can be said to run counter to its geometry: the laws are as if the geometry is other than it is. I shall give a more precise definition of such deviance in a moment. But first it might be best to get our bearings by means of an example.

Imagine the following situation:

(1) Σ is a space which is unbounded, 3-dimensional and Euclidean. Q is a quality which pervades 3-dimensional regions of Σ at times. The only events in Σ are changes over time in the spatial distribution of Q.

(2) R_1 and R_2 are non-overlapping and non-contiguous cubic regions of Σ of the same size. C is a way of 1-1 correlating R_1-points with R_2-points such that

(i) C is distance-preserving, i.e. if x and y are R_1-points and x' and y' are the correlated R_2-points, then the distance between x and y is the same as the distance between x' and y'

(ii)   If we say:

Firstly, that a region x *corresponds to* a region y iff C correlates each x-point with a y-point and each y-point with an x-point

Secondly, that a region x is *characterized* at a time t iff

(a)   any portion of x which lies outside both R_1 and R_2 is Q-pervaded at t

(b)   any portion of x which lies inside R_1 corresponds to an R_2-region which is Q-pervaded at t

(c)   any portion of x which lies inside R_2 corresponds to an R_1-region which is Q-pervaded at t

then the spatiotemporal distribution of Q is governed by:

(a)   A law (L_1) which, for some distance r, ensures that, for any time t, the total portion of Σ which is characterized at t divides exhaustively into non-overlapping spherical regions of radius r.

(b)   A law (L_2) which ensures that all changes over time in the spatial distribution of characterization are spatially continuous.

(c)   A law (L_3) which (to put it loosely, but convenient-ly) ensures that each r-sized sphere of characteri-zation pursues a spatiotemporal path of uniform motion in a straight line, except when obstructed by another sphere of characterization. (To speak of a *mobile* sphere of characterization is just a loose,

but convenient, way of speaking of a spatiotemporally
continuous series of characterized spherical regions.)

The predicate 'characterized' is, of course, somewhat contrived. For
it applies to an R_1-region in virtue of the intrinsic state of the
corresponding R_2-region, and it applies to an R_2-region in virtue of
the intrinsic state of the corresponding R_1-region. The point of
introducing it is to allow a simple formulation of the laws
governing the spatiotemporal distribution of Q.

To illustrate the effect of these laws, suppose that, at a time t_1,
there is an r-sized sphere of Q-pervasion which lies outside both R_1
and R_2 and is (again to put it loosely, but conveniently) moving
along a straight line which passes first through R_1 and then through
R_2. Outside R_1 and R_2, Q-pervasion and characterization are
co-extensive. So the laws ensure that, unless obstructed, the
Q-sphere, coinciding with a sphere of characterization, continues in

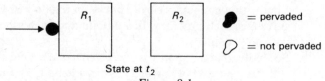

State at t_2

Figure 8.1

uniform motion until it reaches the boundary of R_1 at, say, t_2 (see
Figure 8.1). But now consider what happens after t_2. The laws

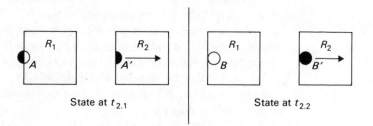

State at $t_{2.1}$ State at $t_{2.2}$

Figure 8.2
The characterized but unpervaded (unshaded) regions A and B in R_1
correspond to the pervaded (shaded) but uncharacterized regions A'
and B' in R_2.

ensure that the sphere of characterization continues in a straight line through R_1. But because, by definition, an R_1-region is characterized iff the corresponding R_2-region is Q-pervaded, the Q-sphere gradually disappears into the boundary of R_1 and, simultaneously, gradually reappears on the other side of the corresponding boundary of R_2 (see Figure 8.2). Thereafter, the

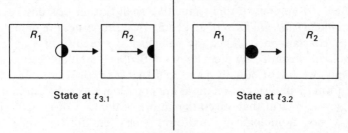

State at $t_{3.1}$ State at $t_{3.2}$

Figure 8.3

Q-sphere continues in uniform motion through R_2 until it reaches the opposite boundary at, say, t_3. At which point the process is reversed: pervasion and characterization gradually re-unite as the Q-sphere disappears into the boundary of R_2 and simultaneously reappears on the other side of the corresponding boundary of R_1 (see Figure 8.3). The Q-sphere now moves towards R_2. When it reaches it, the whole process is repeated, *mutatis mutandis*, the sphere moving into and through R_1 and then out of and away from R_2. Thus the whole course of pervasion and characterization is summarized in Figure 8.4, with the unbroken arrows showing the route of pervasion and the broken arrows showing the route of characterization.

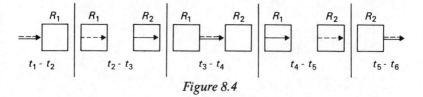

$t_1 - t_2$ $t_2 - t_3$ $t_3 - t_4$ $t_4 - t_5$ $t_5 - t_6$

Figure 8.4

Let me now explain why this is an example of nomological deviance. If S is a space and P is a geometrical property (and here a relation counts as a property), we shall say that P is *nomologically constant in S* iff, given the laws controlling what takes place within *S*, the nomological relevance of *P*, in respect of those laws, is invariant over the whole domain of *S*-items which instantiate it. Thus a distance-relation is nomologically constant in *S* iff its nomological relevance is invariant over the different pairs of *S*-points which are thus related, and a shape-property is nomologically constant in *S* iff its nomological relevance is invariant over the different *S*-regions of that shape. We shall further say that a space is *nomologically uniform* iff all geometrical properties are nomologically constant in it. Since the geometrical structure of a space is wholly determined by the network of distance-relations between its points, we might equally have said that a space is nomologically uniform iff all distance-relations are nomologically constant in it.

Now it is clear that, given the nature of the laws of *Q*-pervasion, Σ is not nomologically uniform. Consider, for example, the property of sphericity. The law L_1 requires that, outside the immediate vicinity of the boundaries of R_1 and R_2, *Q*-pervasion always comes in the form of spherical chunks of radius *r*. But in the vicinity of these boundaries the requirement is different. The requirement is that when a region of pervasion extends along some portion of the boundary of R_1 or R_2, there is a sphere Φ_1 (of radius *r*) overlapping R_1 and a sphere Φ_2 (of radius *r*) overlapping R_2, such that the R_1-region which is part of Φ_1 corresponds to the R_2-region which is part of Φ_2, and such that either (a) *Q* pervades the Φ_1-segment outside R_1 and the Φ_2-segment inside R_2 or (b) *Q* pervades the Φ_1-segment inside R_1 and the Φ_2-segment outside R_2

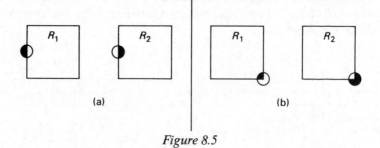

Figure 8.5

(see Figure 8.5). In other words, L_1 requires that, on the boundaries of R_1 and R_2, *Q*-pervasion comes in the form of, as it were, a severed sphere, one of whose segments lies against the boundary of

R_1 and the other against the corresponding portion of the boundary of R_2. So the nomological relevance of sphericity to the distribution of Q-pervasion at a time is not invariant over the whole domain of spherical regions. Its relevance at the boundaries of R_1 and R_2 is different from its relevance in the rest of the space.

Consider next the property of spatial continuity. The law L_2 requires that, away from the boundaries of R_1 and R_2, all changes over time in the spatial distribution of Q-pervasion are spatially continuous. But at these boundaries the requirement is different. The requirement is that the movement of Q-pervasion up to a point on the boundary of one of the regions is immediately followed by its movement (given L_3, movement in the same direction relative to C) away from the correlated point on the boundary of the other, as if the intervening space between the two points is crossed instantaneously (see Figure 8.6). So the nomological relevance of

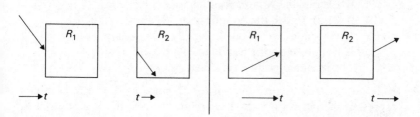

Figure 8.6
Two examples of movement up to the R_1-boundary being immediately followed by movement away from the R_2-boundary.

spatial continuity to changes in the distribution of Q-pervasion is not invariant over all continuous series of points. Its relevance at the boundaries of R_1 and R_2 is different from its relevance in the rest of the space.

In fact, we can see that, quite generally, geometrical properties are not nomologically constant in Σ. For, given any geometrical property, its nomological relevance will vary according to whether its instantiation does or does not involve, for either of the designated regions, the spatial relationship of points inside the region to points outside.

The nomological diversity of Σ (i.e. its lack of nomological uniformity) is part of what makes it nomologically deviant. But there is also a second factor. The geometrical structure of a space is the network of distance-relations between its points. If S is a 3-dimensional Euclidean space, let us say that g is a *co-ordinate function* for S iff g is a function from the points of S to ordered triples of real numbers (both positive and negative) such that, for any two S-points x and y, g correctly represents, relative to the Euclidean metric, the distance between x and y (i.e. if d is the distance between x and y and $g(x) = \langle a,b,c \rangle$ and $g(y) = \langle a',b',c' \rangle$, then $d^2 = (a-a')^2 + (b-b')^2 + (c-c')^2$). Then any co-ordinate function for such a space, by correctly representing the network of distance-relations between its points, correctly represents its geo-metrical structure. Now suppose g_1 is a co-ordinate function for Σ. Let g_2 be that function from Σ-points to triples such that, for any Σ-point x:

(1) if x is outside R_1 and R_2, then $g_2(x) = g_1(x)$;
(2) if x is in (or on the boundary of) R_1 and y is the C-correlated point in R_2, then $g_2(x) = g_1(y)$;
(3) if x is in (or on the boundary of) R_2 and y is the C-correlated point in R_1, then $g_2(x) = g_1(y)$.

g_2 is not a co-ordinate function for Σ, since g_2 does not correctly represent the network of distance-relations in Σ. If x is a point in R_1 and x' the correlated point in R_2, if y is a point in R_2 and y' the correlated point in R_1, and if z is a point outside R_1 and R_2, then the g_2-distance between x and z (i.e. the distance which g_2 attributes to $\{x,z\}$) is the same as the g_1-distance between x' and z, the g_2-distance between y and z is the same as the g_1-distance between y' and z, and the g_2-distance between x and y is the same as the g_1-distance between x' and y'. In short, the network of distance-relations which g_2 attributes to Σ is that network which would obtain if, *per impossibile*, the regions R_1 and R_2 were interchanged. But although g_2 does not correctly represent the geometrical structure of Σ, none the less, given the laws of Q-pervasion, it has a crucial importance. For the geometrical structure which it attri-butes to Σ is, given those laws, the structure which Σ would have to have to be nomologically uniform. The interchange of R_1 and R_2 (in accordance with g_2) is what would be required to render geometrical properties nomologically constant – to give each property an unvarying nomological relevance, in respect of the laws of Q-pervasion, over the whole domain of Σ-items which instantiate it. If R_1 and R_2 were (*per impossibile*) interchanged, L_1, L_2 and L_3 would impose the same constraints on Q-pervasion at the boundaries of R_1 and R_2 as they impose in the rest of the space.

Thus not only does Σ fail to be nomologically uniform, but its failure is so systematic that a certain hypothetical adjustment to its geometrical structure, namely the interchanging of R_1 and R_2, restores uniformity. It is this which makes Σ a case of nomological deviance, a case in which, to some extent, the laws are at variance with the geometry. Thus, taking uniformity as the norm, we can say that the laws of Q-pervasion are as if Σ has the geometrical structure represented by g_2 – as if, in relation to the rest of the space, R_1 has the position initially assigned to R_2 and R_2 has the position initially assigned to R_1. For it is only when we imaginatively interchange R_1 and R_2 in this way that we bring the constraints on what obtains at the boundaries of these regions into line with the constraints on what obtains elsewhere. By the standards operative in the rest of Σ, everything behaves (and is made to behave) at these boundaries exactly as if R_1 were where R_2 is and vice versa. The nomological deviance is so striking that we might express it, figuratively, as a deviation of the *functional* geometry of Σ from its *intrinsic* geometry. We might say that the network of intrinsic distance-relations is as represented by g_1 and that the network of functional distance-relations is as represented by g_2. And, consequently, we might say that R_1 is functionally located where R_2 is intrinsically located and that R_1 is intrinsically located where R_2 is functionally located. The intrinsic geometry is, of course, the actual geometry, and the functional geometry is, in effect, that intrinsic geometry which (set against the norm of uniformity) the laws suggest. The functional geometry is the geometry required for nomological uniformity.

We can derive from the example of Σ a general definition of nomological deviance. A space S is nomologically deviant iff:

(1) S is not nomologically uniform;
(2) there is a hypothetical way of altering the geometrical structure of S which, if, *per impossibile*, it were implemented, would render S nomologically uniform, i.e.:
(2′) there is an internally consistent but false specification of the network of distance-relations between the points of S such

that, *relative to that specification, S* is nomologically uniform, each geometrical property having, in respect of the laws governing what takes place within *S*, an unvarying nomological relevance over the domain of *S*-items which instantiate it.

There are many other forms of nomological deviance in addition to the form exemplified by Σ. There are less radical forms in which the laws are at variance with the network of distance-relations in the space, but not at variance, as in the case of Σ, with its topology. There are more radical forms, in which the laws are at variance not only with the topology of the space but also with its dimensionality. But having elaborated the case of Σ in such detail, I shall continue, in what follows, to focus attention on the form which it illustrates, the form in which there are two congruent regions such that the laws controlling what takes place within the space are as if these regions were interchanged. I shall call this form *reciprocal topological deviance* (RT-deviance).

Now that I have explained and illustrated the concept of nomological deviance, the question I want to consider is this. Is it logically possible that physical space is nomologically deviant? In particular, is it logically possible that physical space is RT-deviant? Could it contain two congruent regions such that, as in the case of Σ, all the laws governing what takes place within it are exactly as if those regions were interchanged?

Suppose someone suggests the following hypothesis:

Despite popular belief, indeed despite all evidence to the contrary, the University Church of St Mary is really situated in Westminster next to the Houses of Parliament and, in compensation, Big Ben is really situated in Oxford next to Brasenose College. The reason we think otherwise (and with perfect justification) is that, in respect of the location of St Mary's and Big Ben, physical space is RT-deviant: everything is made to behave exactly as if St Mary's is in Oxford and Big Ben is in Westminster. Access to St Mary's is from Radcliffe Square and access to Big Ben is from Parliament Square. The bells of St Mary's chime out over Oxford and the strokes of Big Ben resound over Westminster. It is Oxford which is visible from the top of St Mary's and a part of London which is visible from the top of Big Ben. In short, all the laws of physics, whether mechanical, gravitational or electro-magnetic, as well as the psychophysical laws assigning experiential effects to brain-states, are exactly as if the region containing St Mary's and the region containing Big Ben (assuming, for the sake of argument, their congruence) were interchanged.[2] The St Mary's region, though intrinsically located in Westminster, is functionally located in Oxford and the Big Ben region, though intrinsically located in Oxford, is functionally located in Westminster. In this respect, the nomological organization of physical space is at variance with its intrinsic geometrical structure, and, holding constant the laws, it would only be by (as it were) interchanging the two regions that we could restore nomological uniformity and bring the causal processes involving St Mary's and Big Ben in line with what obtains in the rest of physical space.

What are we to make of this hypothesis? Well, even if coherent, it is, presumably, empirically implausible. It is, presumably, vastly less plausible than the accepted theory that St Mary's is in Oxford and Big Ben is in Westminster, since the accepted theory, by representing physical space as nomologically uniform, explains the same data by simpler laws. If physical space is nomologically organized exactly as if St Mary's is in Oxford and Big Ben is in Westminster, the simplest and best explanation is that they are. But the question which concerns us is not whether the hypothesis is plausible, but whether it is coherent. Is it conceivable that, despite the contrary evidence, the hypothesis is true? I shall argue that it is not. I shall argue that physical geometry cannot be logically divorced from nomological organization – that, by our very conception of it, physical space has to be something whose geometrical structure is consonant with the laws which govern what takes place within it.

According to my earlier account, in chapter 5, our conception of physical geometry is topic-neutral: the requirements which must be met for physical space to have a specified geometrical structure can be stated without recourse to any explicitly spatial concepts and without specifying the intrinsic nature of physical points and physical distance. Thus with P as physical space, the claim (call it E) that P is unbounded, 3-dimensional and Euclidean was, in effect, analysed as the claim FS:

For some S, some D, some f and some g

(1) *S* is an uncountable set.

(2) Each *S*-member is simple and contingent.

(3) *D* is an uncountable set of 2-place relations and each of these relations is necessarily irreflexive, symmetric and non-transitive.

(4) For any pair of distinct *S*-members *x* and *y*, there is one and only one *D*-relation *R* such that xRy.

(5) For any *D*-relation *R* and *S*-members *x* and *y*, if xRy, then $\Box\ xRy$, and if $\sim xRy$, then $\Box \sim xRy$

(6) *f* is a 1-1 function from *D* to the set of all real numbers greater than 0.

(7) *g* is a 1-1 function from *S* to the set of all ordered triples of real numbers, both positive and negative.

(8) There is, independently of *f* and *g*, some natural way of ordering *D*-relations in a series such that, for any relations R_1 and R_2, R_1 is prior to R_2 iff $f(R_1) < f(R_2)$.

(9) For any *S*-members *x* and *y*, any *D*-relation *R* and any numbers a, b, c, a', b', c', if xRy and $g(x) = \langle a, b, c \rangle$ and $g(y) = \langle a', b', c' \rangle$, then $(f(R))^2 = (a\text{-}a')^2 + (b\text{-}b')^2 + (c\text{-}c')^2$.

(10) *P* is the aggregate of *S*-members.

To understand the analysis, we are meant to think of *S*-members as forming the points of physical space and the *D*-relations as relations of physical distance. But the analysis does not set any restrictions, beyond the formal requirements, on what these points and distance-relations are.

Now this leads to a certain problem in understanding what it is for physical space to have a unique geometrical structure. Suppose *S* is the set of points of physical space (whatever they may be) and that *D*, *f* and *g* are, respectively, a set of relations and two 1-1 functions which satisfy the conditions specified in the above analysis. If we accept that analysis, we are obliged to accept claim *E*, that physical space is unbounded, 3-dimensional and Euclidean. But in accepting the analysis, we are also, presumably, committed to taking *D*-relations as distance-relations, and, in consequence, to equating the precise geometrical structure of physical space with the network of *D*-relations which hold between its points. But the trouble is that if *D*, *f* and *g* satisfy the relevant conditions, there must be other triples of items (indeed, infinitely many) which satisfy them too. Thus, to stay with the example we have been considering, suppose A is a region containing St Mary's and B is a congruent but non-overlapping region containing Big Ben and C is a way of 1-1 correlating A-points with B-points such that any two A-points instantiate the same D-relation as their correlated B-points. Let I be a function from points to points such that, for any point x, if x is outside A and B, $I(x) = x$, and if x is in A or B, $I(x)$ = the C-correlate of x. And let us say that a relation R' is the I-transform of a D-relation R iff, necessarily, for any points x and y, R' holds for x and y iff R holds for $I(x)$ and $I(y)$. We can introduce a new triple of items, D', f', g', defined thus:

(1) D' is the set of all I-transforms of members of D.
(2) f' is that 1-1 function from D'-relations to positive real numbers such that, if R' is the I-transform of R, $f'(R') = f(R)$.
(3) g' is that 1-1 function from points to triples of numbers such that, for any point x, $g'(x) = g(I(x))$.

It is clear that if D, f and g satisfy the conditions specified in the analysis, then so do D', f' and g'. Indeed, they were defined precisely to achieve that result. So, in terms of that analysis, whatever grounds we have for identifying distance-relations with the members of D, we have the same grounds for identifying them with the members of D'. But we cannot do both. For the network of distance-relations relative to D' is different from the network of distance-relations relative to D. The D'-network is what results from the D-network by interchanging the regions A and B.

One conclusion we can draw from this is that our earlier account of physical geometry, even if on the right lines, is inadequate. According to that account, for physical space to possess a determinate geometrical structure G is simply for there to be *some* network of relations, holding between its points, which exemplifies that structure. This will not do. For, as we have just seen, if there is a network which exemplifies G, then there are other networks (infinitely many) which exemplify other structures – even, as in our example, structures involving different topologies. Obviously, then, the requirements for the possession of a geometrical structure must be more stringent: there must be some further condition which selects from the alternative networks the one which uniquely constitutes the actual network of physical distances. And until we know this further condition, we cannot evaluate the claim that physical space might be nomologically deviant, since we do not know what it means for geometrical structure to be at variance with nomological organization. Given the different networks of relations, what is it for physical space to have one geometrical structure, at variance with the laws, rather than another, which fits them?

One suggestion might be that the genuine distance-relations must be, in themselves, purely general, i.e. relations which do not involve, explicitly or implicitly, any singular reference to members or subsets of the domain of points to which they apply. If we look at the way that, in our example, D'-relations were introduced, it seems that they have this implicit reference. D'-relations were introduced as the I-transforms of D-relations, where R' is the I-transform of R iff, necessarily, for any points x and y, R' holds for x and y iff R holds for $I(x)$ and $I(y)$, and the function I was defined by reference to A and B, i.e. by reference to two particular subsets of the domain of points. Moreover, and as a direct consequence of this, it seems that D'-relations do not have, in any intuitive sense, a unitary relational significance: the same D'-relation can turn out to be different relations when applied to different pairs of points. Thus if x is a point in A and if y and z are points outside A and B, and if R' is a D'-relation, the holding of R' for x and y seems to involve a quite different relationship from its holding for y and z: if R is the D-relation of which R' is the I-transform, then to attribute R' to y and z is to claim that y is R-related to z, while to attribute R' to y and x is to claim that y is R-related to the C-correlate of x in B. All this suggests that we should identify distance-relations with the members of D rather than with the members of D' and take the network of D-relations, not the network of D'-relations, as the genuine geometrical structure of physical space.

This sounds plausible, but when we look more closely, it is not clear in what sense, independently of a chosen system of predicates, D'-relations involve an implicit reference to A and B. It is true that in the perspective of D, D'-relations appear to involve an implicit reference to A and B and their relational significance appears to vary from one pair of points to another. But exactly the same can be said of D-relations in the perspective of D'. If R is a D-relation and R' is its transform, then just as R' can be defined as holding for x and y just in case R holds for $I(x)$ and $I(y)$, so also R can be

defined as holding for *x* and *y* just in case *R'* holds for *I(x)* and
I(y). So if we take *D'*-relations as our starting-point, we can
represent *D*-relations as the ones with an implicit singular reference
and a varying relational significance. If we look at things impartial-
ly, all we are entitled to conclude, it seems, is that each set of
relations is out of line with the other. And this we knew already.

How, then, does our concept of physical distance and physical
topology, together with the ultimate facts, yield a uniquely correct
characterization of the geometrical structure of physical space?
How is there an objective answer to the question of whether the
region containing St Mary's is in Radcliffe Square or in Parliament
Square, if there are alternative networks of relations which meet all
the formal requirements of a 3-dimensional Euclidean geometry
but answer this question in different ways? How can one network
have a privileged status if our physical concepts are topic-neutral
and set no restriction on the intrinsic nature of physical points and
physical distance? The solution, I suggest, is that, from among the
alternative networks, it is nomological organization itself which
selects the physical geometry – nomological organization which
picks out the network of physical distances. Thus, as I see it, it is not
an empirical theory, but a conceptual truth that physical space has,
as its physical geometry, that geometrical structure (that network of
distances) which its nomological organization suggests: it has that
structure which achieves, or comes as close as possible to achieving,
the norm of nomological uniformity – that structure which gives, or
comes as close as possible to giving, distance-relations (and,
thereby, all other geometrical properties) an unvarying nomological relevance over the domain of physical points. In short, it is a
conceptual truth that physical geometry coincides with functional
geometry. St Mary's is genuinely in Radcliffe Square and Big Ben
is genuinely in Parliament Square, because that is where they are
functionally: that is where they are because that is where they have
to be to secure nomological uniformity – to bring the causal
processes leading into and out of the regions containing these
buildings into line, geometrically, with the processes that take place
elsewhere. This, of course, is to exclude the possibility that physical
space is nomologically deviant, since nomological deviance is
precisely the case where the intrinsic and functional geometries
differ.

If this is the right solution, we seem to be well on the way to establishing proposition (1) of the anti-realist argument, as initially sketched – the proposition that the geometrical structure of physical space is essentially linked with its nomological organization. But before we look into this, we must pause to consider a way in which the suggested solution can be challenged and an alternative solution offered in its place. It is to this that we turn in the next chapter.

9

A DEFENCE OF THE NOMOLOGICAL THESIS

I am arguing for the thesis that the geometrical structure of physical space – more precisely, its *physical* geometrical structure – is logically determined, in part, by its nomological organization, i.e. by the laws which govern what takes place within it. Thus suppose S is the set of points of physical space. Then there is a range of uncountable sets $(D_1, D_2, D_3, \ldots)$ of 2-place relations such that, for each set D_i, the network of D_i-relations holding between the members of S satisfies all the formal requirements of a network of distance-relations. Given these different networks, it is, I am claiming, nomological organization which determines the *physical* geometry: the network of *physical* distances is selected as that one which achieves, or comes closest to achieving, nomological uniformity – that one which gives, or comes closest to giving, distance-relations an unvarying nomological relevance over the pairs of points which instantiate them. In short, I am claiming it to be a conceptual truth that physical geometry coincides with functional geometry, and thereby I exclude the possibility that, in respect of its physical geometry, space is nomologically deviant. I shall call this claim the *nomological thesis*.

Before developing my defence of this thesis, I shall, by way of clarification, make three preliminary points:

1   We have been working on the assumption that physical space is unbounded, 3-dimensional and Euclidean, and, in consequence, we have been thinking of the nomological organi- zation as selecting the physical geometry from a somewhat

145

limited range of alternatives, i.e. from those networks of
relations which meet the requirements specified in FS. But
obviously such an assumption and the corresponding restriction
are not required by the nomological thesis as such. Indeed, the
thesis requires that the questions of whether physical space is
bounded or unbounded and whether it is Euclidean or non-
Euclidean are themselves to be settled by nomological considerations. A given network does not qualify as the network of
physical distances merely because, within the range of Euclidean
and unbounded networks, it comes closest to achieving nomological uniformity. To qualify as the physical network, it has,
according to the nomological thesis, to come closest to achieving
nomological uniformity in the *total* range of networks which
meet the formal requirements of a geometry of any sort. This
point, of course, also applies to the *dimensionality* of physical
space. But in this case, there is, presumably, an additional *a
priori* requirement that a physical space be 3-dimensional: i.e. it
is only if their nomologically selected geometry is 3-dimensional
that *S*-members qualify, by the nomological thesis, as the points
of a *physical* space.

2   Even when we confine our attention to those alternative
networks which represent physical space as unbounded, 3-
dimensional and Euclidean, we should, for the purposes of
formulating the nomological thesis, take the range of such
networks to be broader than that defined by FS. By clause (8),
FS requires that the relevant set (*D*) of 2-place relations be
subject to some natural ordering which agrees with the relevant
assignment (*f*) of numbers to relations and which is independent
of both that assignment and the related assignment (*g*) of
co-ordinates to *S*-members. At the time when we formulated it,
this requirement was appropriate, since we wanted FS on its
own to specify the geometrical structure of physical space.
Indeed, without clause (8), the other clauses, apart from (1), (2)
and (10) would have been vacuous, since their truth is guaranteed by the uncountability of *S*. Thus given any assignment of
co-ordinates to *S*-members (any 1-1 function from *S* to the set of
all ordered triples of real numbers), and given the resultant
network of distances which, relative to the Pythagorean principle, this assignment imposes, we can trivially specify a set of
relations whose extension in *S* conforms to that network. It is

simply a matter of selecting, for each real number $d > 0$, the relation of being paired by some member of α, where α is the set of all pairs $\{x, y\}$ of S-members such that, if $\langle a,b,c \rangle$ is assigned to x and $\langle a', b', c' \rangle$ is assigned to y, then $d^2 = (a-a')^2 + (b-b')^2 + (c-c')^2$. However, the requirement is neither needed nor appropriate in fixing the initial range of networks to which the nomological criterion is applied. For the point of applying that criterion is to select the geometry which comes closest to achieving nomological uniformity, irrespective of other considerations. The only natural ordering of distance-relations which is relevant to the nomological thesis is the one which emerges in the framework of their nomological selection. So prior to the application of the nomological criterion, we can count any network of relations as a candidate for the physical geometry, so long as, relative to some assignment of distance-numbers to relations, the network meets the requirements of an unbounded, 3-dimensional and Euclidean space. And still more broadly, when we drop the assumption that physical space is unbounded and Euclidean, we can count any network as a candidate, so long as, relative to some assignment, it meets the requirements of 3-dimensionality.

3   If X is the external item which we take to be a physical space, it is theoretically possible that there are two or more geometries for X which come equally close to achieving nomological uniformity, there being no other geometry which comes closer. Thus, on the one hand, there is the possible case in which the nomological organization is too thin to determine a precise geometrical structure. And, on the other hand, there is the possible case in which different aspects of the organization select different types of geometry, the overall situation being one of swings and roundabouts. These cases are, I must stress, only *hypothetical*: in the actual world, the nomological organization is (I take it) sufficiently rich and coherent to pick out a unique geometry. None the less, it is still worth asking how the nomological thesis would deal with them. Well, let α be the set of geometries which, by the nomological criterion, tie for first place. Then a defender of the nomological thesis can, I think, reasonably accept the following three principles:

(1)   If X qualifies as a physical space, its physical geometry is

indeterminate with respect of α. Put another way, any determinate description of the physical world must be relative to an arbitrary choice of one α-member as the geometrical frame of reference.

(2)   *X* does not qualify as a physical space unless each α-geometry is 3-dimensional.

(3)   The greater the discrepancy between the different α-geometries, the less case there is for taking *X* to qualify as a physical space.

These three principles do not, of course, yield a definite answer for every case, since the third principle does not say *how* similar the α-geometries must be for *X* to qualify as a physical space. But I do not see any point in trying to make the nomological thesis, in its general form, any more precise. Certainly, it is easy to envisage extreme cases where the appropriate answer is obvious. But there are also likely to be cases where a defender of the thesis would want to say that the question of whether *X* does or does not qualify as a physical space could be argued either way. It is not an objection to the nomological thesis if there are some hypothetical cases where it leaves the status of *X* indeterminate, any more than it is an objection if there are some hypothetical cases where, construing *X* as a physical space, it leaves its physical geometry indeterminate.

These three points have helped to clarify the nomological thesis. None the less, there remain a number of importantly different ways in which the thesis can be developed or interpreted. Two of the alternatives will emerge at the end of this chapter, and one of these alternatives will be subject to a further distinction in the next. But I want to begin by considering a possible objection to the thesis in all its forms – an objection which offers a quite different criterion for selecting the physical geometry. The objection runs like this:

It is true that there are many, indeed infinitely many, networks of relations, holding between the points of physical space, each of which meets all the formal requirements of a geometrical structure. But it is not on the basis of nomological organization that the network of physical distances is to be selected. Rather, what distinguishes the physical network from the others is that it is the one which, if we knew the intrinsic nature of physical space, without knowing its nomological organization, we would find it *natural* to select: it is that one which, independently of nomological considerations, would be conspicuous to someone who knew what the points of space were like in themselves. Thus while, from our actual viewpoint, nomological organization, in so far as we can infer it from our empirical evidence, is our only guide to physical geometry, it is not logically decisive. It could be that the real geometry differs from what the laws suggest and could be seen to differ if, *per impossibile,* we could look at things *sub specie aeternitatis* – look at things from the most objective, i.e. the transcendental, viewpoint. For example, if physical space is a sense-field, then, whatever its nomological organization, its physical geometry is determined by the relations of sensible distance between places in the field; for it would be this sensual geometry that was conspicuous to one who knew the intrinsic nature of physical space – who knew that physical points were sense-field places. Consequently, it is, after all, logically possible that physical space is, in respect of its physical geometry, nomologically deviant – possible that its nomological organization is at variance with its geometrical structure. Thus it is logically possible that St Mary's, while functionally located in Oxford, is physically located in Westminster and that Big Ben, while functionally located in Westminster, is physically located in Oxford. For if physical space is a sense-field, it could be that, in terms of the field-relations, the St Mary's region is in Westminster and the Big Ben region is in Oxford, although the laws controlling processes within the field, and controlling the effects of these processes on human experience, are, by the standard of nomological uniformity, exactly as if the positions of these regions were reversed. And it is the intrinsic sensual geometry of the field, not its nomological organization, which determines where the regions are physically located.

I shall call this the *transcendental objection,* and the positive thesis it offers, of the determination of physical geometry, I shall call the *transcendental thesis.* It should be noted that the transcendentalist is not merely offering a transcendental version of clause (8). He is requiring more of the physical geometry than that its distance-relations should have some natural and pre-nomological ordering in line with their geometrical interpretation. Otherwise, he would be offering no solution to the problem of the alternative geometries, as posed in the previous chapter – the problem of different networks which satisfy the requirements of FS. The transcendental criterion is intended to be something which, amongst other things, will decide between these alternatives.

How should we respond to the transcendental thesis? Well, we should begin by noting two obvious difficulties with it. The first difficulty is that, since we have no way of inspecting things from the transcendental viewpoint (the viewpoint of one who knows the intrinsic nature of physical space), the thesis renders the physical geometry of space empirically inscrutable. All we can discern from our actual (i.e. empirical) viewpoint is the functional geometry – the geometry, topic-neutrally specified, which meets (or comes closest to meeting) the requirements of nomological uniformity. And while the network of relations which constitutes this geometry obtains independently of the laws, we have no grounds for supposing that, independently of the laws, there is any basis for selecting it. We have no grounds for supposing that this functional geometry coincides with the transcendentally natural intrinsic (TNI) geometry – the geometry it would be natural to select, independently of nomological considerations, from the transcendental viewpoint. It might be objected that we do have such grounds – the same grounds as we have, quite generally, for (*ceteris paribus*) favouring a nomologically simple theory over one that is nomologically complex. After all, if the two geometries coincide, we avoid nomological deviance in respect of the TNI-geometry and thus have simpler laws at the transcendental level. And surely it is reasonable to postulate a TNI-geometry which yields the simplest laws compatible with our empirical data. Is not this just a case of 'inference to the best explanation', with nomological simplicity as an explanatory merit? But the objection is misconceived. For there is no way in which the supposition of a *transcendental* nomological simplicity could, as such, serve any explanatory purpose. The only theory we can empirically justify is one which, being topic-neutral, leaves unspecified the intrinsic nature of the distance-relations it postulates. Considerations of simplicity contribute to the choice of this theory, but to claim that these distance-relations are transcendentally conspicuous in some pre-nomological way adds nothing to its explanatory power. Of course, we could seek a basis for this claim in a richer theory which provided an explanation of the laws themselves. Thus we might hypothesize that the laws are imposed by God and chosen so as to display to us, empirically, a structure which is already and distinctively conspicuous to Him. But, apart from the problem of justifying such a hypothesis, I assume that the transcendentalist does not want the acceptability of his thesis to depend on a theological position of this sort. Failing this, the supposition that the functional and TNI-geometries coincide would have to rest on an allegedly self-evident principle that coincidence is objectively more probable than deviance. But I cannot see how such a principle could be seriously entertained.

The transcendentalist might reply that this problem for his thesis is only epistemological and that a thesis should not be rejected simply on the grounds that it leaves us with less knowledge or well-grounded belief than we ordinarily suppose ourselves to possess. This is true. But at least we are going to need a very powerful argument in favour of the transcendental thesis, before we would be willing to put physical geometry beyond the scope of empirical appraisal. On the face of it, the epistemological problem is a symptom of some substantial error in the account of how the physical geometry is to be selected.

The second difficulty for the transcendental thesis is that there seems to be no guarantee that physical space has a TNI-geometry at all – no guarantee that, independently of nomological considerations, the transcendental viewpoint affords a natural way of selecting a geometry for physical space. It does, of course, afford such a way if physical space is a sense-field; for in such a case, the sensual geometry would be transcendentally conspicuous. But, presumably, physical space might be something quite different – something whose intrinsic nature is of a less intuitively spatial kind – where, even from the transcendental viewpoint, there is no natural way of choosing between the alternative geometries except in terms of nomological organization. The transcendentalist might try to avoid this problem by claiming that the possession of a TNI-geometry is a requirement of something's qualifying as a physical space. But given its epistemological consequences, such a claim would be hard to defend. For, since we have no way of achieving the transcendental viewpoint, the alleged requirement would deprive us of any reason for supposing that the external item which we call 'physical space' qualifies as a physical space in the relevant sense, i.e. qualifies as the sort of item which could form part of the subject matter of our ordinary physical discourse. This consequence, indeed, is so intolerable that, even if the requirement obtained (and I do not think that it does), we would be justified in revising our concept of a physical space so as to eliminate it. (There is a parallel here with the case of NMR.[1]) It seems, then, that rather than press the requirement, the transcendentalist would do better to modify his position by restricting the range of cases to which the transcendental criterion applies – by taking the transcendental criterion to be decisive in those cases where physical space has a TNI-geometry, but the nomological criterion to be decisive in those cases where it does not. In other words, it seems that he should retain his original thesis, but with the qualification that if the transcendental viewpoint affords no natural way of choosing between the alternative networks, except in terms of nomological organization, then it is nomological organization which determines the physical geometry. But the trouble with this is that, thus modified, the transcendental thesis is beginning to look somewhat contrived. For why should the nomological criterion fail in those cases where there is a TNI-geometry if it succeeds in those cases where there is not? Once we have conceded so much to the nomological criterion, it is hard to see any rationale for denying its universal applicability.

These difficulties with the transcendental thesis are serious. But perhaps they are not enough to remove the challenge to the nomological thesis altogether. For the transcendentalist can still claim, with some initial plausibility, that there is at least one case where our intuitions are on his side, namely where we suppose physical space to be a sense-field. Thus if physical space is a sense-field, there does seem to be a *prima facie* case for equating its physical geometry with its sensual geometry, irrespective of its nomological organization. If, sensually, the St Mary's region is in Westminster and the Big Ben region is in Oxford, there seems to be a case for saying that our ordinary beliefs about their physical locations are mistaken and that physical space is, even in respect of its physical geometry, nomologically deviant. Before we reject the transcendental thesis altogether, we should examine the sense-field case more closely, to make sure that even here, where the transcendentalist has his best chances, the nomological criterion gives the right results. Obviously, we must focus on examples in which the sensual geometry is nomologically deviant, since it is for these examples that the nomological and transcendental criteria conflict.

So far, we have only considered a very restricted form of nomological deviance in which the sensual and functional geometries coincide except in respect of the locations of two regions. Thereby, we have ensured that, although the nomological and transcendental criteria give different results, they at least agree in characterizing physical space as a unitary 3-dimensional continuum. We will be in a better position to assess the relative merits of the nomological and transcendental theses, in the chosen area, if we consider cases in which the nomological deviance, and hence the conflict between the rival criteria, is of a more radical kind. In fact, I shall consider two such cases, where what is at issue is, in the one case, the unity of physical space and, in the other, its dimensionality.

The first case I want to consider is a development of the original case of RT-deviance. In the original case, there is a single sense-field and a pair of sensually congruent field-regions whose interchange is required for nomological uniformity – each region being functionally located where the other is sensually located. In the new case, there is also a pair of regions whose interchange is required for nomological uniformity, but the two regions belong to different sense-fields. In effect, then, the new case is also a case of RT-deviance, but in a trans-field form, in which each of the relevant regions is intrinsically located in one field and functionally located in the other.

In detail, the case to be considered (*case 1*) is this. There are two sense-fields, F^a and F^b, of the same intrinsic type – each being unbounded, 3-dimensional and Euclidean, and each being a medium for the same range of sense-qualities. The two fields are quite separate – if you like, suppose them to belong to different minds – so that there are no relations of sensible distance between places in one and places in the other. F^a exhaustively divides into two portions F^a_1 and F^a_2 which lie on opposite sides of an unbounded plane A. Likewise, F^b exhaustively divides into two portions F^b_1 and F^b_2 which lie on opposite sides of an unbounded plane B. (Incidentally, the planes are not sensibly marked, anymore than the equator is marked on the earth.) The significance of this division is twofold. In the first place, physical space is the sum of F^a_1 and F^b_2. That is, physical space exhaustively divides into two portions, the points in one portion being the field-places of F^a_1 and the points in other being the field-places of F^b_2. Thus when a material object moves (if we can still speak of movement here) from one portion to the other, the underlying path of quality-pervasion is discontinuous: it disappears into the boundary A of F^a_1 and re-emerges on the other side of the boundary B of F^b_2 – the whole process being divided between the two fields. Secondly, and in line with this, the nomological organization is such as to yield a case of trans-field RT-deviance, in which the interchange of F^a_1 and F^b_1 (or F^a_2 and F^b_2) is required for nomological uniformity. Everything is nomologically constrained exactly as if, by the standard of uniformity, F^a_1 is sensibly continuous with F^b_2 and F^a_2 is sensibly continuous with F^b_1. (To envisage the details, turn back to the case of Σ, elaborated in the previous chapter, and adapt it to the trans-field form.) Thus F^a_1 and F^b_2, while portions of different sense-fields, are functionally continuous – organized as the contiguous portions of a single space. This, of course, is why we, the subjects whose experiences the processes in F^a_1 and F^b_2 control, receive no empirical indication of the underlying discontinuity. Because the only empirically conspicuous geometry is one which the standard of uniformity itself selects, we interpret the two portions of physical space as forming a single undivided continuum. The fact that F^a_1 and F^b_2 are portions of different sense-fields is empirically concealed.

How, then, is *case 1* to be interpreted? What consequences does it have for the physical geometry of space? Consider first the transcendental criterion. According to this criterion, the physical geometry is that geometry which would be conspicuous, independently of nomological considerations, from the transcendental viewpoint – that geometry which it would be natural to select if we knew the intrinsic nature of physical space, without knowing its nomological organization. This criterion, therefore, will yield the result that what we call physical space is really the sum of two physical spaces, with no relations of physical distance connecting the points in one with the points in the other. Thus if x is a point in F^a_1 and y is a point in F^b_2 then, on this account, it is a mistake, even in terms of physical geometry, to speak of the *distance* between x and y or of the *spatial route* from x to y or of an object *moving along a continuous path* from x to y. For according to the transcendental criterion, the physical geometry is fixed by the sensual geometry, and, in the sensual geometry, places in F^a_1 and places in F^b_2 stand in no geometrical relations. This consequence of the transcendental thesis is, it seems to me, manifestly absurd. For, irrespective of its other geometrical properties, what we call physical space must surely be, in terms of its *physical* geometry, a unitary space, even if, so to speak, its substance – the points which compose it – is drawn from two sense-fields. It may be that whenever I cross the High Street, the process which underlies the movement of my body is divided between two fields, but it is certain that, at the level of physical geometry, my body pursues a continuous path in a single space. This means that for *case 1*, it is only the nomological criterion which yields the correct results. The physical geometry coincides with the functional geometry. F^a_1 and F^b_2 are contiguous portions of the same physical space, in line with their uni-spatial organization.

The second case I want to consider involves a nomological deviance of a quite different kind, in which the sensual and functional geometries differ in respect of dimensionality. More specifically, it is a case in which physical space is a sense-field which is sensually 2-dimensional but functionally 3-dimensional. It will be easiest (though the assumption is not necessary) if we assume that the sense-field (F), though unbounded, is only *finitely* grained, each F-place being sensually adjacent to four other places, two along one of the dimensions and two along the other. We could then represent the sensual geometry mathematically by a 1-1 function s from the set of F-places to the set of all ordered pairs of integers (both positive and negative) such that two places x and y are adjacent iff, if $s(x) = \langle a,b,\rangle$ and $s(y) = \langle a',b'\rangle$, then either (1) $a = a'$ and $b-b' = \pm 1$ or (2) $b = b'$ and $a-a' = \pm 1$.

Given this assumption, let us suppose that there are two sense-qualities Q_1 and Q_2 such that it is logically necessary that, for each F-place x and each time t, x is either characterized by Q_1 or characterized by Q_2, but not both.[2] It is also necessary, whether logically or nomologically, that every episode of characterization is temporally extended, so that if a place is Q-characterized at t, where either $Q = Q_1$ or $Q = Q_2$, it is Q-characterized throughout some t-containing period. Let us say that g is a *3-dimensional assignment* iff g is a 1-1 function from the set of F-places to the set of all ordered triples of integers (both positive and negative). And let us say that two places x and y are *g-adjacent* iff g is a

3-dimensional assignment such that if $g(x) = \langle a,b,c \rangle$ and $g(y) = \langle a',b',c' \rangle$, then either (1) $a = a'$ and $b = b'$ and $c-c' = \pm 1$ or (2) $a = a'$ and $c = c'$ and $b-b' = \pm 1$ or (3) $b = b'$ and $c = c'$ and $a-a' = \pm 1$. Then each 3-dimensional assignment represents a possible 3-dimensional arrangement of F-places, two assignments being geometrically equivalent iff they are equivalent with respect to adjacency. We can now state in what sense F is functionally 3-dimensional. Let L be the set of laws controlling the F-time distribution of Q_1 and Q_2 and the effects of this distribution on human experience. Then there is a 3-dimensional assignment g^* such that, if A is the arrangement of F-places (i.e. the network of adjacencies) represented by g^*, and by all geometrically equivalent assignments, then out of all the possible geometrical arrangements, of any dimensionality, A is unique in achieving nomological uniformity in respect of L (e.g. we may suppose that while there is no other arrangement in which adjacency has a constant nomological relevance, the laws ensure, in the case of A, that all changes in the distribution of Q_1 and Q_2 are made up of 'minimal' movements of Q_1-characterization against a background of Q_2-characterization, where a *minimal* movement is a movement from one F-place to an adjacent [= g^*-adjacent] place). Because it is this 3-dimensional arrangement which uniquely achieves nomological uniformity, it is this arrangement which we, from our empirical viewpoint, discern as the physical geometry (though for reasons which I shall not elaborate, concerning the precise character of the nomological organization, we construe the arrangement as a continuum, rather than as finitely grained). The underlying 2-dimensional arrangement, because it runs counter to the nomological organization, remains, like the sensible discontinuity of F^a_1 and F^b_2, empirically concealed.

This, then, is *case 2*. And, like *case 1*, it tells against the transcendental criterion. For it is surely indisputable that physical space is *physically* 3-dimensional, even if its points are drawn from a 2-dimensional sense-field. But the transcendental thesis, by equating the physical geometry with the sensual geometry, would be forced to deny this. Once again, it is only the nomological criterion which yields the correct results. The physical geometry of F is to be equated, not with its sensual, but with its functional geometry – with the 3-dimensional arrangement which achieves nomological uniformity and is, thereby, empirically conspicuous.

On the face of it, then, these two cases constitute decisive counter-examples to the transcendental thesis even in that area (where we suppose the TNI-geometry to be sensual) where the thesis appeared to stand its best chance of success. And this seems to leave the nomological thesis as the only viable position.

However, the transcendentalist could still try to salvage something from his position in the following way:

Of course, physical space must, whatever its intrinsic nature, be physically unitary and 3-dimensional. It would not qualify as a physical space if it were not. But just because of this, we need to be more careful in how we express the cases which supposedly refute the transcendental thesis. Thus, while we can certainly suppose that the ultimate reality is as envisaged in *case 1* (a pair of sense-fields with trans-field RT-deviance) and can do so compatibly with our acceptance of a physical world, we cannot *identify* physical space with the sum of F^a_1 and F^b_2. We cannot do so precisely because (a) if physical space were identical with $F^a_1 + F^b_2$, its physical geometry would have to coincide with its sensual geometry, (b) in the sensual geometry, F^a_1 and F^b_2 are portions of distinct spaces, and (c) physical space has to be, in respect of its physical geometry, a single space. Likewise, while we can certainly suppose that the ultimate reality is as envisaged in *case 2* (a 2-dimensional sense-field F with a 3-dimensional organization) and can do so compatibly with our acceptance of a physical world, we cannot identify physical space with F. We cannot do so precisely because (a) if physical space were identical with F, its physical geometry would have to coincide with its sensual geometry, (b) in its sensual geometry, F is 2-dimensional, and (c) physical space has to be, in respect of its physical geometry, 3-dimensional. In both cases, the right conclusion to draw is that, if the ultimate reality is as envisaged, physical space, rather than being an ingredient of that reality, is ontologically derivative. Its existence, together with its physical geometry, is logically sustained by the way the underlying sensory items are nomologically organized. Thus, in *case 1*, it is not that physical space is identical with $F^a_1 + F^b_2$ (how could it be if F^a_1 and F^b_2 are portions of different fields?), but, rather, that it is something which, together with its unitary physical geometry, the uni-spatial organization of F^a_1 and F^b_2 logically

157

creates. And, in *case 2*, it is not that physical space is identical with *F* (how could it be if *F* is only 2-dimensional?), but, rather, that it is something which, together with its 3-dimensional geometry, the 3-dimensional organization of *F* logically creates. In short, if physical space is ontologically primitive, its physical geometry is that geometry which would be conspicuous, independently of nomological considerations, from the transcendental viewpoint. But for this very reason, if the transcendentally conspicuous geometry of the ontologically primitive item does not meet the requirements of a physical geometry, physical space is ontologically derivative and falls outside the scope of the transcendental criterion.

In certain respects, this reply anticipates the anti-realist position which I shall eventually adopt. In particular, I think the transcendentalist is right to claim that, in the cases envisaged, physical space is ontologically derivative. For I think that physical space, if it exists at all, has to be ontologically derivative, whatever the nature of the ultimate reality. And I shall try to establish this in due course. However, I do not think the reply will serve as an effective defence of the transcendental thesis. For it concedes too much to the nomological thesis to leave, in any rational form, a role for the transcendental criterion. This becomes clear if we set the two new cases, which concern the unity and dimensionality of physical space, side by side with the original case (of intra-field RT-deviance), which concerns the relative location (in a unitary 3-dimensional space) of two physical regions. The new cases seemed to constitute a decisive objection to the transcendental thesis, since we are unwilling to conclude that, in line with its sensual geometry, space is physically divided or physically 2-dimensional. To meet this objection, the transcendentalist now claims that, in these cases, physical space is ontologically derivative: it is true, he concedes, that the physical geometry is determined by the nomological organization of the sense-field(s), but only because that nomological organization logically creates the very space whose geometry is thus determined. Such a claim, in a sense, protects the transcendental criterion by removing these cases from its scope. We cannot say that the physical geometry of space differs from its sensual geometry, since the space itself does not have a sensual geometry. Rather, we must say that the physical geometry of space differs from the sensual geometry of that which underlies it. But to protect the transcendental criterion in this way is, implicitly, to abandon it altogether. For if the functional geometry is what is physically relevant in the new cases, it must also be what is physically relevant in the original case, where the conflict between the nomological and transcendental criteria first arose. If it is right to take space as physically undivided when what underlies it are the functionally contiguous portions of separate sense-fields, and right to take space as physically 3-dimensional when what underlies it is a 2-dimensional sense-field with a 3-dimensional organization, then it must also be right to let nomological considerations determine the physical location of the St Mary's region and the Big Ben region in the original case – right, that is, to locate the former region in Oxford and the latter region in Westminster, even when, contrary to the nomological organization, the sensual locations of the corresponding field-regions are reversed. Moreover, if it is right, in the new cases, to construe physical space as ontologically derivative – as something whose existence is logically sustained by the nomological organization of the sense-field(s) – it must also be right in the original case. It is true, of course, that in the original case, unlike the new ones, the sensual geometry meets the requirements of a *possible* physical geometry, since the sense-field is unitary and 3-dimensional. But this can hardly be relevant to determining the *actual* physical geometry, if the nomological organization is decisive in the other cases. It would be absurd, since quite devoid of rationale, to let the sensual topology outweigh the functional topology when the RT-deviance is confined to a single sense-field, if the functional topology is logically decisive when two fields are involved. The upshot of this is that the transcendentalist cannot press his reply without forgoing the transcendental criterion altogether. For if he does, he has to concede that it is always the functional and not the sensual geometry of the underlying reality which determines the physical geometry of space. Once he makes this concession, the only thing which distinguishes his position from the nomological thesis, in its original form, is the claim that where the physical geometry differs from the sensual geometry, the two geometries belong to different items – the physical geometry being the geometry of physical space and the sensual geometry being the geometry of that ontologically primitive item by whose nomological organization the physical space is logically created. Whether or not this claim is correct, it is one which, if necessary, a defender of the nomological thesis could happily accept – indeed, accept with alacrity, if, like the author, he sees the defence of this thesis as a step in the argument for physical anti-realism.

It is clear, then, that the transcendental objection fails. Even if we assume that there is a transcendentally natural geometry – a geometry which it would be natural to select, independently of nomological considerations, from the transcendental viewpoint – it is not this, but the nomological organization, which logically determines the physical geometry of space. Even if physical space, or what underlies it, is a sense-field, it is the functional, not the sensual, geometry of the field which is physically relevant. From now on, therefore, I shall take it that, in some form, the nomological thesis is correct.

But in *what* form? As originally formulated, the thesis asserts the logical dependence of the physical geometry of space on its nomological organization. It assumes that there is a framework of natural law governing the distribution of certain intrinsic properties over point-moments and the effects of this distribution on human experience; and it claims, as a conceptual truth, that, out of the range of alternative networks of relations between points, each of which meets the formal requirements of a geometrical structure, the physical geometry of space is constituted by that network which achieves, or comes closest to achieving, nomological uniformity in respect of that framework. Now in this form the nomological thesis permits (at least, prior to any further philosophical argument) a realist view of physical space, in which physical points are taken as ontologically primitive. It permits us, for example, to envisage physical space as *identical with* a sense-field, so long as we equate the physical geometry of the field (the network of physical distances between field-places) with its functional geometry, irrespective of whether this coincides with or differs from its sensual geometry. But, as our recent considerations show, the nomological thesis can also assume a radically different form, in which a realist view of physical space is explicitly excluded. In this anti-realist form, the thesis claims that physical space is the logical creation of something else: the physical geometry is logically determined by nomological organization, but the organization not of space itself, but of something which underlies it. On this version of the thesis, it remains a conceptual truth that the physical geometry of space coincides with its functional geometry – the geometry which achieves, or comes closest to achieving, nomological uniformity. But the coincidence is to be explained by the fact that physical space, together with its geometry, derives its very existence from the nomological organization in the underlying reality. On this version, we cannot *identify* physical space with a sense-field. At most, we can only suppose that it is the nomological organization of an underlying sense-field (or set of sense-fields) which logically sustains the existence of physical space and, as part and parcel of the sustainment, logically determines the physical geometry.

The distinction between these two versions of the nomological thesis promises to be of crucial importance. Since our discussion of the problem of occupancy in chapter 5 (the problem of how to characterize the role of physical space as a medium for physical objects), our strategy has been to construe the occupants of physical space as ontologically derivative – as the logical creation of the distribution of intrinsic properties over point-moments together with laws which ensure the kinds of distributive uniformity and continuity characteristic of space-occupying continuants. It is clear that, combined with the anti-realist version of the nomological thesis, this strategy is incompatible with physical realism in any form. For if the physical occupants are the logical creation of facts about physical space and if physical space is the logical creation of facts about something else, then there are no ontologically primitive physical entities – nothing left of the physical world at the level of ultimate reality. It follows, of course, that if we are to retain physical realism in any form, we must either endorse the realist version of the nomological thesis, retaining the ultimacy of physical space, or adopt a new strategy for occupancy, retaining the ultimacy of physical occupants. My policy will be to argue that neither of these alternatives is acceptable and that physical realism must be rejected.

10

SPATIAL ANTI-REALISM

As we have just seen, there are two versions of the nomological thesis. There is a realist version, which takes physical space (more precisely, the points of physical space) to be ontologically primitive and claims that its physical geometry is determined by its nomological organization. And there is an anti-realist version, which takes physical space (i.e. the points of physical space) to be ontologically derivative and claims that its physical geometry is determined by the nomological organization of something else – something in that underlying reality of which the space itself is a logical creation. I shall call these two versions, respectively, the *realist nomological thesis* (RNT) and the *anti-realist nomological thesis* (ANT). We have already established that the nomological thesis is true in some form. So the question to be considered is: which version should we adopt? And this question has a crucial bearing on the issue of physical realism itself. For if, as we have been assuming, the occupants of physical space are ontologically derivative – logically created by the distribution and organization of intrinsic properties of points at times – we can only retain physical realism if we take physical space to be ontologically primitive, thus rejecting the nomological thesis in its anti-realist form.

Before we can decide between the realist and anti-realist versions of the nomological thesis (between RNT and ANT), we need to draw a further distinction – a distinction between two different ways in which the realist version can be developed. In explaining this distinction, I shall, for simplicity, assume that any physical

162

geometry has to be Euclidean and that, in respect of its physical geometry, physical space is unbounded. I also take it to be a conceptual truth that any physical geometry is 3-dimensional.

Let P be physical space. Let us say that f is a P-assignment iff f is a 1-1 function from the set of P-points to the set of all ordered triples of real numbers, both positive and negative. In conjunction with a Euclidean metric, we can think of a P-assignment as imposing a network of distances on physical points: thus, for any P-assignment f, two P-points x and y have the f-distance d iff, if $f(x)$ = $\langle a,b,c \rangle$ and $f(y)$ = $\langle a,'b',c' \rangle$, then $d^2 = (a\text{-}a')^2 + (b\text{-}b')^2 + (c\text{-}c')^2$. Two P-assignments f_1 and f_2 are geometrically equivalent iff they impose the same relative distances, i.e. iff, for any P-points x, y, w, and z, the ratio of the f_1-distances for x and y and for w and z is the same as the ratio of the corresponding f_2-distances. Let us call each total set of geometrically equivalent P-assignments a *G-set*. Then the range of alternative G-sets represents the range of alternative 3-dimensional Euclidean geometries of P. We will say that a G-set is *law-selected* iff the geometry it represents coincides with the functional geometry of P, i.e. achieves, or comes closest to achieving, nomological uniformity.

Now RNT makes two claims. In the first place, it claims that P-points are ontologically primitive – are ingredients of ultimate reality. Secondly, it claims, and claims as a conceptual truth, that, irrespective of the intrinsic nature of P (irrespective of what P-points are like in themselves), its physical geometry is that geometry represented by the law-selected set. It is this second claim – the distinctively nomological claim – which can be developed in alternative ways.

I shall start with an example. Let us use the term 'centred' to apply to any set of points which are equidistant from some other point. More specifically, let us speak of a set of P-points as *physically centred* when there is a P-point from which all the members of the set are physically equidistant. And, for any P-assignment f, let us speak of a set of P-points as *centred for f* when there is a P-point from which all the members of the set stand at the same f-distance. Likewise, for any set α of P-assignments, let us speak of a set of P-points as *centred for α* when it is centred for each member of α. Now RNT claims that the physical geometry of P is that geometry represented by the law-selected G-set. So, in particular, it claims that a set of P-points is physically centred iff it is centred for the law-selected set. But this claim is compatible with two different accounts of what the property of physical centredness is. On the one hand, it is compatible with saying that physical centredness is the property of being centred for whatever set happens to be law-selected. On the other hand, it is compatible with saying that, given α as the law-selected set, physical centredness is whatever intrinsic property is essential to, and distinctive of, those sets of P-points which are centred for α. (If nothing else is available, this intrinsic property would simply be the property of being centred for α.) On both accounts, it is the laws that determine which sets of P-points are physically centred. But the method of determination is subtly different in the two cases. On the first account, physical centredness, wherever it obtains, is itself an aspect of the nomological organization: a set's being physically centred *consists in* its meeting the conditions of centredness (the equidistance of its members from the same P-point) in whatever geometry achieves, or comes closest to achieving, nomological uniformity. But on the second account, physical centredness is a property which, in itself, is logically independent of nomological organization, and the laws are only relevant in determining which non-nomological property it turns out to be.

This is only an example, dealing with just one geometrical property. But the distinction it illustrates is perfectly general. Thus, for each geometrical predicate 'ϕ', RNT leaves us with a choice between alternative accounts of the nature of ϕ-ness in its physical form. On the one account, physical ϕ-ness is the nomological property of being ϕ for whatever G-set the laws select (i.e. ϕ in whatever geometry achieves, or comes closest to achieving, nomological uniformity). On the other account, given the G-set which the laws select (given the geometry which achieves, or comes closest to achieving, nomological uniformity) physical ϕ-ness is whatever intrinsic property is essential to, and distinctive of, those P-items which are ϕ for that set (ϕ in that geometry). In consequence, we can see that RNT, when properly developed, divides into two versions – a version which systematically construes physical geometrical properties in the first way and a version which systematically construes them in the second way. I shall call these two versions, respectively, the *A-thesis* and the *B-thesis*.

These two theses agree, of course, on the specification of the physical geometry of P *in the actual world*. Both accept that, in the actual world, the network of physical distances is that network which accords (under the Euclidean metric) with the law-selected G-set, i.e. that network which achieves, or comes closest to achieving, nomological uniformity. (This is what makes each thesis a version of RNT.) Thus, although they construe physical geometrical properties in different ways, they assign them, in the actual world, the same extensions. Where the two theses differ is in the specification of the physical geometry of P in a relevantly different possible world – the specification of the physical geometry which P would possess if it were nomologically organized in a relevantly different way. Thus according to the A-thesis, the physical geometry of P is separately fixed, for each possible world, by the laws which obtain in that world, so that the geometry varies from world to world with variations in the nomological organization. But according to the B-thesis, the physical geometry of P is fixed, once for all, by the laws which obtain in the actual world, so that the geometry remains constant through all worlds in which P exists, irrespective of variations in the organization.

We can illustrate this by considering the case of physical centredness. According to the A-thesis, physical centredness is the property of being centred for whatever G-set is law-selected. Thus the A-thesis is committed to claiming:

(a) It is logically necessary, i.e. true in all possible worlds, that, for any set x of P-points: x is physically centred iff, for some G-set α, α is law-selected and x is centred for α.

According to the B-thesis, given the law-selected G-set, physical centredness is whatever intrinsic property (perhaps merely the property of being centred for that set) is essential to and distinctive of those items which are centred for that set. Thus the B-thesis is committed to claiming:

(b) For any G-set α, if α is law-selected, then it is logically necessary, i.e. true in all possible worlds, that, for any set x of P-points: x is physically centred iff x is centred for α.

Now let α_1 be the G-set which is law-selected in the actual world. And let W be a possible world with different laws, but containing P, in which a different G-set α_2 is law-selected. Finally, let β be some set of P-points which is centred for α_1 but not centred for α_2. It is a consequence of claim (a) that a set of P-points is physically centred in W iff it is centred for whatever G-set is law-selected in W. It is a consequence of claim (b) that, given the G-set which is law-selected in the actual world, a set of P-points is physically centred in W iff it is centred for that set. So according to the A-thesis, β, being non-centred for α_2, is *not* physically centred in W, while, according to the B-thesis, β, being centred for α_1, *is* physically centred in W. Generalizing from this, we can see that the A-thesis entails that, for each possible world, the physical geometry of P in that world accords with the G-set which is law-selected in that world, while the B-thesis entails that, for each possible world, the physical geometry of P in that world accords with the G-set which is law-selected in the actual world. Thus, on the A-thesis, the physical geometry of P varies from world to world with variations in the nomological organization. But, on the B-thesis, it holds constant through all worlds in which P exists.[1]

My reason for distinguishing these two versions of RNT is not so that we can decide between them. Rather, I want to use the distinction to show that RNT is unacceptable in any form. I want to show that a defender of RNT finds himself, in virtue of different aspects of his position, committed to accepting both versions and, thereby, because of their incompatibility, to abandoning his position altogether. In other words, I want to show that, by taking account of the distinction between the A-thesis and the B-thesis, we can come to see that it is the anti-realist form of the nomological thesis (ANT) which is correct. I shall begin by showing how RNT commits one to an acceptance of the A-thesis.

On either version, RNT takes physical space, or, more strictly its points, to be ontologically primitive – to be ingredients of ultimate reality. If physical space *is* ontologically primitive, then it has an intrinsic character which, as it were, lies beneath the surface of its physical character: the description of the physical geometry of P and the specification of its role as a medium for physical occupants do not reveal what P-points are like in themselves. It is because of this that we can, on the realist view, entertain the hypothesis that P is a sense-field – that its points are, in themselves, field-places. Now according to the B-thesis, whatever the intrinsic nature of P, its physical geometry (the network of physical distances between P-points) is fixed, once for all, by the laws which obtain in the actual world, and thus holds constant, irrespective of variations in the nomological organization, through all possible worlds in which

P exists. This claim may seem to have some plausibility when we confine our attention to cases in which, in the actual world, the functional geometry coincides with the TNI-geometry – with the geometry which it would be natural to select, independently of nomological considerations, from the transcendental viewpoint. Thus suppose we equate P with a 3-dimensional sense-field F and, as in the original sense-field theory[2], we stipulate that there is no nomological deviance: the functional geometry of F, and thereby its physical geometry, coincides with its sensual geometry. Now envisage a possible world in which the nomological organization of F is different. In particular, if R_1 and R_2 are sensually congruent F-regions containing, respectively, St Mary's and Big Ben (more precisely, containing the sensory processes which underlie them), envisage a possible world W which is just like the actual world except that the sensual locations of St Mary's and Big Ben are reversed and everything is organized exactly as if R_1 and R_2 were interchanged. There is at least some temptation to say, of this case, that F retains the same physical geometry in W, although its organization has changed. For its physical geometry in the actual world, although running counter to the organization in W, coincides with something, namely its sensual geometry, which it retains in *all* worlds. The change in organization seems, as it were, to be compensated by the transcendentally natural character of the geometry which the original organization selects. However, the B-thesis has no such plausibility in those cases where, in the actual world, the functional and TNI geometries conflict. Thus suppose we alter the original supposition in such a way that the sensual geometry is RT-deviant in the actual world and nomologically uniform in W. It is hard to see any rationale, in this case, for attributing to F in W the physical geometry which achieves uniformity in the actual world. For in W this geometry is out of line with both the functional and the sensual geometries. If W obtained, there would be nothing either in the intrinsic nature of F or in its nomological organization to make this geometry appropriate. The point becomes even clearer if we consider cases in which, in the actual world, the conflict between the functional and TNI geometries is more radical. Thus suppose (as in *case 2* of the previous chapter) we take P to be a 2-dimensional sense-field F' with a 3-dimensional organization. Now envisage a possible world in which, restoring nomological uniformity, F' has a 2-dimensional organization. There is nothing here to tempt us to say that F' retains, in such a world, a 3-dimensional physical geometry. Indeed, there is nothing which tempts us to say that it retains a *physical* geometry at all or that it remains, in any sense, a *physical* space. If P is a 2-dimensional sense-field, then its 3-dimensional organization is essential to its possession of a 3-dimensional geometry and hence essential to its qualifying as a physical space. To envisage circumstances in which it loses its 3-dimensional organization is just to envisage circumstances in which it ceases to be physical. (The same remarks apply, *mutatis mutandis*, to the case (*case 1* of the previous chapter) in which we take P to be the sum of two field-portions drawn from different sense-fields.) The clear consequence of all this is that the B-thesis must be rejected altogether. We cannot even retain it for those cases where, in the actual world, the functional and TNI geometries coincide. For even here, the initial plausibility of the thesis, such as it is, only stems from some residual attraction towards the transcendental thesis, which has already been discredited. It is clear that, in all cases, the physical geometry of the ontologically primitive item, whatever it is, is determined in each world by its nomological organization in that world.

This conclusion commits the spatial realist to accepting the A-thesis. But the trouble is that the A-thesis itself is vulnerable to an even simpler, but equally decisive, objection. Whether or not physical space is ontologically primitive, it is uncontroversial that it is a genuine space. But, for any genuine space (whether physical or non-physical), its particular geometrical structure is something which it possess non-contingently: its geometrical structure is essential to the very identities of the points and regions which compose it. If S is a space and N is the network of distance-relations holding between its points, it is logically impossible for those same points to be characterized by a different network of distance-relations. For to be characterized by a different network, they would have to move to different spatial positions in S and thus to become different points. Depending on the nature of S, it may be more natural to think of the network of distances as logically flowing from the identities of the points or more natural to think of the identities of the points as logically flowing from the network of distances. But there can be no denying that the two are essentially connected in such a way that we cannot have the same points without the same network. Now if we apply this essentialist doctrine to the case of *physical* space, we get the result that its physical geometry is the same in all worlds in which it (i.e. the same collection of physical points) exists. Of course, it is logically possible for there to be a physical space with a different physical geometry, since it is logically possible for there to be a numerically different physical space. But given P as our actual space, it is logically impossible for P to have a different physical geometry. There is no possible world in which P-points form a pattern of physical distances differing from their pattern in the actual world, since to form a different pattern they would have to become different points. It follows that we can accept the A-thesis only if the nomological organization of P cannot vary, in geometrically relevant ways, across different possible worlds. For the A-thesis insists that the physical geometry of P is determined, in each world, by its organization in that world. But if P is ontologically primitive – an ingredient of ultimate reality – its nomological organization must be purely contingent. There must be a possible world in which the same primitive item is governed by quite different laws (or no laws at all) and thus has, according to the A-thesis, a different physical geometry (or no physical geometry at all). We are forced to conclude, therefore, that the A-thesis is wrong. The actual physical geometry of P is essential to its identity and hence, as the B-thesis claims, holds constant through all possible worlds in which P exists, however much the laws may vary.

It might be objected, in reply, that this argument simply ignores the fact that physical space, being (according to RNT) ontologically primitive, has an intrinsic character beyond what is expressed by a specification of its physical geometry. If physical points were nothing more than geometrical positions, the argument against the A-thesis would hold: we could not alter the network of physical distances without destroying the points. But if the points have an intrinsic nature which transcends their geometrical role, then we have something else on which to anchor their identities when envisaging a variation in their physical positions. Thus if physical points are field-places, the identity of each point is simply the identity of a certain field-place, and although the actual network of sensual distances is essential to them, the actual network of physical distances is not: the same places (*ergo*, the same points) could take on different positions in the physical geometry by being subject to a different nomological organization. However, what this shows is merely that if we are going to allow the physical geometry to vary with variations in the nomological organization, we cannot *identify* physical points with field-places. We can suppose that what *underlies* physical space is a sense-field and that physical points, as it were, *coincide with* and are *ontologically mediated by* places in the field. But unless we identify the physical geometry with the sensual geometry – thereby keeping the physical geometry invariant through changes in the organization – the physical points cannot *be* sensual points. For, whatever their intrinsic nature, physical points just *are* positions in physical space and cannot survive an alteration in the network of physical distances, just as sensual points (field-places) are positions in a sense-field and cannot survive an alteration in the network of sensual distances. This is not to deny that, if the ontologically primitive item is a sense-field, variations in its organization entail corresponding variations in the physical geometry. It is just that we cannot think of the geometrical variations as occurring in the same physical space – as variations in the network of physical distances over the same domain of physical points.

However, there is a further and more sophisticated way in which my argument against the A-thesis might be challenged. In chapter 5, I rejected the Kantian view that we can know *a priori* that physical space is Euclidean. On this basis, I went on to allow for the further possibility that its geometrical structure, instead of being homogeneous and static, varies, in detail, from place to place and from time to time. Moreover, I claimed that such variations are not only possible, but, in effect, what the General Theory of Relativity postulates. 'For' as I put it 'in giving a purely geometrical account of gravitational fields, the General Theory postulates a 4-dimensional space-time continuum whose curvature varies from region to region (indeed, from point to point) with the varying density of matter.'[3] But if the geometrical structure of physical space can vary over time, surely this means that the very same physical points can be characterized by different networks of physical distances at different times and, consequently, that no one network holds essentially. Moreover, if we must allow for the case in which the same points are characterized by different networks at different times, we cannot exclude the case in which the same points are characterized, at a time, by different networks in

170

different possible worlds. It seems, therefore, that unless my earlier claims were wrong, the essentialist doctrine of geometry is mistaken and, in consequence, the argument against the A-thesis is misconceived.

Even if this objection were sound, however, it would not dispose of the essentialist doctrine altogether. Nor would it undermine it sufficiently to leave the A-thesis intact. For while we may be willing to allow a degree of flexibility in the geometrical structure of physical space, we could not allow the radical flexibility required by the A-thesis. It is one thing to claim that there could be a variation in the *metrical* properties of points over time, and another to claim that there could be, whether over time or over possible worlds, a variation in the *topology*. But the A-thesis allows for geometrical variation of any kind – within the limits imposed by the *a priori* requirements of a *physical* geometry. It allows for a case in which, if *W* is a possible world with an appropriately different set of laws, a region which is in Oxford in the actual world is in Westminster in *W* and a region which is in Westminster in the actual world is in Oxford in *W*. Even if we modified the essentialist doctrine, we would hardly be willing to modify it sufficiently to permit this result. But, in any case, the challenge to the essentialist doctrine is misconceived. For to say that physical space varies in geometrical structure over time is either incoherent or just a loose way of saying that there are different geometrical structures in the *different* momentary cross-sections of the 4-dimensional space-time continuum. If we think of physical space as persisting through time, so that the very same points exist at different times, we must also think of its geometrical structure – the network of physical distances – as necessarily static. Conversely, if we accept the possibility of changes in geometrical structure, as in the General Theory, we must take the 4-dimensional continuum as the primary object of geometrical specification and re-construe what we call 'physical space' as the collection of distinct 3-dimensional spaces obtained by appropriately slicing this continuum. Either way, there is, in the final analysis, no space, whether 3-dimensional or 4-dimensional, whose geometrical structure varies over time, and hence no challenge to the essentialist doctrine. Of course, it is only because I accept the essentialist doctrine that I interpret the situation in this way. I construe any temporal variation of geometrical structure in terms of the static 4-dimensional continuum in order to avoid the consequence that the very same physical points are characterized by different networks of physical distances at different times. But I can hardly be accused, in this, of begging the question. Prior to the challenge, the essentialist doctrine appeared self-evident. All I am showing is how the considerations which led to the challenge can be adequately handled in the framework of that doctrine. And, needless to say, this is how they are handled in the General Theory: it is the regions of space-time, not the regions of space *at* times, to which the curvatures are assigned.

The position we have reached, then, is this: there are two principles which are individually undeniable but irreconcilable from the standpoint of RNT. The first, which we may call the *principle of variability*, is that, for any ontologically primitive item, the physical geometry of that item, if it has one, is essentially linked with its nomological organization and is subject to variation, through different possible worlds, with variation in the relevant laws. The second, which we have called the essentialist doctrine, but which we may now re-label, appropriately, the *principle of constancy*, is that, for any genuine space, the geometrical structure of that space is essential to its identity and holds constant through all possible worlds in which the space exists, whatever the variations in nomological organization. These two principles are, clearly, jointly incompatible with the claim that physical space is ontologically primitive. For if physical space is ontologically primitive (i.e. if physical points are ontologically primitive), then, by the one principle, its geometrical structure varies from world to world according to its nomological organization, while, by the other principle, its geometrical structure remains constant with the constancy of its identity. By the principle of variability, the same physical points form different patterns of physical distances in relevantly different possible worlds. By the principle of constancy, the same physical points form the same pattern of physical distances in every possible world. So, in combination, the two principles refute the nomological thesis in its realist form. By the principle of variability RNT entails the A-thesis, and, by the principle of constancy, it entails the B-thesis. Since these two theses are incompatible, we must reject RNT altogether and, thereby, reject spatial realism.

It follows that, if we accept the existence of a physical space at all, we must adopt the nomological thesis in its anti-realist form (i.e. ANT). We must take physical space to be ontologically derivative and say that both its existence and its essential geometry are the logical product of an underlying reality which does not contain it. We must distinguish between the essential geometrical structure of physical space – a structure which, governed by the principle of constancy, holds constant through all possible worlds in which that space exists – and the contingent physical (i.e. physically relevant) geometry of the underlying primitive item – a geometry which, governed by the principle of variability, logically depends on and varies with the laws. And we must likewise distinguish between the nomological organization of physical space – an organization which, to the extent that it is essential to the geometry of that space, is also essential to its existence – and the nomological organization of the underlying item – an organization which, though required for its physical geometry and for the existence of physical space, is purely contingent.

To illustrate how this works in detail, let us, once again, focus on the case where the ontologically primitive item is a sense-field. And to bring out, in its sharpest form, the contrast between the primitive item and the derivative physical space, we will suppose that the sense-field (F) is, in terms of its sensual geometry, 2-dimensional, though subject to a 3-dimensional organization. We will suppose, that is, that there is a 3-dimensional assignment of co-ordinates to F-places (i.e. a 1-1 function from the set of F-places to the set of all ordered triples of real numbers) such that, in respect of the laws controlling the F-time distribution of sense-qualities and the effects of this distribution on human experience, the network of distance-relations which this assignment attributes to F-places, on the basis of the Euclidean metric, uniquely achieves, or comes closest to achieving, nomological uniformity. (Here, I am continuing to assume, for simplicity, that physical space is Euclidean.) This uniformity-achieving network (N) constitutes the physical (i.e. the physically relevant) geometry of F – the network of physical distances between F-places. It is only contingent that N constitutes the physical geometry of F. In a possible world in which a different network achieves uniformity, a different network constitutes the physical geometry, if there is a physical geometry at all. Thus the physical geometry of F varies, from world to world, with variations in its nomological organization, and in a world where it lacks a 3-dimensional organization, it lacks a physical geometry altogether.

Because *F* possesses its physical geometry only contingently, *F* itself is not a physical space: if it is a space at all, it is a sensual space whose essential geometrical structure is defined by the network of sensual distances between field-places. Rather, physical space (*P*) is logically created by the 3-dimensional organization of *F*, and it inherits, as it were, *F*'s contingent physical geometry as its own essential geometrical structure – a structure which it retains, as its physical geometry, in all worlds in which it exists. This means that in a world in which *F* has a different physical geometry, there is a numerically different physical space – a different set of physical points. And it means that in any world in which *P* exists, it retains those aspects of the nomological organization of *F* by which, in the actual world, its existence and essential geometrical structure are logically sustained. In this way, by adopting ANT, we reconcile the twin principles of variability and constancy. Physical geometry is subject to the principle of variability at the level of ultimate reality and to the principle of constancy at the derivative level of physical space. *F* varies in its physical geometry from world to world with relevant changes in its nomological organization. But the geometrical structure of *P* holds constant in all worlds in which *P* exists.

I have already indicated how the acceptance of ANT calls in question the viability of physical realism in any form. This is an issue which we must consider, in detail, in the next chapter. But I want to conclude our present discussion by noting something which, if not crucial, is at least of some interest, given the line of argument that has brought us to this point.

In chapter 5, I argued, as part of the argument for the topic-neutrality thesis, that, beyond a specification of its geometrical structure, we cannot specify the intrinsic nature of physical space in physical terms, since any physical description leaves unrevealed the intrinsic nature of physical points and physical distance. It was this claim, moreover, which, by generating the problem of the alternative networks (each with a *prima facie* claim to count as the physical geometry), led us to the nomological thesis as the solution. However, in adopting the anti-realist version of this thesis, we can now see that the topic-neutrality of physical description has to be understood in a new way. It is true that, beyond a specification of its geometrical structure, we cannot specify the intrinsic nature of physical space in physical terms. But this is because the space itself has no intrinsic nature beyond what the geometrical specification specifies. The underlying primitive item has a further intrinsic nature and one which may be specifiable, though not in physical terms. But physical space itself, which is logically created by the organization of that item, does not. Physical space itself is no more than the contingent realization of a pure geometrical structure – a structure which acquires, as it were, a concrete existence by the nomological organization of something else. From the standpoint of ANT, to speak of the intrinsic nature of physical points is only a loose way of speaking about the intrinsic nature of certain ontologically primitive entities (not themselves physical points) whose nomological organization creates the physical space. And to speak of the intrinsic nature of physical distance is only a loose way of referring to that network of relations, in the underlying reality, whose selection by the nomological criterion determines the physical geometry. To wonder what physical space is like in itself – to look for a possible specification of that spatial substance or content for which the formal geometry provides the structure – is, from the standpoint of ANT, totally misconceived, unless it is re-construed as a question about the nature of the underlying reality. By ceasing to be ultimate, the space itself has, one might say, become topic-neutral.

11

FULL ANTI-REALISM

We have established the nomological thesis in its anti-realist form (ANT), which holds that physical space is ontologically derivative and that its essential geometrical structure is logically determined by the nomological organization of something else, which underlies it. The question we must now consider is whether ANT leaves room for any form of physical realism. In rejecting the primitiveness of physical space, can we retain anything physical as an ingredient of ultimate reality?

One thing is clear. If we are to retain some form of physical realism, we must alter our account of the nature of occupancy. For since our discussion in chapter 5, we have taken the occupants of physical space to be themselves ontologically derivative – to be the logical creation of the distribution of intrinsic properties over points at times, together with laws which ensure the kinds of distributive uniformity and continuity characteristic of space-occupying continuants. It is clear that, combined with ANT, such a position excludes physical realism. For if the physical occupants are the logical creation of facts about physical space and if physical space is the logical creation of facts about something else, then there are no ontologically primitive physical entities and hence nothing left of the physical world to form an ingredient of ultimate reality. If we are to retain some form of physical realism, we must adopt some new account of the relationship between space and its occupants – an account which takes the occupants to be ontologically primitive. We already know, from the earlier chapter, the broad outline of the account we require. Instead of construing material objects as logically created by the distribution and nomological organization of properties of points at times (an organization which ensures those distributive uniformities and continuities characteristic of space-occupying continuants), the physical realist must construe physical space as logically created by the distribution and nomological organization of properties of material objects at times (an organization which ensures those distributive uniformities and continuities characteristic of a 3-dimensional spatial medium). Instead of taking material objects to be ontologically constituted as the derivative occupants of a primitive space, he must take physical space to be ontologically constituted as a derivative medium for primitive objects. In short, he must develop a matter-selective realism in place of a space-selective realism. Only thus can he, accepting ANT, retain something of the physical world as an ingredient of ultimate reality.

A matter-selective realism could be developed along the following lines:

1 We begin by assuming that, however much or little of it is included in the ultimate reality, the physical world is composed of:
   (1) Time.
   (2) Physical space (unbounded, 3-dimensional and Euclidean).
   (3) A stock of mutually impenetrable spherical material particles (atoms), all of the same size and of the same physical type.
   (4) A set α of physical laws governing the motion of atoms.
   We will also assume that there is an additional set β of psycho-physical (strictly, physio-psychical) laws, whereby certain types of spatial and spatiotemporal configuration of atoms (intuitively, brain-states and brain-processes) are causally sufficient for the simultaneous or immediately subsequent occurrence of certain types of experience in human minds.

2 Let γ be the set of all ordered triples of real numbers, both positive and negative. We will think of γ-members as collectively forming the points of an abstract, 3-dimensional Euclidean space (S). That is, we will speak of such triples as S-points and we will fix the distance between any two S-points in accordance with the Euclidean metric:

d is the distance between $\langle a,b,c \rangle$ and $\langle a',b',c' \rangle$ iff $d^2 = (a-a')^2 + (b-b')^2 + (c-c')^2$.

3   We postulate an uncountable set E of atomic states, a set α' of laws controlling the realization of E-states and a set β' of laws controlling the effects of such realization on human experience, such that

(a) Ultimate reality (or the relevant portion of ultimate reality) is composed of
   (1) Time.
   (2) Human minds.
   (3) Atoms.
   (4) The realization of E-states by atoms at times.
   (5) α' and β'.

(b) There is a 1-1 function f from E-states to S-points such that, if we say that an atom x is *located at* an S-point $f(y)$ at time t iff x is in E-state y at t, then, for some number n greater than 0 (a number representing the atomic radius):
   (1) α' ensures that, for any atom x and any time t, x is located at one and only one S-point at t.
   (2) α' ensures that no two atoms are located at the same S-point at the same time. Indeed, more strongly,
   (3) α' ensures that, for any distinct atoms x and y, any S-points w and z, and any time t, if x is located at w at t and y is located at z at t, then the distance between w and z is no less than $2n$.
   (4) α' ensures that all changes in the location of an atom in S are S-time continuous. Indeed, more strongly,
   (5) α' imposes exactly the same constraints on the 'motion' of atoms in S as α imposes on their motion in physical space.
   (6) β' assigns the same experiential effects to atom-configurations in S and S-time as β assigns to the corresponding configurations in physical space and space-time.

(c) Physical space is just the logical creation of this quasi-spatial organization of the atoms. It is just the concrete realization, by the laws controlling E-states, of the

abstract geometrical structure of S. α' creates a space
for the atoms by controlling their intrinsic states in a
way that mirrors the structure of S – by ensuring that
everything behaves exactly as if each atom, by realizing
a particular E-state, occupies (so as to exclude all other
atoms) a particular spherical region of a 3-dimensional
Euclidean space and, by passing through a continuous
series of E-states, pursues a spatially continuous path.

I shall call this version of matter-selective realism the *states-version*
(SV).

SV combines ANT with physical realism. It retains atoms as
ontologically primitive, thus maintaining a physical presence in the
ultimate reality, and it construes physical space as the logical
creation of the underlying organization, thus satisfying the nomological thesis in its anti-realist form. Moreover, by going mentalistic,
we can provide a concrete example of what the E-states might be.
Thus let us assume that the dimension of phenomenal pitch is
continuous and unbounded and that h is a 1-1 function from
pitches to real numbers (both positive and negative) which
represents the topology and metric of the dimension in an
intuitively acceptable way (e.g. if we take a tone as the unit of
distance and $h(x) = 0$, then, for each positive integer n, $h(y) = n$ iff
y is n tones higher than x, and $h(y) = -n$ iff y is n tones lower than
x, the non-integral values of the intervening pitches being fixed
proportionately). Let us say that an auditory sensation is *simple* iff
it is the realization of a unique pitch at a certain loudness. And,
selecting three loudness-degrees X, Y and Z, let us define A as that
set of auditory states such that, for any s, s is a member of A iff for
some triple of (not necessarily distinct) pitches x, y and z, to be in
state s is to have a total auditory sensation consisting of a simple
sensation of x at X, a simple sensation of y at Y and a simple
sensation of z at Z. Then, to provide a mentalistic version of SV, we

(a) construe atoms as minds (conscious subjects) of some
    distinctive, though unspecified, kind K;
(b) identify E with A;
(c) define f (the function from E-states to S-points) in such a
    way that, for any A-state s and any pitches x, y and z, if x, y
    and z are the pitches respectively linked in s with X, Y and
    Z, then $f(s) = \langle h(x), h(y), h(z) \rangle$.

It would then turn out that α' is a set of laws controlling the realization of auditory states in *K*-minds and that β' is a set of laws controlling the effects of auditory sensations in *K*-minds on human experience. And it would turn out that physical space is the logical creation of auditory facts about *K*-minds together with these laws. If you like, taking *X, Y* and *Z* as the axes of a co-ordinate system and pitch-values as co-ordinates, we can think of *A*-states as collectively forming the points of an abstract 3-dimensional auditory space (*A**) and of *K*-minds as located, at any time, at those *A**-points which they realize. In effect, it is the fact that this spatial model exactly fits the nomological organization of the auditory states which creates the physical space and which arranges the atoms in physical space-time in a way which matches their pitch-arrangement in A*-time. Let us call this mentalistic version of SV the *auditory states-version* (ASV).

ASV is not the only mentalistic version of SV. There are indefinitely many other versions on the same general lines. Nor is SV the only version of matter-selective realism. It is possible to construct an alternative version which focuses on the *relations* between atoms rather than on their intrinsic states – a version which takes physical space to be the logical creation of certain contingent relations between atoms at times, together with the laws which control the obtaining of these relations.[1] But we need not concern ourselves with these alternatives, since they shed no further light on the issue we have to discuss.

The issue is this: is matter-selective realism, however developed, a genuine option? Can we coherently suppose that while physical space is ontologically derivative, its material occupants, in the form of atoms, are ontologically primitive? I shall argue that we cannot.

The first point to be made is that, as we noted in our earlier discussion,[2] matter-selective realism is in radical conflict with our ordinary understanding of the relationship between physical space and its occupants. We ordinarily think of material objects as *essentially* spatial – as objects of which spatial location and spatial extension are logically essential attributes. Indeed, we think of such objects as existing by and through their occupancy of space: we think of spatial occupancy as constituting the very form of their existence – as constituting their mode of being. And, in consequence, we think of physical space, in conjunction with time, as providing the framework of their identity: we think of a portion of matter as individuated, at a time, by the region it occupies, and as persisting, through time, by following a spatiotemporally continuous path. This way of understanding the relationship between matter and physical space cannot be retained if we take matter as ontologically primitive and space as logically created by the nomological organization of matter. For if matter is ontologically primitive, its nomological organization will be purely contingent. Given the material items in the actual world, there will be a possible world in which the same items are organized in a quite different and non-space-creating way. So if matter is ontologically primitive and physical space is a logical creation, material objects are not entities of which spatial location is a logically essential attribute.

The matter-selective realist might try to undermine this point by focusing on the distinction between a necessity which is *conceptual* (or *de dicto*) and one which is *objective* (or *de re*) – in the present case, between what is logically required for something to qualify as a material object, and what, given some material object, is logically required for the existence of that thing. Thus he might concede that physical space is logically required for the existence of material objects, in the sense that nothing would qualify as material unless it had a position and an extension in space. But, at the same time, he could deny that location in physical space is a logically essentially attribute of the material objects themselves – at least, of those he selects as ontologically primitive. Endorsing SV, for example, he might concede that the atoms only qualify as atoms (as particles of matter) in virtue of being located in physical space, but insist that they have such location only contingently, in virtue of the nomological organization of their pre-spatial states. Moreover, he might claim that when we think of material objects as, in themselves, essentially spatial, we are failing to notice or give due weight to the distinction he draws – that we mistakenly interpret a condition which is necessary for the satisfaction of the concept *material* as one which is essential to the objects to which the concept applies. Such a mistake, he might argue, is hardly surprising, given that the intrinsic nature of matter lies beyond the scope of empirical knowledge: we think of material objects as essentially spatial because their sub-spatial intrinsic character is empirically concealed.

However, this reply does not carry much conviction. For even when we take everything into account, including both the distinction between conceptual and objective necessity and the limits on empirical knowledge, our original intuitions remain. We continue to hold that occupancy of space is not only a necessary condition of something's being material, but also an essential attribute of those things which are material. If we envisage a case in which the ontologically primitive items are only contingently spatial (e.g. the K-minds of ASV) – spatial in virtue of their nomological organization – we see the contingency as precluding an identification of these items with material objects and as leaving us, at best, with the option of saying that these items and their quasi-spatial organization form the underlying reality of which material objects, along with their arrangement in physical space, are the logical creation. Given our actual material objects, the suggestion that these same objects could exist without spatial location seems, even all things considered, to be as absurd as the suggestion that, given our actual physical space, the same points could exist with a different geometrical structure.

This point may well be decisive. But even if it is not, there is a further argument which clinches the issue. A little earlier, I presented a mentalistic version (ASV) of matter-selective realism, in which atoms were construed as minds and physical space was taken to be logically created by the nomological organization of their auditory states. As I said, we can think of the auditory states (the A-states) as collectively forming the points of an abstract 3-dimensional space (A^*) and the minds (the K-minds) as located, at any time, at those A^*-points which they realize. The laws ensure that, at each time, each K-mind is located at just one A^*-point and distinct K-minds are located at distinct A^*-points, and that, through time, each K-mind pursues an A^*-time continuous path. Let us call the type of ultimate reality here envisaged U_1. For the purposes of assessing matter-selective realism, I shall assume that a U_1-reality would suffice for the existence of a physical world of space and atoms, whether or not, given such a reality, atoms would (as ASV requires) be ontologically primitive.

Let us now envisage a second type of ultimate reality (U_2) which is exactly like U_1 except that (1), for some A^*-distance d, the laws permit any two K-minds to exchange their A^*-positions at any moment when they are d-related and (2) a certain number of such nomologically permissible exchanges take place. (To say that two minds M_1 and M_2 exchange their A^*-positions at t is to say that the A^*-path of M_1 after t is from the A^*-position of M_2 at t and the A^*-path of M_2 after t is from the A^*-position of M_1 at t.) We will further suppose that, whenever such exchanges occur, the laws ensure that each mind assumes not only the position, but also the velocity and direction of the other, so that each subsequently behaves in exactly the way the other would have behaved if the exchange had not occurred (see Figure 11.1). Thus whenever two

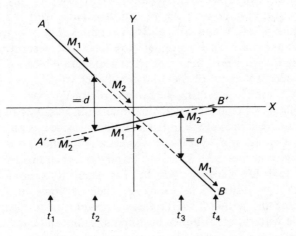

Figure 11.1

The figure shows a 2-dimensional cross-section of A^* (using the loudness-degrees X and Y as spatial axes). Within this cross-section, it depicts two positional exchanges, at t_2 and t_3, between the mind M_1 (represented by unbroken lines) and the mind M_2 (represented by broken lines). Notice how, when the exchanges occur, each mind continues on the original course of the other.

minds exchange their A*-positions, they also exchange all their physically relevant properties. This means that such exchanges do not alter the character of the physical world described in physical terms. Thus if we were to suppose that it is a U_2-reality which actually underlies the physical world, we need not and should not abandon our ordinary beliefs about the behaviour of atoms. Rather, we should continue to accept that each atom pursues a continuous path in physical space, corresponding to a continuous path in A^*, even when what follows the continuous path in A^* is not a single K-mind, but a causally continuous sequence of auditory sensations connecting the phases of different minds.[3] In other words, if we re-construe Figure 11.1 as depicting a cross-section of physical space, each continuous line, AB and $A'B'$, shows the path of a single atom, the unbroken portions showing the phases associated with the auditory sensations of M_1 and the broken portions showing the phases associated with the auditory sensations of M_2. When, at t_2 and t_3, the minds change places in A^*, the atoms retain their original positions and dispositions, but exchange, as it were, their underlying mental substance. Because the minds exchange *all* their physically relevant properties, each exchange leaves everything the same in physical terms.

It follows, of course, that if the underlying reality is of type U_2, atoms and K-minds are not identical. For suppose a is an atom and M is a K-mind. If a and M are numerically identical, it is logically necessary that they coincide in A^* throughout their history. But this is not logically necessary in U_2. For since it is nomologically possible for K-minds to exchange their A^*-positions, without disturbing the paths of the atoms, each atom has the capacity to coincide with different minds at different times and each mind the capacity to coincide with different atoms at different times. Even if a and M in fact coincide throughout their history, the coincidence is not logically or even nomologically guaranteed. It is possible for M to exchange positions with some other mind and thus possible for the coincidence to cease. And this is enough to show that a and M are numerically distinct.

U_2 differs from U_1 both in its nomological organization (the U_2-laws permit positional exchanges in appropriate circumstances) and in its A^*-time arrangement of K-minds (certain permissible exchanges occur). But to complete the picture, let us envisage a third type of ultimate reality (U_3), which is exactly like U_2 except that, by chance, no positional exchanges occur. Thus in terms of composition, U_3 falls between U_1 and U_2. It is like U_2 in its more permissive laws (the A^*-positional exchanges being nomologically possible), but like U_1 in its A^*-time arrangement of minds (each mind following an A^*-time continuous path). This means that, as in the case of U_1, each atom coincides throughout its history with a unique mind and each mind coincides throughout its history with a unique atom. But it also means that, as in the case of U_2, atoms and K-minds are numerically distinct, since none of the coincidences is logically guaranteed.

Now all three types of ultimate reality yield physical worlds of the same physical character. The replacement of U_1 by U_2 makes no difference to the spatiotemporal arrangement of atoms, nor to the physical and psychophysical laws, since the paths of the atoms are not affected by the positional exchanges of the K-minds. Likewise, of course, there is no alteration, physically, in arrangement and laws when U_1 is replaced by U_3. However, while all three types of reality yield physical worlds of the same physical character, the matter-selective realist cannot allow that they yield physical worlds of the same ontological status. For the realist wants to use U_1 as an example of a reality in which atoms are retained as ontologically primitive. It is crucial to this example – as an example of matter-selective realism – that atoms and K-minds be numerically identical, since only thus do we get atoms as ingredients of the ultimate reality. But, as we have seen, atoms and K-minds are not identical in either U_2 or U_3. And, since K-minds are the only ontologically primitive continuants, this means that, in the cases of U_2 and U_3, atoms are ontologically derivative: they are entities whose existence is logically sustained by the way the K-minds are nomologically organized. Thus the matter-selective realist is forced to say that if U_1 is replaced by either U_2 or U_3, the K-minds cease to be atoms and a new set of atoms is created, and that if U_2 or U_3 is replaced by U_1, the K-minds become atoms and the original set of atoms disappears. These are strange consequences of the realist's position. The ontological alterations at the physical level seem out of all proportion to the marginal alterations in the ultimate reality.

In fact, if we focus on the comparison of U_1 with U_3, we can see that the realist's position is incoherent. Let us suppose that, in the actual world, the underlying reality is of type U_3. On this supposition, the actual laws permit K-minds to exchange their A^*-positions in appropriate circumstances, though, purely by chance, no such exchanges occur, even when the appropriate circumstances obtain. As we have seen, this means that atoms and K-minds are numerically distinct, even though, throughout their history, each atom coincides with a single mind and each mind coincides with a single atom. Let us call the set of atoms Γ and the set of K-minds Δ. Now, given the permissive laws, each atom has the nomological capacity to coincide with different K-minds at different times and each K-mind has the nomological capacity to coincide with different atoms at different times. But it is clearly not logically essential either to the members of Γ or to the members of Δ that they should have this capacity. Holding Γ and Δ constant, we can envisage a possible world W which is exactly like the actual world except that, with stronger laws, this nomological capacity is removed – a world which contains the very same atoms and the very same minds, but in which positional exchanges between K-minds are nomologically excluded. In other words, we can construct around Γ and Δ a counterfactual situation in which the physical world remains the same but the underlying reality is of type U_1. Now, obviously, just as Γ is the set of atoms in the actual world, so also it is the set of atoms in W. Moreover, since Γ-members and Δ-members are numerically distinct in the actual world, they remain numerically distinct in W. So by envisaging W, we have envisaged a world in which a U_1-reality obtains but in which atoms are ontologically derivative. But, according to matter-selective realism, such a reality is one in which the atoms are identical with K-minds and thus ontologically primitive.

The realist might object that the possibility of a U_1-world in which atoms are ontologically derivative does not entail the impossibility of a U_1-world in which atoms are ontologically primitive. Thus he might claim that given the actual world (a U_3-world), as specified, there are two different ways of transforming it into a U_1-world according to how much of the ontology we hold constant: if we retain both Δ and Γ, we reach a U_1-world in which atoms are derivative; but if we just retain Δ, we reach a U_1-world in which the K-minds become atoms and hence in which atoms are primitive. In each case, he would say, what we retain or discard is a matter for stipulation – a question of choosing our entities and then constructing the counterfactual situation around them. Alternatively, he might claim that, even if, given our supposition about the actual world, there is no way of envisaging a U_1-world in which the members of Δ are atoms, none the less there is no incoherence in supposing that the *actual* world is one in which a U_1-reality obtains and in which the K-minds are atoms. But neither of these claims is defensible. In the first place, while it is true that a merely qualitative description of a possible world leaves some freedom to stipulate the identities of the objects it contains, it is clearly incoherent to suppose that there are two possible worlds in which the ultimate realities are of exactly the same type and contain exactly the same primitive objects, but in which there are ontological differences at the physical level. For there cannot be differences at the physical level unless there is some difference in the ultimate reality to generate them. Consequently, we cannot make sense of the suggestion that, given an actual U_3-world, we can, *holding Δ constant*, reach different U_1-worlds according to whether we retain or discard Γ. Granted that we can envisage a U_1-world containing Γ and Δ, we cannot also envisage a U_1-world containing Δ alone and thus cannot envisage a U_1-world in which Δ-members are atoms. Moreover, for the same reason, we cannot coherently postulate an actual U_1-world in which atoms are ontologically primitive. For given an actual U_1-world W_1, we can, holding the K-minds constant, envisage a possible U_3-world W_2 in which atoms are ontologically derivative, and thence, holding both the K-minds and the atoms constant, envisage a possible U_1-world W_3 in which atoms are ontologically derivative. W_1 and W_3 will then turn out to be the same world, since there is nothing to distinguish them at the level of ultimate reality. Consequently, W_1 will be a world in which atoms are ontologically derivative.

The upshot of this is that ASV is incoherent. Even if we suppose the ultimate reality to be as ASV postulates, we cannot identify atoms with K-minds, since we can envisage the same atoms and minds in different circumstances (a U_3-world) where they are clearly distinct. So even in the case of a U_1-reality we must take the atoms, like the physical space, to be ontologically derivative – to be the logical creation of the K-minds and the nomological organization of their auditory states. But, clearly, the same considerations apply, *mutatis mutandis*, to any version of matter-selective realism. Thus whatever ontologically primitive continuants the realist postulates, we can envisage a possible world, containing the same primitive entities and the same material objects, but in which, with more permissive laws, the 1-1 coincidence of primitive and material items is only accidental. And by focusing on this possibility, we can see that, even in the postulated world, the items are not identical. Consequently, there is no way of constructing a coherent version of matter-selective realism – no way in which, accepting physical space as a logical creation, we can retain material objects as ontologically primitive.

This conclusion is, in any case, what our modal intuition requires – our intuition that the occupancy of space is an essential attribute of material objects. All that remains is to show how nicely the conclusion and the intuition fit together. We have already established that physical space (if it exists at all) is ontologically derivative. We know, moreover, that if physical space is ontologically derivative and if, as our intuition requires, material objects are essentially spatial, then material objects too are ontologically derivative. But it is also true that by taking material objects to be ontologically derivative, we can explain why they are essentially spatial. They are essentially spatial because they are ontologically constituted as occupants of space. This holds whether or not space is taken as primitive. If, as we originally supposed, space were primitive, material objects would derive their existence from the distribution and organization of the intrinsic states of points at times. If, as we now know, space is derivative, space and material objects derive their existence from a common source, in such a way that the creation of the objects logically requires the creation of their spatial medium. Thus, in the examples we have been considering, the A^*-time arrangement of the K-minds and its nomological organization suffice to create the atoms only because the organization, by, as it were, embodying a 3-dimensional structure, creates a space to contain them. Quite generally, whatever the ontological status of physical space, material objects are essentially spatial because their spatial character is the inevitable consequence of their mode of creation.

Obviously the considerations which require us to assign a derivative status to material objects (if they exist) also require us to assign a derivative status to any other occupants of physical space (e.g. sub-atomic particles, if these count as non-material). In consequence, since neither physical space nor its occupants are ontologically primitive, we are forced to accept that ultimate reality is wholly non-physical. In other words, we are forced to reject physical realism altogether. From now on our concern will be to work out, in more detail, what we should put in its place. Should our anti-realism be nihilistic or reductivist? And if reductivist, what form of reduction should we accept? These are the questions to be considered in Part IV.

PART IV

THE CASE FOR PHENOMENALISM

12

THE REJECTION OF THE ISOMORPHISM-REQUIREMENT

We have established, and established *a priori*, that ultimate reality is wholly non-physical. So physical realism is false – indeed, incoherent. But a realist could still try to salvage something from this conclusion. In the first place, as we saw at the outset,[1] anti-realism admits of two versions, namely *nihilism*, which denies the existence of a physical world altogether, and *reductivism*, which accepts its existence, but as the logical product of something else. Obviously, while both these positions are anti-realist, reductivism is closer than nihilism to physical realism, since, like realism, but unlike nihilism, it retains the existence of a physical world. Moreover, reductivism itself admits of different versions, according to the type of reduction involved, and some of these versions are closer to realism than others. Thus reductivism moves closer to realism if it sees the creation of the physical world as necessarily involving an ultimate reality which is predominantly external to human minds. It moves still closer if it requires this external reality to be similar, in structure and laws, to the physical world it creates. And it comes closest of all if it requires the physical world and this reality to be isomorphic. So it is possible to retain much of the realist's position within the framework of anti-realism. Incidentally, when I speak of the *existence* of a physical world, I mean this to cover both the existence of physical entities *and* the obtaining physical facts. And, correspondingly, when I speak of the logical *creation* of a physical world, I mean this to cover both the creation of physical entities *and* the sustainment of physical facts. In the second case, I could have spoken, instead, of the logical *production* of the physical world, since, in chapter 1, I introduced the predicate 'logical product of' to cover both sustainment and creation. But, for some reason, I have a stylistic preference for the term 'creation' in the present context.

How much of the realist's position, then, should we retain? How close to or far from physical realism should our anti-realism go? I am going to divide our discussion of this question into two stages. In the first stage, which will cover this chapter and the next, I shall be exclusively concerned with the relative merits of different versions of reductivism. I shall, in effect, take the existence of a physical world for granted and simply try to establish the principles of its creation. In the second stage, covering chapters 14 and 15, I shall return to the issue between reductivism and nihilism – the issue of whether, given our anti-realism, there is or could be a physical world at all.

The version of reductivism which is furthest from physical realism – the version which is, one might say, on the brink of nihilism – is that which takes the physical world to be logically created by the character of and (natural) constraints on the course of human experience. We already have a label for this position: *reductive phenomenalism*. Leaving aside the challenge of nihilism (to be considered later), it is this position which I shall try to defend, though with two modifications. The first modification is simply a narrowing of the phenomenalist thesis to read: 'The physical world is the logical creation of (merely) the *constraints* on human experience.' (Thus the character of human experience is treated as physically irrelevant except in so far as it reflects the constraints.) From now on, I shall take 'reductive phenomenalism' to signify this narrower thesis. The second modification will emerge at the end of chapter 13, but I think it best, for the time being, to leave it concealed.

To avoid any confusion, there are two preliminary points which must be borne in mind. Firstly, as we noted in chapter 1,[2] *reductive* phenomenalism is not the same as and does not entail *analytical* phenomenalism. In claiming that the physical world is the logical creation of the constraints on human experience, it is not committed to claiming that statements about the physical world can be analysed into statements about the experiential constraints. I feel the need to emphasize this yet again because I am conscious of using the term 'reductive' in what may be, in philosophical circles, an unusual sense. Secondly. reductive phenomenalism does not, as such, deny the existence of an external reality, nor even deny it a role in the creation of the physical world. For in claiming that the physical world is the logical creation of the constraints on human experience it does not deny that these constraints are imposed by something external to the human minds. What it claims is that the constraints, on their own. suffice for the creation of the physical world, irrespective of what, if anything, lies behind them – that if there is an ultimate external reality, it contributes nothing to the existence of the physical world except what it contributes to the obtaining of the constraints. The phenomenalist does not even have to deny that the existence of such a reality is logically necessary for the creation of a physical world. For he may be prepared to concede that, without something to impose them, there could be no constraints of a world-creating type. Such a concession would not undermine his claim that it is these constraints, on their own, which create the physical world, and that anything else contributes only indirectly, by contributing to the constraints.

It will be easiest if we begin by considering the claims of reductive phenomenalism in the framework of a particular, and by now familiar, example. Let us assume that the physical world (PW) is composed of the following elements:

(1)   time;
(2)   a 3-dimensional Euclidean space;
(3)   a stock of spherical material particles, these particles having an arrangement, in space-time, of determinate type A;
(4)   a set α of laws governing the motion of particles in the normal Newtonian way.

In addition, we will assume that there is a set β of psychophysical laws, assigning experiential effects in human minds to particle-configurations. More precisely, we will assume that there is a function f, from configuration-types to experience-types, and 1-1 correlation between human minds and non-overlapping groups of particles, such that β ensures that, for any time t, mind m and correlated particle-group g, m has an experience of type ψ at t iff, for some c, g has a configuration of type c at t and $f(c) = \psi$. Thus β correlates each human mind with a particular group of particles (intuitively, the group which forms its neural embodiment) in such a way that the configuration of this group, at any time, determines (in accordance with f) the simultaneous experiential state of the mind.[3] The total physical reality, $PW + \beta$, I shall designate by P. Needless to say, these assumptions about the composition of the physical world and its nomological links with human experience are a considerable over-simplification of the truth. But, as I have emphasized on other occasions, this sort of simplification is required for the purposes of philosophical clarity.

Along with these assumptions about the nature of the physical reality, we will begin by envisaging an ultimate reality (U) consisting of the following elements:

U
- Human minds/subjects
- External reality (E)
  - External component (EC)
    - (1) Time.
    - (2) A 3-dimensional Euclidean sense-field F, existing in some non-human mind.
    - (3) An F-time distribution, of determinate type D, of two sense-qualities Q_1 and Q_2.
    - (4) A set α' of laws governing the distribution of Q_1 and Q_2.
  - A set β' of laws assigning experiential effects in human minds to quality-configurations in F

We will assume that, for some F-distance r, α' ensures, amongst other things, that (a) at any time, the total portion of F which is Q_1-pervaded divides exhaustively into non-overlapping spheres of radius r (every other region of F being Q_2-pervaded), and (b) all changes in Q_1- pervasion are F-time continuous. Because of this, we will often find it convenient, when describing events in F, to speak as if the spheres of Q_1-pervasion were mobile continuants – each sphere preserving its identity through an F-time continuous series of region-moments. Adopting this way of speaking, we will assume that P and E are isomorphic, i.e. that the F-time arrangement of Q_1-continuants matches the space-time arrangement of particles (both being of determinate type A) and that α' and β' (in respect of Q_1-continuants) match α and β (in respect of particles). This means, in particular, that β' correlates each human mind with a particular group of Q_1-continuants (just as β correlates it with a particular group of particles) in such a way that the configuration of this group, at any time, causally determines the simultaneous experiential state of the mind in accordance with f.

Now, for each mind m and time t, the F-time distribution of Q_1 and Q_2 up to and including t (or more intuitively, the arrangement, velocities and directions of Q_1-continuants at t), together with α' and β', sets a certain constraint on the course of m's experience at and after t. It does so in two ways: firstly, by causally determining, according to the t-configuration of the group of Q_1-continuants which is correlated with m, the experience of m at t; secondly, by causally influencing the subsequent configurations of this correlated group and, thereby, influencing the course of m's experience after t. (If the laws of motion (α') are, like the laws of experiential effect (β'), deterministic, then the distribution of qualities up to t determines their distribution subsequent to t and, thereby, determines the subsequent course of m's experience. But even if it does not determine the subsequent course of m's experience, it at least narrows the range of possibilities.) This constraint on the course of m's experience, imposed by the F-time distribution up to t, we may call the *mt-constraint*. The totality of constraints on human experience is then the totality of these specific constraints collected from each mind-time pair. I shall call this constraint-totality CT. In the framework of this example, the reductive phenomenalist claims that the physical world PW (indeed, the total physical reality P) is the logical creation of CT. As I have already indicated he does not deny the relevance of the external reality (E) to the creation of PW, since it is this reality ($EC + \beta'$) which generates the experiential constraints. What he claims is that E has relevance only as the generator of these constraints: any alteration to the external reality which makes no difference to the constraints makes no difference to the existence or character of the physical world. According to the phenomenalist, there would still be a derivative physical world of the same type as PW if the constituents of CT were the direct result of divine volition or (if this is possible) obtained without the backing of any external reality at all.

Unlike E, CT is, in structure, quite unlike the physical reality (P) which, according to the phenomenalist, it logically sustains. Each element in CT is, for a certain mind and time, a constraint on the course of experience in that mind from that time – a constraint which is specified by distinguishing, within the class of logically possible courses, those which are causally permissible from those which are not. Such elements do not have, either individually or collectively, anything like the structure of a physical world. We cannot directly see in them, as we can in E, a replica of physical space or replicas of material particles. But, obviously, if reductive phenomenalism is correct, there must be some way in which the structure of P is implicit in, encoded by, the structure of CT; otherwise, there would be no sense in which the physical reality was the logical product of the constraints. So the first task of the phenomenalist must be to state the form which this encoding takes. His answer is that the structure of P is implicit in CT by being explicit in that which makes CT systematic. What makes CT systematic is not that it forms a uniform system of natural necessity when taken on its own, but that, by postulating a certain kind of external reality, we can envisage it as part of something whose natural necessities do form a uniform system. What makes the constraints systematic is not something we can state solely in terms of their location in the framework of time and human minds: we cannot, for example, say that different minds are always constrained in the same way at the same time; nor can we even say that different minds are always constrained in the same way at the same time provided that their previous experiential biographies have been exactly similar. What makes the constraints systematic is their capacity for absorption into the uniform nomological organization of a more extensive reality – a reality in which all events, both in the realm of human experience and outside it, are uniformly controlled by the same general laws. It is not that the organization of human experience is uniform in its own terms, but that, by expanding our ontology, we can subsume it under the uniform organization of something larger. The relevance of this to the phenomenalist is that any such larger nomologically uniform reality which absorbs CT would (we may reasonably assume) exemplify the structure of P. (This is not quite true, but I shall leave the refinements, e.g. concerning nomological *relevance*, till later.) We discern the structure of P in CT by asking 'What sorts of ultimate external reality, with a uniform organization, would generate those constraints on human experience?' and by finding the P-structure exemplified in each of the possible answers. In some answers, admittedly, the exemplification involves a slight shift in ontological perspective. Thus in an external reality of type E, we find, as the ultimate counterparts of the physical particles, not continuants, but F-time continuous paths of Q_1-pervasion. Again (and in contrast), in the external reality we envisaged in the previous chapter (the world of K-minds), we find, as the ultimate counterpart of physical space, not a space, but the quasi-spatial organization of auditory experience. But, subject to such adjustments in ontological perspective, it is isomorphism with P which defines the relevant range of possible external realities, i.e. those realities which have a uniform nomological organization and yield CT. In this sense, the structure of P is implicit in the constraints on human experience and can be extracted from them by, as it were, applying the requirements of organizational uniformity. Put succinctly, the structure of P is implicit in the constraints because the constraints are, by the standard of uniformity, exactly as if an ultimate external reality with that structure obtained.

The fact that the structure of P is, in this way, implicit in CT does not, of course, make reductive phenomenalism true. It does not entail that P is logically sustained by CT – that the constraints, on their own, suffice for the existence and determine the character of the physical world. Moreover, our initial inclination is to deny the phenomenalist's claim. Our inclination is to say that, without the backing of an external reality, the constraints would be insufficient. Indeed, our inclination is to say that, for the existence of a physical world, the ultimate reality must contain an external item with approximately the same structure. Thus we are far from inclined, initially, to accept that the external reality contributes nothing to the physical world save what it contributes to the constraints. But at least we must concede to the phenomenalist that the constraints on human experience play a crucial role in the creation of a physical world and that the contribution of the external reality is, in some sense, mediated by them. If the external reality imposed no constraints on human experience, it would contribute nothing to the creation of a *physical* world, since it would contribute nothing to the creation of a world-for-us, a world-from-our-viewpoint. If the ultimate reality consisted merely of EC and human minds, with no bridging laws, such as β', whereby the quality-arrangements in F affect the course of human experience, then there would be no physical world – just as, if the ultimate reality consisted of human minds and two external components, EC_1 and EC_2, each of which had a physically appropriate structure, but only one of which, EC_1, was nomologically linked with human experience, then there would be, at most, one physical world, i.e. that which was constituted as *our* world through the constraints imposed, by EC_1, on our experience. Moreover, if the external reality is to contribute something to the creation of a physical world, not only must it impose constraints on human experience, but the structure of such a world must be, at least to some significant degree, reflected in the character of the constraints. Thus if the ultimate reality consisted of EC, human minds and a different set of bridging laws, β^*, such that β^* assigned the same type of experiential effect to every configuration-type, again there would be no physical world, since there would be no encoding of the structure of a physical world in the character of the constraints. (Thus we would not need to envisage an external 3-dimensional structure in order to see the constraints as forming, or forming part of, a nomologically uniform system.) The fact that the external component has a physically appropriate structure only contributes to the creation of a physical world if that structure is, as it were, projected, through the constraints, on to the human viewpoint – translated, by the nomological links with human experience, into a world *for us*. And this structure is only projected on to the human viewpoint to the extent that it is implicit in, encoded by, the relevant constraints, i.e. to the extent that the constraints it imposes on human experience are, by the standard of organizational uniformity, exactly as if an external reality with that structure obtained. (Incidentally, in focusing, here and subsequently, exclusively on the constraints on *human* experience, I am, for simplicity, assuming that there are no other minds whose experiential constraints are relevant in a similar way. Strictly speaking, we must allow for the possibility of there being other (non-human) subjects who are involved in the creation of the physical world in the same way as we are or who are involved in the creation of another physical world in the way that we are involved in the creation of ours.)

This point is an extension of something which would hold even if physical realism were true. Of course, if realism were true, the physical world, being ontologically primitive, would be something whose existence was logically independent of the constraints on human experience. The constraints, indeed, would just be consequences of the physical world together with certain psychophysical laws. In terms of our example, PW would be identical with EC, and

EC could exist without β' (= β) or any other laws linking configurations in *F* with human experience. But it would at least be true that, whatever its intrinsic nature, it was only because of the constraints it imposed on human experience that the physical world qualified as a *physical* world. The reason for this is that, given the topic-neutrality thesis, there would be nothing in the intrinsic character of the physical world, other than its structure and laws, which was relevant to its being physical (there would be nothing distinctively physical in the substances and qualities which were thus structured and organized). And, clearly, structure and laws would not be enough. We could not say, for example, that a sense-field qualified as a physical space simply in virtue of having a geometry and internal organization of a physically appropriate sort, nor that *K*-minds qualified as material particles simply because of the physically appropriate organization of their auditory states. Even if realism were true, an external item would qualify as a physical world only if it constituted a world for us, and it would constitute a world for us only if, through the appropriate psychophysical laws, it imposed appropriate constraints on our experience. In acknowledging the role of the experiential constraints in the creation of the physical world, we are merely adapting this result to the needs of anti-realism, in which the physical world and the external item are no longer identified.

What we have conceded to the phenomenalist does not commit us to saying, as he does, that the constraints on human experience suffice, on their own, for the creation of a physical world and that the external reality contributes nothing to the physical world save what it contributes to these constraints. Indeed, we can still insist, staying as close as possible to realism, that, for the existence of a physical world, two things are necessary: first, that, within the total ultimate reality, there should be some external component (external to human minds) which exemplifies the relevant physical structure; secondly, that, together with the appropriate bridging laws, this external component should impose constraints on human experience which encode the relevant physical structure. This position gives equal weight to the external reality and to the experiential constraints. And it makes the effectiveness of each factor, in the creation of a physical world, depend on its reinforcement by the other, so that the structure of the external component is physically effective only if it is projected through the constraints, and the encoding in the constraints is physically effective only if it is the projection of an external structure. In effect, the position is that, without the constraints, the external component would be irrelevant, and without the external backing, the constraints would be illusory. On the face of it, this seems to be a very plausible view.

This position agrees with reductive phenomenalism in requiring that the structure of the physical world be implicit in (encoded by) the constraints on human experience. It differs in further requiring that this structure be explicit in (exemplified by) some ultimate external reality by which the constraints are generated. This additional requirement, of external exemplification, I shall call the *isomorphism-requirement* (IR). I call it this because it requires that, subject, perhaps, to some difference in ontological perspective, the physical reality and the underlying external reality be isomorphic. We have already seen how this requirement is satisfied in our example, where (if we treat Q_1-spheres as continuants) E is isomorphic with P. It is this which makes the example so easy to accept. For although the example is reductivist and, hence, anti-realist, it is almost as if we have retained the physical world as an ingredient of ultimate reality, the specification of EC revealing those aspects of its intrinsic nature which fall beyond the scope of physical description and empirical discovery.

However, although IR has some initial plausibility, our argument for anti-realism already commits us to rejecting it. It was a crucial principle, in that argument, that if S is that ultimate external item which corresponds to physical space, the physically relevant geometry of S is to be equated with its *functional* geometry, i.e. with that geometry which achieves, or comes closest to achieving, nomological uniformity, in which each distance-relation has (in respect of the laws controlling processes within S and the effects of these processes on human experience) a constant nomological relevance over all the pairs of points which instantiate it. On the basis of this principle – what we may call the *principle of geometrical uniformity* (PGU) – we established that physical space cannot itself be an ingredient of ultimate reality, i.e. cannot be identical with the corresponding ultimate item. For while physical space, like any genuine space, possesses its geometrical structure *essentially*, the corresponding ultimate item possesses its physical (i.e. physically relevant) geometry only contingently: its physical geometry, being its functional geometry, is determined by its nomological organization and will, therefore, vary, across different possible worlds, with variations in the laws which are attached to it. Physical space and the ultimate item cannot be identified, since the network of physical distances which are essential to the one are not essential to the other.

All this, of course, we have already covered in detail in earlier chapters. What matters for present purposes is that, given PGU, there is no necessity for the external reality to exemplify the structure of the physical reality it underlies. For there is no guarantee that the functional geometry of the external component coincides with its intrinsic geometry. And where the two geometries differ, i.e. in the case of what we earlier called *nomological deviance*, there is a corresponding difference between the intrinsic structure of the component and the intrinsic structure of the physical world. We can illustrate this, very simply, in the framework of our example, by subjecting the sense-field to the familiar case of reciprocal topological (RT) deviance. Thus suppose that R_1 and R_2 are congruent regions of F and that E_1 is what we obtain from E by making two alterations: (1) we interchange the R_1-time and R_2-time quality-distributions; (2) we correspondingly alter the laws α' and β' so that everything is organized, with respect to both quality-distribution and effects on human experience, exactly as if R_1 and R_2 were interchanged – the network of distance-relations which would emerge by switching the locations of these regions being what is required for nomological uniformity. To characterize E_1 more precisely, let Φ_1 be that property which applies to any F-region R at any time t iff (a) any portion of R which lies outside R_1 and R_2 is Q_1-pervaded at t, (b) for any portion x of R which lies within R_1, the R_2-region which corresponds to x is Q_1-pervaded at t, and (c) for any portion x of R which lies within R_2, the R_1-region which corresponds to x is Q_1-pervaded at t. And let Φ_2 be the property associated in an exactly analogous way with Q_2-pervasion. Then E_1 is what we obtain from E by substituting Φ_1 for Q_1-pervasion and Φ_2 for Q_2-pervasion throughout, so that the F-time distribution of Φ_1 and Φ_2 is of type D (thus matching the F-time distribution of Q_1 and Q_2 in E) and the laws for Φ_1 and Φ_2 have the same form as α' and β' (thus formally matching the laws for Q_1 and Q_2 in E). Now while in E the intrinsic and functional geometries of F coincide, in E_1 they differ. In E_1, R_1 is functionally located where R_2 is sensually located and is sensually located where

R_2 is functionally located. For the functional geometry of F is that geometry which achieves nomological uniformity, and, in E_1, the geometry which achieves nomological uniformity is that which results from the sensual geometry by interchanging the locations of R_1 and R_2. Since it is the functional geometry of F which constitutes its physical (physically relevant) geometry, it follows that E_1 does not exemplify the structure of the physical reality it sustains. The physical reality is isomorphic not with E_1 as it actually is, but with E_1 as it would be if its structure were adjusted to meet the requirements of uniformity. Put another way, the physical reality is isomorphic with E_1 *relative to* its characterization in terms of Φ_1 and Φ_2 – the characterization whose form conceals the nomological deviance. In other words, the physical reality sustained by E_1 remains, as in the original example, isomorphic with E, and, in particular, the physical world remains isomorphic with EC.

Despite its initial plausibility, then, the isomorphism-requirement must be rejected. The structure of the physical world need not be exemplified by the external reality, and it will not be exemplified if the functional geometry of the external component differs from its intrinsic geometry. The case of RT-deviance is just one example. There are other examples in which the deviance relates to the metric of the external component, but not to its topology. And, as we have seen, there are cases in which the deviance relates to the topology in a more radical way (e.g. if the component is intrinsically 2-dimensional but its functional geometry is 3-dimensional). Moreover, by increasing the number of pairs of regions involved, we can develop the case of RT-deviance so as to undermine the isomorphism more extensively. Thus we can envisage a case in which F divides into a vast number of pairs of congruent regions such that nomological uniformity is only achieved relative to a geometry which interchanges the members of each pair. To this extent, the phenomenalist is right in his interpretation of the original example. There are at least *some* ways in which, preserving the same constraints on human experience, we can alter the structure of E without affecting the existence or the character of the derivative physical world. The isomorphism of P and E (and, in particular, of PW and EC) is not an essential feature of the original example.

This point can be further developed in two ways. In the first place, if the physically relevant geometry of the external component is determined by the requirements of nomological uniformity, it is clear that the same requirements must determine physical relevance in other respects. To take just one example, let R be some region of F and let E_2 be what we obtain from E by (1) interchanging Q_1-pervasion and Q_2-pervasion in R, and (2) altering the laws α' and β' so that everything is organized, with respect to both quality-distribution and effects on human experience, exactly as if Q_1-pervasion in R was really Q_2-pervasion, and Q_2-pervasion in R was really Q_1-pervasion. To characterize E_2 more precisely, let Ψ_1 be that property which applies to any F-region x at any time t iff any part of x which lies inside R is Q_2-pervaded at t and any part of x which lies outside R is Q_1-pervaded at t. Likewise, let Ψ_2 be that property which applies to any F-region x at any time t iff any part of x which lies inside R is Q_1-pervaded at t and any part of x which lies outside R is Q_2-pervaded at t. Then E_2 is what we obtain from E by substituting Ψ_1 for Q_1-pervasion and Ψ_2 for Q_2-pervasion throughout, so that the F-time distribution of Ψ_1 and Ψ_2 is of type D (thus matching the distribution of Q_1 and Q_2 in E) and the laws for Ψ_1 and Ψ_2 have the same form as α' and β' (thus formally matching the laws for Q_1 and Q_2 in E). To get a concrete picture of how things work in E_2, imagine a moving sphere of Q_1-pervasion which, if α' obtained, would pass through R between the times t_1 and t_5. Because the E_2-laws for Ψ_1 and Ψ_2 formally coincide with the E-laws for Q_1 and Q_2, the sequence of events would be as in Figure 12.1, where Q_1-pervasion is represented by shading and Q_2-pervasion by no shading. Thus the sphere, being, as it were, a Ψ_1-continuant, changes into a Q_2-sphere as it enters R on the left and changes back into a Q_1-sphere as it leaves it on the right. And quite generally, the behaviour and experiential effects of Q_1-continuants in E are exactly replicated by the behaviour and experiential effects of Ψ_1-continuants in E_2.

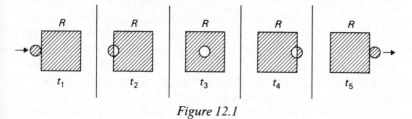

Figure 12.1

Now like E_1, E_2 exhibits a form of nomological deviance: there is a conflict between nomological organization and intrinsic structure. Just as, in E_1, everything is organized exactly as if, in respect of each quality, pervasion in R_1 were really pervasion in R_2, and vice versa, so, in E_2, everything is organized exactly as if, in respect of R, Q_1-pervasion were really Q_2-pervasion, and vice versa. But in the case of E_2 the deviance relates not to geometrical, but to qualitative structure. What is needed to restore nomological uniformity is not the interchange of two regions (or any other alteration of the geometry), but the interchange of two qualities in respect of a region. But, clearly, in determining the physically relevant structure, considerations of the same kind apply in both cases. Whether it is the geometrical or the qualitative structure which is nomologically deviant, the physical reality is to be modelled, not on the external reality as it is, but on the external reality re-structured to meet the requirements of uniformity. The physical reality which E_2 sustains is isomorphic, not with E_2, but with what results from E_2 when Q_1-pervasion-in-R and Q_2-pervasion-in-R are interchanged throughout both the distribution and the laws. Or put the other way, the physical reality which E_2 sustains is isomorphic with E_2 *relative to* its characterization in terms of Ψ_1 and Ψ_2 – the characterization whose form conceals the nomological deviance – just as the physical reality sustained by E_1 is isomorphic with E_1 relative to its characterization in terms of Φ_1 and Φ_2. Whichever way you look at it, the replacement of E by E_2 (like the replacement of E by E_1) makes no difference to the existence or character of the derivative physical world. The material particles retain their original arrangement and organization (as in PW), material occupancy being correlated with Q_2-pervasion inside R and with Q_1-pervasion outside it, and vice versa for emptiness.

Secondly, nomological deviance is not the only organizational factor which undermines isomorphism. Just as the structure of the physical reality conceals any nomological deviance in the external reality which underlies it, so also it conceals distinctions which are nomologically irrelevant. Thus let us envisage a case in which the external reality (E_3) contains *two* sense-fields, F_1 and F_2, each being 3-dimensional and Euclidean, such that the laws controlling quality-distribution and effects on human experience, draw no distinction between locations in F_1 and the corresponding locations in F_2. To be more precise, suppose that G is a 1-1 correlation between F_1-places and F_2-places such that the places in each field stand in the same (sensual) distance-relations as their correlates in the other. And suppose S is the complex space whose points are pairs of G-correlated places, one drawn from F_1 and the other drawn from F_2. If we say that an S-point x is Q_1-*characterized* iff at least one element of x lies, in its own field, on a region of Q_1-pervasion, and that an S-point x is Q_2-*characterized* iff each element of x lies, in its own field, on a region of Q_2-pervasion, and if we say that an S-region x is Q_1-*pervaded* (Q_2-*pervaded*) iff all its points are Q_1-characterized (Q_2-characterized), then E_3 is such that we can obtain E from it by substituting F-places for S-points throughout, so that the S-time distribution of Q_1 and Q_2, though divided between the two fields, matches the F-time distribution of Q_1 and Q_2 in E, and the laws for Q_1 and Q_2 in respect of S (both distributive and experiential) match the E-laws, α' and β', in respect of F. Now E_3 does not exhibit any kind of nomological deviance: we cannot say that the qualities or the modes of geometrical arrangement vary in their nomological significance between the two fields or from one region to another within a single field. The principles of organization are uniform throughout the whole system. None the less, there is still a sense in which the organization of E_3 belies its structure. For the organization is exactly as if F_1 and F_2 were numerically identical. If R_1 is a region in F_1 and R_2 the correlated region in F_2, the laws permit us to replace any instance of the Q_1-pervasion of R_1 by a simultaneous instance of the Q_1-pervasion of R_2, and vice versa, without having to alter the quality-distribution or course of human experience in any other respect. The distinction between location in F_1 and location in F_2 is, we might say, a distinction without a nomologically relevant difference. This, in turn, affects the structure of the physical reality which E_3 sustains. For it is the nomologically relevant structure of E_3 which constitutes its physically relevant structure. Because the distinction between F_1-location and F_2-location is nomologically irrelevant, the distinction is not preserved at the physical level. At the physical level, there is a single space whose simple points correspond to the complex points of S. The physical reality which E_3 sustains is isomorphic not with E_3 as it is, but with E_3 as it would be if (to eliminate the nomologically irrelevant distinction) its two sense-fields were fused, all instances of Q_1-pervasion being preserved. In other words the physical reality which E_3 sustains remains (as in the case of E_1 and E_2) isomorphic with E.

A different example, concerned with qualitative structure, would be that in which there are two sense-qualities which are nomologically indistinguishable. Thus consider the case of an external reality, E_4, which is just like E except that Q_1 is replaced by, as it were, a disjunction of qualities, Q_a and Q_b, between which the laws do not distinguish. (To be precise, let Φ be that property which applies to any F-region R at any time t iff R is exhaustively divisible into parts each of which is, at t, either Q_a-pervaded or Q_b-pervaded. Then E_4 is such that we can obtain E from it by substituting Q_1-pervasion for Φ throughout.) Then once again, because the distinction between Q_a and Q_b is nomologically irrelevant, it is not reflected at the physical level. The only distinction at the physical level is between regions which are materially occupied and regions which are empty, although at some region-times material occupancy is correlated with Q_a-pervasion and at other region-times with Q_b-pervasion. The physical reality which E_4 sustains is isomorphic with E, i.e. is isomorphic with E_4 as it would be if (to eliminate the nomologically irrelevant distinction) Q_a and Q_b were the same quality.

We can see, then, that there are at least two general ways in which the physical reality can fail to be isomorphic with the external reality which underlies it. Firstly, where the external reality is subject to some form of nomological deviance, the physical reality takes on the structure required for nomological uniformity. Secondly, where the external reality involves distinctions which are nomologically idle, the physical reality assumes the simpler structure required for nomological relevance. In both cases, the underlying structure is, as it were, transformed into the physical structure by being adjusted to meet a certain nomological standard – adjusted, in effect, to be as the nomological organization suggests. Thus in each of the examples we have considered, apart from the original example of E, there is a sense in which the organization of the external reality fails to reflect its intrinsic structure (whether, as in the case of E_1 and E_2, by making the same property vary in its nomological relevance, or merely, as in the case of E_3 and E_4, by giving different properties the same nomological relevance), and, in each case, the physical reality is modelled on the underlying reality as the organization represents it, rather than as it actually is. In each case, the external reality is, either by the standard of uniformity or the standard of relevance, organized exactly as if its structure were such and such, and the physical reality it sustains is then structured to match the way things are *as if*, rather than the way they *are*.

None of this, of course, establishes the truth of reductive phenomenalism. It does not establish that the physical reality is sustained solely by the constraints on human experience. It does not establish that any replacement of *E* which does not alter the experiential constraints does not affect the existence or character of the physical world. But the rejection of IR does at least remove one obstacle to the phenomenalist's position. We shall see in the next chapter just how important the removal of this obstacle is. For the principles which underlie the rejection of IR are ones which the phenomenalist can further exploit. Indeed, they are principles which, given the acceptance of a physical reality, will oblige us to accept, almost in full, the phenomenalist's account of its sustainment.[4]

THE PRINCIPLES OF CREATION

Reductive phenomenalism claims that the physical world is the logical creation of the constraints on human experience. In claiming this, the phenomenalist need not deny that the relevant constraints are imposed by something external to human minds and hence need not deny that an external reality plays some role in the creation of the physical world. What he claims is that the constraints, on their own, suffice for the creation of the physical world, irrespective of what (if anything) lies behind them: that if there is an external reality, it contributes nothing to the existence of the physical world save what it contributes to the obtaining of the constraints; that any alteration of the external reality which makes no difference to the constraints makes no difference to the physical world, or, indeed, to the total physical reality comprising both the physical world and the psychophysical laws.

Reductive phenomenalism is not an intuitively plausible position. But we have been forced to make two important concessions to it (in addition, of course, to the acceptance of anti-realism itself). In the first place, we have acknowledged that, assuming the existence of a physical world, the constraints on human experience play a crucial role in its creation. The creation of a physical world necessarily involves the encoding of a physical structure by the experiential constraints. However physically appropriate its own structure, an external reality which imposed no constraints on human experience, or none from which a physical structure could be extracted, would contribute nothing to the creation of a physical world, since it would contribute nothing to the creation of a world-for-us. The physical appropriateness of the external structure is operative in the creation of a physical world only if that structure is projected, through the experiential constraints, on to the human viewpoint. Secondly, in rejecting the isomorphism-requirement, we have conceded that the underlying external reality need not exemplify the structure of the physical reality it sustains. Where the external reality is nomologically deviant, the physical reality assumes the amended structure required for nomological uniformity, and where the external reality involves distinctions which are nomologically idle, the physical reality assumes the simplified structure required for nomological relevance. In both cases, the underlying structure is transformed into the physical structure by being adjusted to meet a certain nomological standard – adjusted to be as the nomological organization represents it. And this means that there are at least some ways in which, preserving the constraints on human experience, the external reality can be altered in structure without affecting the existence or character of the physical world, or, indeed, of the total physical reality. Thus in terms of our example, E can be replaced, on the one hand, by E_1 or E_2, and, on the other, by E_3 or E_4, while retaining a physical reality of exactly the same type as P. For, in each case, the physical reality, being fashioned to meet the standards of uniformity and relevance, retains its isomorphism with E.

These two concessions do not, as such, amount to an endorsement of the phenomenalist's position. They do not commit us to saying that the experiential constraints, on their own, suffice for the creation of the physical world, irrespective of what (if anything) lies behind them. We could still hold, and it seems quite plausible, that the creation of a physical world requires the ultimate existence of some external item, and one in which the structure of the created world is discernible either directly or through those adjustments demanded by the standards of uniformity and relevance. However, as we shall now see, the points which the phenomenalist has gained are ones which he can develop into a more powerful case.

One thing which suggests that there may be a smooth transition to the phenomenalist's position is that the principles which determine the physically relevant structure of the external reality are similar to those which cover the encoding of a physical structure by the experiential constraints. To discern the physically relevant structure of the external reality, we have to ask: 'How, if at all, would the intrinsic structure of that reality need to be modified to achieve (or maximize) nomological uniformity and relevance?' To discern the physical structure encoded by the constraints, we have to ask: 'What structure would be exemplified by any nomologically uniform and relevant external reality which yielded those constraints?' In both cases, the physical structure is discernible in a certain item (whether external or experiential) as that structure which is needed to meet certain nomological requirements – as that structure which, in the perspective of those requirements, the nomological organization suggests. In both cases, the item encodes the physical structure (in the limiting case, the encoding takes the form of exemplification) by being, in nomological organization, exactly as if, by the standards of uniformity and relevance, an external reality with that structure obtained. This means that to accept the phenomenalistic creation of a physical world, i.e. its creation by the constraints on human experience, we only have, it seems, to extend the principles which we already acknowledge. If E_1 (or E_2) and E_3 (or E_4) suffice for the sustainment of a physical reality with the structure of P, because it is this structure which we extract from each of them by applying, respectively, the standards of uniformity and relevance, why not accept, analogously, that CT suffices for the sustainment of a physical reality with this same structure, because it is this structure which we extract from it by applying the same standards? Why not say in both cases that there is a derivative physical reality modelled on that hypothetical external structure which yields the specified constraints on experience and meets the requisite nomological standards?

In fact, however, the connection between the phenomenalist's position and the principles of uniformity and relevance goes much deeper than this. It is not just that these principles might be extended to cover the phenomenalistic case; it is also that these very principles, applied to the case of an external reality, are founded on considerations of a phenomenalistic kind. For what gives the principles their validity – what provides their rationale – is that they tie the structure of the physical reality to the perspective of the human viewpoint. The physical reality is structured to meet (as far as possible) the requirements of nomological uniformity and nomological relevance only because it is as thus structured that the external reality represents itself in human experience. Deviance and irrelevance disappear from the physical structure because, in the nature of things, there can be no record of them, however implicit, in the experiential constraints – no way in which they can feature in the world which is empirically available to us.

Thus consider again the case of E_1 in which the underlying sense-field (F) is subject to an RT-deviance in respect of the regions R_1 and R_2. Here, the functional (i.e. uniformity-achieving) geometry of F differs from its intrinsic (i.e. sensual) geometry: R_1 is functionally located where R_2 is sensually located and is sensually located where R_2 is functionally located. But why should the functional geometry be the one which is physically relevant – the one which determines the arrangement of occupancy and emptiness in physical space? After all, looking at E_1 *sub specie aeternitatis*, it is the sensual geometry which is conspicuous: the functional geometry is seen only as a vivid representation of the nomological deviance, of the way in which, as it were, the real geometry and the nomological organization conflict. The answer is that it is the functional geometry which is conspicuous at the human (i.e. empirical) viewpoint. The functional geometry only qualifies as the physically relevant geometry because *we*, the human subjects, in our empirical theorizing, have to employ the standard of uniformity to gauge the structure of the external reality. All we can do is to seek for some theory of the external reality, in topic-neutral terms, which explains the course of our experience in the simplest way, and the quest for simplicity involves, amongst other things, postulating a reality whose nomological organization is, or comes as close as we can get it to being, uniform.[1] In our empirical theories, we are forced to fit the external structure to the organization, since we have no direct access to the underlying reality as it is in itself. And it is this which gives the functional geometry of F its physical relevance: in effect, the functional geometry is physically relevant because it is this geometry, projected through the constraints on human experience, which is relevant to the creation of a world-for-us. Obviously, the same considerations apply in the other cases. Thus in the case of E_3 there are two sense-fields which are nomologically organized as a single space, location in one field being nomologically indistinguishable from location in the other. Here again, though now by reference to the standard of nomological relevance, we can

211

distinguish between the *intrinsic* bi-spatial structure of E_3 and the *functional* uni-spatial structure reflected in its organization. Here again, it is the functional structure which constitutes the physically relevant structure: there is only one physical space, in line with the uni-spatial organization of the fields rather than their intrinsic duality. And here again, what makes the functional structure physically relevant is that it is this structure which is discernible at the human viewpoint. The duality of the fields drops out at the physical level because, being nomologically irrelevant, it leaves no traces in the experiential constraints, and, leaving no traces, it contributes nothing to the creation of a world-for-us. (All that we have said about E_1 extends, of course, to the parallel case of E_2 and all we have said about E_3 extends to the parallel case of E_4.)

The principles of uniformity and relevance, therefore, rest on the more general and overtly phenomenalistic principle that the physically relevant structure of the underlying external reality is that structure under which the reality is empirically represented at the human viewpoint – that structure under which the reality is disposed to reveal itself, in the topic-neutral terms of empirical theory, through the constraints on human experience. I shall call this the *principle of representation*. As well as providing the rationale for the principles of uniformity and relevance, the principle of representation is more powerful than their conjunction, since it covers cases which they do not. Thus consider the case of an external reality, E_5, which is just like E except that: (a) E_5 contains two external components, EC_1 and EC_2, each of which is qualitatively identical (in both quality-distribution and distributional laws) to EC, and (b) the bridging laws, β^* ,while preserving the β'-correlations between configuration-types and experience-types, correlate each human mind with two groups of Q_1-continuants, a group in EC_1 and the corresponding group in EC_2, such that it is causally necessary for both groups to instantiate the relevant configuration-type if an experience is to occur in the correlated mind. Now E_5 does not exhibit any kind of nomological deviance, for its organization is, like that of E, perfectly uniform. Nor, looked at *sub specie aeternitatis*, does it involve distinctions which are nomologically irrelevant. For although the two components are qualitatively identical, corresponding events in the two fields are nomologically distinguished by the fact that, apart from human experience, the causes and effects of each lie exclusively in its own field. What we have are two fields separately organized in the same way, not, as in the case of E_3, two fields organized in combination as a single field. None the less, we still want to say, in this case, as in the case of E_3, that the duality drops out at the physical level – that, together with β^*, the two fields combine to create a single physical space. This result, while not covered by the principles of uniformity and relevance, is both covered and explained by the principle of representation. By this principle, the physically relevant structure of E_5 is that in which the two fields are fused into a single space. For it is as a single space that the fields project themselves, through the experiential constraints, on to the human viewpoint. The duality disappears at the physical level because it receives no empirical representation: anything in the character of or the constraints on human experience which might be explained by postulating a pair of parallel external spaces could be explained on similar lines, but more simply, by postulating a single space.

It might seem we already have, in the principle of representation, a full endorsement of the phenomenalist position. For if the physical reality assumes that structure under which the underlying external reality is empirically represented at the human viewpoint, and if the representation at the human viewpoint is determined by the character of the constraints on human experience, it seems that the constraints alone determine the character of the physical world, irrespective of what imposes them. The structure encoded by the constraints will always, it seems, be the physically relevant one, however much it differs from the actual intrinsic structure of the external reality. But we must be careful here. Certainly we are very close to the phenomenalist position, but there is still a gap. The extent of the gap is measured by the difference between the following two things:

(1) The encoding by the experiential constraints of a certain type of external structure (not necessarily realized).
(2) The representation by the experiential constraints of an actual external reality as possessing a certain type of structure (not necessarily a structure which it does possess).

Now (2) certainly involves (1). The experiential constraints can represent an actual external reality as possessing a certain type of structure only if that type of structure is the one which they encode. But (1) need not involve (2). All that is necessary for the encoding of a certain type of external structure is that it should be that type whose realization would provide the simplest explanation of the constraints. And, obviously, this condition does not require that there actually be an underlying external reality which, by such encoding, the constraints represent as structured in the relevant way. It is not even necessary that, if there is an underlying external reality (a reality which imposes the constraints), it is one which the constraints represent as having the type of structure which they encode. Thus we could hardly say that if the constraints are directly imposed by a single act of divine volition ('And God said, "let there be such and such constraints".') and encode a certain physically appropriate type of structure, they represent the volitional act as structured in that way. For even allowing that the representation of an external reality need not be wholly veridical, there is not enough structural similarity between the volitional act and what is encoded by the constraints to see the constraints as a representation of the act in any sense at all. To take an analogy, if I look at a stick which is half-immersed in water, my visual experience represents it (non-veridically) as bent. But if a blow on my head causes me to 'see stars', my visual experience does not represent the blow, nor the instrument which effects it, as star-like. My visual experience is a hallucination (with no external object) rather than a misrepresentation of an object which I actually perceive.

It follows that, accepting the principle of representation, we could avoid the full phenomenalist position by insisting that the sustainment of a physical reality requires not only the appropriate experiential constraints, but also the existence of an external reality by which the constraints are imposed and which they (however non-veridically) represent. This position would be phenomenalistic in as much as it claims that, provided there is some underlying external reality which the constraints represent, the character of the physical reality is determined solely by the character of the constraints, however non-veridical their representation. But it would fall short of *full* reductive phenomenalism in denying that the constraints, on their own, suffice for the sustainment of a physical reality – in insisting that the constraints need to be supplemented by an external reality which, whether correctly or incorrectly, they represent as structured in the appropriate way. Let us call this position, the *representational thesis*.

One of the problems for the representational thesis is how to find an objective basis for distinguishing between cases in which the external reality is empirically represented and cases in which it is not. How do we decide whether something is a case of *mis*-representation or *non*-representation? The problem is not just one of where to draw the line in a spectrum, like the problem of deciding how many people are needed to constitute a *crowd* or how much hair someone must lose to qualify as *bald*. The problem is rather that we have yet to isolate the relevant variables – the variables in terms of which we might come to think of something as constituting a borderline case.

One fact which promises to be significant, in this connection, is that in all the examples we have so far considered and which we have construed as cases of *mis*-representation, it has been possible to find, for the underlying external reality, a characterization *relative to which* it exemplifies the structure of the physical reality it sustains.[2] Thus in the case of E_1 we introduced a pair of properties Φ_1 and Φ_2 whose application coincides with the application of Q_1-pervasion and Q_2-pervasion relative to an interchange of location in R_1 and location in R_2. (Thus Φ_1 applies to any region R at any time t iff (a) any portion of R which lies outside R_1 and R_2 is Q_1-pervaded at t, (b) for any portion x of R which lies within R_1, the R_2-region which corresponds to x is Q_1-pervaded at t, and (c) for any portion x of R which lies within R_2, the R_1-region which corresponds to x is Q_1-pervaded at t. And Φ_2 is analogously associated with Q_2.) In terms of these properties we can characterize E_1 in a way which formally conceals its nomological deviance, since the F-time distribution of Φ_1 and Φ_2 in E_1 coincides with the distribution of Q_1 and Q_2 in E, and the laws for Φ_1 and Φ_2 in E_1 have the same form as the laws (α' and β') for Q_1 and Q_2 in E. Relative to this characterization, E_1 exemplifies the nomologically uniform structure under which it is empirically represented at the human viewpoint and thus exemplifies the structure of the physical reality (of the same type as P) which it sustains. Again, in the case of E_3, we introduced a space S whose points are formed by pairs of correlated places drawn, respectively, from the two fields (F_1 and F_2), and, for each time, we assigned Q_1 to any S-point one of whose elements lies on a region of Q_1-pervasion, and Q_2 to any S-point each of whose elements lies on a region of Q_2-pervasion. In these terms, we can characterize E_3 in a way which formally conceals its intrinsic, but nomologically irrelevant, spatial duality. And relative to this characterization, E_3, exemplifying the structure under which it is empirically represented, exemplifies the structure of the physical reality it sustains. In fact, for each of the cases we have considered, there is a characterization relative to which the external reality exemplifies the structure encoded by the constraints and exemplifies the structure of the physical reality which, applying our principles, we have taken it to sustain.

Now someone who wants to stay with the representational thesis and avoid the full phenomenalist position, might see in this point a basis for distinguishing between *mis*-representation and *non*-representation – between cases in which the external reality is empirically represented, but non-veridically, and cases in which it is not represented at all. Thus he might say that an external reality X is empirically represented under (or as possessing) a certain type of structure T iff three conditions are satisfied:

(1) The experiential constraints imposed by X encode T (i.e. the theory that T is ultimately realized, whether true or false, provides the simplest explanation of the constraints).

(2) There is a characterization K of X relative to which X exemplifies T.

(3) The encoding of T systematically depends on this K-relative exemplification of T, in that, for each aspect A of T, the encoding of A by the constraints at least partly depends on the K-relative exemplification of A by X.

Fed into the representational thesis, these conditions reinstate a kind of isomorphism-requirement. It is not that, under its most natural characterization (selected *sub specie aeternitatis*), the external reality has to be isomorphic with the physical reality it sustains. But at least there must be some characterization, however contrived, which achieves isomorphism and which explains why the physical reality has the structure it has. There must be some way of imposing the encoded structure on the external reality and of seeing the encoding as systematically grounded on the reality thus structured. This requirement is satisfied in the cases of E_1 - E_5. But it would not be satisfied if the experiential constraints were either autonomous (not imposed by an external reality) or directly imposed by a single act of divine volition.

This gives substance to the notion of empirical representation.

But it does not, I think, lead to an acceptance of the representational thesis in preference to the more extreme position of reductive phenomenalism. The reason will become clear if we consider a further case. In developing this new case, I make the assumption that the distributional laws (α') in E are deterministic, in the sense that, for any time t, the F-distribution of Q_1 and Q_2 at t is deducible from α' together with some portion of the F-time distribution preceding t. The point of this assumption will emerge presently.

Suppose R is some region of F and T is some period of time. Then let E_6 be the external reality we obtain from E by:

(1) Eliminating at all times within T the regions of Q_1-pervasion in R;

(2) altering the laws α' and β' so that (a) it is a law that R-T is wholly Q_2-pervaded, and (b), apart from (a), everything is organized, with respect to both quality-distribution and effects on human experience, exactly as if the R-T distribution in E and the E-laws, α' and β', obtained.

To see how things work in E_6, imagine a sequence of events in E in which, all within the period T, two Q_1-spheres, A and B, enter R, collide at a certain point p and are thence deflected, like billiard balls, with the velocities and directions prescribed by α'. We shall suppose the sequence to be as depicted in Figure 13.1, with Q_1-pervasion represented by shading, and Q_2-pervasion by no

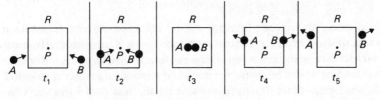

Figure 13.1 The E-sequence

shading. Now in the case of E_6, the process is the same except that, since t_1-t_5 fall within T, R remains Q_2-pervaded throughout, so that the spheres are gradually annihilated over the period in which, in E, they pass into R and are gradually reconstituted over the period in which, in E, they re-emerge. Thus in E_6, the sequence of events is as depicted in Figure 13.2: R remains Q_2-pervaded throughout, but the laws of distribution ensure that the relation

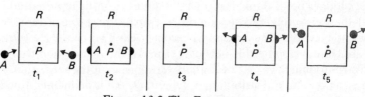

Figure 13.2 The E_6-sequence

between the directions and velocities of the spheres at t_1 and t_5 is the same as it would have been if the spheres had collided at p and been deflected in accordance with α'. Thus apart from their annihilation within R, the constraints on the behaviour of A and B are the same as the constraints in E. Likewise, we have the same constraints on human experience. Thus suppose that, in E, A and B are members of the group of Q_1-spheres correlated with the human mind M and that their collision at p at t_3 would (given the rest of the E-configuration of this group at t_3) suffice, under β', to produce a simultaneous experience in M. Then in E_6, the same type of experience is ensured in M at t_3, even though the collision does not occur. In short, apart from the unchanging state of R, everything is organized, both in the field and in human minds, exactly as if A and B followed their original uninterrupted courses, as in E, in the framework of the original laws α' and β'. (As an alternative illustration, we could imagine a sequence of events in which, all within the region R, two spheres enter, collide within and re-emerge from the period T.)

Like E_1 and E_2, E_6 exhibits a kind of nomological deviance. Its organization is not uniform with respect to its intrinsic structure. Uniformity can only be restored by re-inserting in R-T the eliminated spots of Q_1-pervasion, thus eliminating the law that R-T is wholly Q_2-pervaded, and subsuming the rest of the organization under the general laws α' and β' – in short, by converting E_6 back into E. Thus the functional (uniformity-achieving) structure of E_6, like that of E_1 and E_2, coincides, not with its intrinsic structure, but with the intrinsic structure of E. Moreover, as in the case of E_1 and E_2, the functional structure seems to be what is physically relevant. Following the precedent of those earlier cases, our inclination is to say that, in the physical world which E_6 creates, the space-time distribution of material occupancy and emptiness matches the F-time distribution of Q_1 and Q_2 in E (so that, although R-T is wholly Q_2-pervaded, material particles follow uninterrupted courses through the corresponding region of physical space over the same period), and that, quite generally, the physical reality has the character we attributed to P in the original example.

Now this conclusion is not incompatible with the representational thesis. Nor is it incompatible with this thesis when the notion of empirical representation is defined in the suggested way. Quite the reverse. The conclusion follows from the thesis construed in terms of that definition. For we can find a characterization of E_6 which meets all the requirements. Thus let us say that an F-region x is Q_1-*associated* at a time t iff some portion of the pre-t distribution of Q_1 and Q_2 (i.e. of the total F-time distribution preceding t) would, if α' obtained, necessitate the Q_1-pervasion of x at t. Notice that to ascribe Q_1-association to a region x at a time t says nothing about how x is *pervaded* at t; nor does it say anything about the laws which obtain. It only says something about the quality-distribution prior to t. It claims that the prior distribution is such that from it, together with the assumption of α', the Q_1-pervasion of x at t is deducible (whether or not α' actually obtains and whether or not x is actually Q_1-pervaded at t). Let us next, in terms of Q_1-association, introduce two further properties X_1 and X_2. X_1 applies to a region x at a time t iff (a) if t falls outside T, then x is Q_1-pervaded at t, and (b) if t falls within T, then every part of x which lies outside R is Q_1-pervaded at t and every part of x which lies inside R is both Q_2-pervaded and Q_1-associated at t. X_2 applies to a region x at a time t iff x is Q_2-pervaded at t and no part of x is Q_1-associated at t. Then E_6 is what we obtain from E by substituting X_1 for Q_1-pervasion and X_2 for Q_2-pervasion throughout, so that the F-time distribution of X_1 and X_2 in E_6 matches the F-time distribution of Q_1 and Q_2 in E and the laws for X_1 and X_2 in E_6 have the same form as the laws, α' and β', for Q_1 and Q_2 in E.[3] Let us call this characterization of E_6, in terms of X_1 and X_2, K. Now we are assuming that (relative to its natural characterization, in terms of Q_1 and Q_2) E exemplifies the type of structure encoded by the experiential constraints (CT) which it generates. Consequently, since E and E_6 generate the same experiential constraints, it is also true that, *relative to K*, E_6 exemplifies the type of structure encoded by the constraints it generates. Moreover, the encoding of this structure systematically depends on the K-relative exemplification in the required way: that is to say, for each aspect A of the structure, the K-relative exemplification of A is at least part of what accounts for the encoding of A by the constraints. So E_6 meets all the conditions of empirical representation as we defined it: there is a type of structure (the one it exemplifies relative to K) under which E_6 is empirically represented at the human viewpoint. Since this is the type of structure which P exemplifies, it follows from the representational thesis that E_6 sustains a physical reality with the same character as P. In other words, the thesis endorses our original inclination, following the precedent of E_1 and E_2, to take the functional structure of E_6 as what is physically relevant.

How, then, might we see this case as undermining the representational thesis? The answer is that it forms a kind of bridge with cases which meet the phenomenalistic conditions but not the representational requirement. The point is that, in E_6, the region-period R-T has been rendered physically irrelevant: because it is a law that R-T is wholly Q_2-pervaded, the physical consequences are the same as if (perhaps, *per impossibile*) the region did not exist over that period – the field being, throughout T, internally bounded by an R-shaped hole in which no sense-qualities were, or could be, realized. It is true, of course that the attribution of X_1 and X_2 to regions within R at times within T plays a crucial role in K: it is in terms of these properties that we get an F-time distribution matching the space-time distribution of matter and get laws of distribution and experiential effect matching the physical and psychophysical laws. But, whatever the R-T distribution of X_1 and X_2, all we can deduce from it about the *intrinsic* state of R-T is that R-T is wholly Q_2-pervaded. Anything else we can deduce concerns the distribution of the sense-qualities over F at *earlier* times. (It is this, of course, which makes the K-characterization contrived, in the same way that the characterization of E_1 in terms of Φ_1 and Φ_2 is contrived – the ascription of Φ_1 (Φ_2) to a region of R_1 is really the ascription of Q_1-pervasion (Q_2-pervasion) to the corresponding region of R_2, and vice versa.) We might just as well eliminate R throughout T and make up the loss to the domain of X_1 and X_2 with an appropriate portion of some purely abstract space – a portion corresponding to the R-shaped hole in F.

The significance of this is that as we increase the size of R and T, so, even by the standards of the representational thesis, E_6 comes steadily closer to the phenomenalistic case, in which the physical reality is sustained by the experiential constraints alone. For as we increase the size of R and T, so we diminish the portion of the external component which is operative in the sustainment. And we can make R and T as large as we like, so long as we retain some pre-T period by which to fix the R-T distribution of X_1 and X_2. Even if we make R equal to F and make T cover everything after the first few seconds of the 'big bang', we still have the same constraints on human experience and the same K-relative exemplification of the structure which these constraints encode. And, consequently, we still have, by the representational thesis, a sustainment of the same physical reality. But if the operative portion of F-time can be thus diminished, without affecting the existence or character of the physical world, it is hard to stop short of the full phenomenalist position. If, without revising our physical beliefs, we can coherently suppose that the ultimate external reality has remained unchanged over the last million years and will remain unchanged until the end of time, it is hard to avoid the conclusion that the physical reality is the product of the experiential constraints alone and that the external reality, whatever form it takes, has relevance only as the determinant of the constraints. If E_6 suffices for P, however extensive (preserving some pre-T period) we make R and T, it is hard to see the representational requirement as anything but arbitrary.

It may be objected that the moral to be drawn from this is not that phenomenalism is correct, but that, contrary to what we supposed, E_6 does not sustain a physical reality with the structure of P. But, on closer inspection, it is clear that such a conclusion is not available. If E_6 does not sustain a physical reality with the structure of P, there are only two possibilities:

(1) that E_6 sustains no physical reality at all; and
(2) that E_6 sustains a physical reality with a different type of structure – presumably a reality isomorphic with E_6 itself.

The first alternative is highly counter-intuitive in the case where R and T are very small. Just as E_6 approaches the phenomenalistic case as R and T are increased, so it approaches the case of E as R and T are decreased. Unless we can find some quite general reason for being nihilistic – a reason which applies even when, relative to its natural characterization, the external reality has a physically appropriate structure – it seems impossible to deny that, for a sufficiently small R-T, E_6 suffices for a physical reality of some kind. On the other hand, the second alternative is incompatible with the principles we have already established. If E_6 has an empirical representation at all, it is represented under the structure of P, since it is this structure which is encoded by the experiential constraints. So if we take E_6 to sustain a physical reality with a different structure – a reality (presumably) in which the distribution and organization of matter coincide with the distribution and organization of Q_1 – we abandon the principle of representation and undermine the principles of uniformity and relevance for which this principle provides the rationale. Ultimately, there is no way of pursuing the second alternative without reinstating the full-blooded isomorphism-requirement which we have already refuted.

The only way of avoiding the phenomenalist position would be to draw a line through the spectrum of R-T sizes, so that, for all sizes below a certain limit, E_6 sustains a physical reality with the structure of P and, for all sizes above that limit, it sustains no physical reality at all. This would be to retain the principle of representation, since wherever there is a physical reality, it has that structure under which the underlying external reality is empirically represented. But it would fall short of full-blooded phenomenalism, since there would be no physical reality at all if the intrinsic structure of the external reality deviated too radically from the structure encoded by the constraints. Of course, the exact location of the line is bound to be arbitrary, since the spectrum of R-T sizes is continuous: there is bound to be, as it were, a range of borderline cases whose status, as sufficing or not sufficing for a physical reality, is irresolvably arguable. But this, it might be said, is just the familiar problem of vagueness which we encounter in so many other cases. At what point, for example, does a table cease to exist if we remove its atoms one by one? However, in the case of E_6, the problem goes deeper than this. When we remove an atom from a table, we are altering, if only marginally, its shape and size. It may be difficult to see any particular atom-removal as decisive in destroying the table; but, at the same time, we are forced to acknowledge that a sufficient number of atom-removals adds up to an alteration which is decisive, since, at each stage, it is only in virtue of possessing a tabular shape and size that the residual collection of atoms could qualify as a table. It is precisely because the removal of one atom alters the shape and size of the table that the removal of sufficiently many atoms destroys it altogether. But, in the case of E_6, a marginal increase in the size of R-T is not matched by any alteration, however marginal, in the character of the physical reality. For, so long as some physical reality remains, its character is determined (in accordance with the principle of representation) by the character of the experiential constraints, and these constraints remain unchanged. So what we have to envisage in this case, unlike the case of the table, is that a way of altering the underlying reality which makes *no* physical difference can be extended to a point where it makes *all* the difference. Such an interpretation of E_6 may be logically coherent; but it is devoid of any rationale. Why even think of drawing a line through the spectrum if the size of R-T is physically irrelevant up to the selected point? To do so would just be to succumb to the influence of our original anti-phenomenalist intuitions, which, by now, have been totally discredited.

It seems to me, therefore, that, once we have endorsed the principle of representation (that the physically relevant structure of the ultimate external reality is that structure under which the reality is empirically represented at the human viewpoint), we cannot, if we accept the existence of a physical world at all, stop short of the full phenomenalist position. Having said this, I must now add a qualification. For I think there is one respect in which the phenomenalist position needs to be modified – though not in the direction of the representational thesis. As things stand, the phenomenalist claims that the physical world is the logical creation of the constraints on human experience, where each constraint is a causal limitation on the subsequent course of experience for a particular mind at a particular time. What I think he should claim is that the physical world is the logical creation of these constraints, *together with* the fact that their fitting together, to encode a physical structure, is non-accidental. More precisely, I think that, for the sustainment of a physical reality, two conditions are necessary and (assuming there is no *a priori* argument for nihilism) jointly sufficient:

(1) The totality of constraints encodes a physical structure, i.e. encodes a type of structure which could be the structure of a physical reality.

(2) The fact that the different constraints, for different mind-time pairs, harmonize, so as jointly to encode a physical

structure, is guaranteed by the general method of constraint-generation – a method which thus preserves the harmony through possible variations in the specific external conditions which obtain and the consequent variations in the constraints these conditions impose.

To illustrate, here are two types of case which fail to meet the second condition:

(a) There is a 1-1 correlation between human minds and external sense-fields such that (i) the course of experience in each mind is controlled by the configurations of qualities in the correlated field, (ii) each field has its own internal organization, but there are no nomological links between different fields, and there is no other external item on which processes in different fields are nomologically dependent, and (iii) purely by chance, the quality-distributions in the different fields harmonize in such a way as to generate, in the framework of the laws, constraints which fit together, across different minds, to encode a single physical structure.

(b) There is a 1-1 correlation between times and external sense-fields such that (i) at each time, human experience is controlled by the quality-configurations in the correlated field, (ii) each field has its own internal organization, but there are no nomological links between different fields, and there is no other external item on which processes in different fields are nomologically dependent, and (iii) purely by chance, the quality-distributions in the different fields harmonize in such a way as to generate, in the framework of the laws, constraints which fit together, across different times, to encode a single physical structure.

In neither of these cases does the ultimate reality qualify, by my conditions, as sustaining a physical reality, since the fit between the different constraints, whether across minds or across times, depends on a harmony between the fields which is merely coincidental. We cannot say that the fit is guaranteed by the general method by which the constraints are generated, since it would disappear if the quality-distributions were altered in some random way, the method of constraint-generation remaining the same. My reason for requiring such a guarantee is that, without it, the constraints would not be sufficiently connected to combine in the creation of a single physical world. If there is to be a public and persistent world – the same world for different minds, the same world at different times – then surely the harmony of encoding across both minds and times must be ensured by certain fundamental aspects of the underlying external reality (e.g. its laws) independently of what particular constraints are, in accordance with the specific external conditions, imposed. This requirement is, of course, met by each of the cases E, E_1, … E_6.

It should be noted that this modification to the phenomenalist position does not reinstate any kind of isomorphism-requirement. It does not require that the underlying reality exemplify the structure of the physical reality it sustains, nor even that it does so relative to a suitable characterization. My conditions would be satisfied if the constraints were directly imposed by God with the intention of securing their fit. For such an intention, together with the omnipotence of God, would constitute that fundamental aspect of the underlying reality which ensured the harmony of encoding, across both minds and times, independently of the particular constraints imposed.

From now on, I shall take the label 'reductive phenomenalism' to signify the phenomenalist position as thus modified. And if I usually, for brevity, characterize this position as the thesis that the physical world is the logical creation of the constraints on human experience, it must be understood that the modification, though not expressed, still applies.

14

THE CHALLENGE OF NIHILISM

As I have often emphasized, anti-realism is compatible with two contrasting positions; it is compatible with *reductivism*, which accepts the existence of a physical world, though one which is logically created by an underlying non-physical reality, and it is compatible with *nihilism*, which denies the existence of a physical world altogether. The argument I have developed in the last two chapters does not establish which of these positions we should adopt. The argument shows what form reductivism must take, if reductivism is correct; but it does not show that reductivism is correct. It establishes that the physical world, if there is one, is the logical creation of the constraints on human experience; but it does not establish that there is, nor even that there could be, a physical world. It is time to examine the issue between reductivism and nihilism more closely.

There are three ways in which a nihilist position, or something approximating to it, might be defended. Firstly, it might be argued that our belief in the existence of a physical world, while coherent, cannot be empirically justified and that, in consequence, it would be irrational to retain it. This, of course, would be an argument for scepticism rather than for full-blooded nihilism. Secondly, and more strongly, it might be argued that our very concept of a physical world is inherently realist and that, consequently, the refutation of realism is a proof that this concept has, and can have, no application. If successful, this argument would show reductivism to be incoherent and establish nihilism *a priori*. Thirdly, and in a similar vein, it might be argued that, whether or not it is inherently realist, our concept of a physical world is at least inherently anti-phenomenalist, and that, consequently, we should look on the argument of the last two chapters not as a defence of phenomenalism, but as a *reductio* of reductivism. This argument too, if successful, would establish nihilism *a priori*. The second and third arguments, which dispute the coherence of reductivism, are clearly more central to our concern. But I shall begin by saying something about the first, partly because it has an important bearing on the more central issues to be considered later.

It might seem that the sceptical argument, while possibly threatening to other forms of reductivism, has little force against the phenomenalistic form which I have been defending, since this form minimizes the logical gap between our experiential evidence and our physical beliefs. The phenomenalist, after all, construes the physical world as the logical creation of the constraints on human experience, the physical realization of a certain structure being nothing over and above the encoding of that structure by the constraints. To establish the existence and character of the physical world, we have, it seems, merely to decipher the code, and this presumably we can do, at least to some considerable degree, by looking for the simplest topic-neutral theory which explains the actual course of our experience. Of course, even on a phenomenalist account, the physical facts transcend our experiential evidence: at no time do we have, either individually or collectively, a complete record of human experience, and even if we did, it would not conclusively establish the obtaining of certain experiential *constraints*. None the less, it could be claimed that our evidence is enough to *justify* our physical beliefs, and that the grounds for scepticism are considerably less for the phenomenalist than for someone who makes the physical facts depend more crucially on the nature of the ultimate external reality. Admittedly, given my modification (at the end of the last chapter), there is one respect in which even the phenomenalist has to take account of this external reality. For the creation of a physical world requires that the harmony of encoding, across minds and times, is ensured by the general method of constraint-generation. But once the harmony is discovered, it seems reasonable to infer that it is non-accidental in this way, just as it seems reasonable to attribute an inherent bias to a coin which, over a long series of tosses, consistently turns up heads.

However, this way of representing our epistemological situation is doubly misconceived, and, once the misconceptions are exposed, it will be seen that, even in the case of phenomenalism, there is a sceptical challenge to be met. In the first place, and here I endorse an earlier suggestion,[1] most of our information about the course of human experience is itself evidentially grounded, in one way or another, on our information about the physical world. This is obviously so in the case of one subject having information about the experiences of another. For such information is only available to the extent that the character of the experiences can be inferred from the behaviour (including the verbal behaviour) and physical circumstances of the subject who has them. But it is also true in the case of a subject's knowledge of his own past experiences. I believe that my past experiences have collectively exhibited a certain coherence and thematic character – the sort which would be most simply explained by postulating an external reality with a physically appropriate structure. But I hold this belief only because I already accept the existence of a physical world and accept a certain account of the way in which my experiences and physical circumstances are systematically linked. It is true that I can directly recall a number of experiences – at least I think I can. But even here I rely heavily on my recollection of physical circumstances in fixing their temporal order, the temporal distances between them and their remoteness from the present. Divorced from my physical knowledge, the evidential value of these acts of recall would be very slight. This is not to deny that my current knowledge of the physical world (if it is knowledge) is in some way grounded on my past experiences. Presumably, it is only because they are causally derived from and rationally appropriate to (what is from a God's eye view) the accumulated evidence of past experience, that my current physical beliefs, if true, qualify as knowledge. But this does not mean, nor is it the case, that my current access to this evidence is independent of the physical knowledge it has supplied. Without relying on this knowledge, I cannot, to any significant degree, survey the course of my past experience to see whether the physical beliefs it has implanted are ones which it objectively warrants. In consequence, phenomenalism provides no automatic defence against the sceptic's challenge. For while phenomenalism construes the physical world as the logical creation of the constraints on human experience, we depend on our physical knowledge to establish what experiential constraints obtain.

The second misconception is more subtle and concerns the nature of reductive phenomenalism itself. To appreciate it, we must start by taking a closer look at the relation of logical sustainment. As stated in the original definition,[2] one fact or set of facts F is logically sustained by another fact or set of facts F' iff F obtains wholly in virtue of F' in the following sense:

(a) F is a logical consequence of F', i.e. it is logically necessary that if F' obtains, then F obtains.

(b) F is mediated by F', i.e. the obtaining of F is achieved through the obtaining of F'.

(c) F is exhausted by F', i.e. the obtaining of F is nothing over and above the obtaining of F'.

But there is a distinction to be drawn between two kinds of sustainment – kinds which, to mark the difference, I shall call *prospective* and *retrospective*. Thus let us suppose that F is logically sustained by F', in accordance with the definition. Then I shall say that the sustainment is *pro*spective iff someone who knew that F' obtained could, on that basis alone, establish its sustainment of F. In contrast, I shall say that the sustainment is *retro*spective iff it could only be established by someone who, in addition to knowing that F' obtained, had independent knowledge of the obtaining of F. Obviously, there is a parallel distinction between prospective and retrospective *creation*. An entity x is the logical creation of the fact or set of facts F iff the existence of x (the fact that x exists) is logically sustained by F. So the creation of an entity is prospective or retrospective according to whether its existence is prospectively or retrospectively sustained.

To construct an example of prospective sustainment, suppose that John weighs 14 stone and Mary weighs 10 stone. Then the fact (F_1) that John weighs 14 stone and the fact (F_2) that Mary weighs 10 stone jointly sustain the fact (F_3) that John is heavier than Mary. For F_3 obtains wholly in virtue of F_1 and F_2 in accordance with the definition. Moreover, the sustainment is clearly prospective. For anyone who knew the specific weights of John and Mary could, on this basis alone, establish their weight-relation (F_3) and establish it as something which those specific weights (F_1 and F_2) logically sustain. The sustainment is prospective because it is discernible through a knowledge of the sustaining facts alone. But not all cases of sustainment are prospective. Thus consider the case in which, prior to the rejection of realism, we take the existence and arrangement of material continuants to be logically sustained by the spatiotemporal distribution and nomological organization of a certain quality. Assuming material continuants to come in the form of spherical particles, of the same size and type, we suppose that, for some quality Q, the underlying physical reality consists of a spatiotemporal distribution of Q, together with certain laws which ensure, amongst other things, that (1) at each time, the spatial distribution of Q divides into non-overlapping spheres of the appropriate (particle) size, and (2) over time, all changes in the spatial distribution of Q are spatiotemporally continuous. The distribution and laws are chosen in such a way as to allow us to construe the particle-continuants as constituted by the spatiotemporally and causally continuous paths of spherical Q-pervasion. But the derivative ontology of continuants is not something which would be discernible through a knowledge of the underlying reality alone. If our only information concerned the distribution and organization of Q, we could not, on that basis alone, establish the existence of any genuine continuants. We could recognize that, in a sense, things are organized as if there were continuants. And we might even, for convenience, speak as if there were – speak of mobile spheres of Q-pervasion which preserve their identity through the sequences of Q-pervaded region-moments. But this would only be a *façon de parler*, devoid of ontological commitment. To recognize the creation of the continuants, we have to know of their existence independently of what sustains it: we have to begin by acknowledging the particles and then envisage the distribution and organization of the quality as what underlies them. In other words, the postulated sustainment is retrospective – one which could only be established by someone who, in addition to knowing the sustaining facts, had independent knowledge of the facts sustained.

It might be objected that, given the definition of sustainment, the very notion of retrospective sustainment is incoherent. According to the definition, if F is logically sustained by F' then F is a logical consequence of F'. But how can F be a logical consequence of F' unless the obtaining of F is deducible from the obtaining of F'? And if the obtaining of F is deducible from the obtaining of F' and all the other conditions of sustainment are satisfied, then surely the sustainment will be prospective – one which could be established from a knowledge of F' alone. But the objection is misconceived. For it is simply not true that whenever one fact is a logical consequence of another, the obtaining of the first is deducible from the obtaining of the second. It is easy enough to find counter-examples from other areas. Thus suppose 'p' is short for 'this glass contains H_2O' and 'q' is short for 'this glass contains water'. Then it is logically (i.e. a stronger-than-naturally[3]) necessary that if p then q. For since water and H_2O are the same substance, there is no possible world in which a glass contains the one but not the other.[4] Consequently, the fact that q is, in the relevant sense, a logical consequence of the fact that p (indeed, each is a logical consequence of the other). But the proposition that q cannot be deduced from the proposition that p. The proposition that q can only be deduced from the proposition that p together with the additional premise that water and H_2O are the same substance. And, given the difference in the concepts *water* and H_2O, this additional premise, though logically necessary, cannot be established *a priori*. It can only be established empirically, by conducting the appropriate chemical analysis of the liquid we call 'water'.

Now the phenomenalist claims that the physical world is the logical creation of the constraints on human experience. But, presumably, the creation he envisages is only retrospective. For, clearly, a knowledge of the experiential constraints (and of the non-accidental character of the harmony of encoding) would not, on its own, suffice to establish the existence of a physical world. On the basis of such knowledge alone, we could at best introduce the locutions of a physical ontology as a *façon de parler* – a way of conveniently recording the fact that the constraints are, by the standard of explanatory simplicity, exactly as if there were an external reality with the appropriate structure. We could see, on such a basis, why the acceptance of a physical theory would be natural and useful for those subjects whose experiences are thus constrained, but we could not, on that basis, establish the theory as correct. It is only when we take the physical facts for granted that we can go on to assert their phenomenalistic sustainment. Admittedly, I am here assuming that, even if reductive phenomenalism is true, statements about the physical world cannot be analysed, with the preservation of factual meaning, into statements about experiential constraints. If they could, then a knowledge of the constraints would suffice to establish the existence of a physical world. For while, on the basis of such knowledge alone, we could at best introduce the locutions of a physical ontology as a *façon de parler*, recognizing the existence of a physical world would amount to no more than recognizing the truth of what, as a *façon de parler*, such locutions express. But it is clear, I take it, that the ontological commitment of physical statements cannot be analysed away in this fashion, and that, in consequence, the phenomenalistic creation (if it obtains at all) has to be retrospective.

We can now identify the second misconception in the earlier reply to the sceptical challenge. It was assumed, in that reply, that to establish the existence and character of the physical world, we merely have to establish that the constraints on human experience encode the appropriate structure, since (given our phenomenalistic approach) the physical realization of a certain structure is nothing over and above its being encoded by the constraints. We can now see that this assumption is wrong, since, if there is a physical world, its creation is only retrospective – a creation which can only be established by someone who already and independently knows of the existence of the created item. Thus the original account of our epistemological situation was doubly misconceived. In the first place, information about the experiential constraints is only available through knowledge of the physical world. And secondly, even if such information could be obtained in some other way, it would not suffice to establish the existence of a physical world, given that the phenomenalistic creation has to be retrospective. In short, even if the physical world is the logical creation of the constraints on experience, it is only through prior knowledge of the physical world that we can discover the constraints or recognize the creation. And this means that, even against the phenomenalist, the sceptical challenge retains its force.

Is there, then, some other way in which the sceptical challenge can be met? Well, certainly, there is no way of justifying our physical beliefs from scratch. If we were to discard the beliefs, we could find no rational way of re-acquiring them on the basis of what remained. This much, at least, we must concede to the sceptic. But it does not follow from this that, once we have the beliefs, it is irrational to retain them. The sceptic has not provided any evidence against them. Nor has he shown that they are not objectively warranted by the course of past experience. Moreover, there are two respects in which our physical beliefs are self-endorsing. In the first place, they are, by and large, mutually coherent. And secondly, they confirm the claim that they are objectively warranted: for by relying on the beliefs, we can go on to establish the systematic way in which their acquisition is controlled by, and appropriate to, our sensory evidence. All this, of course, leaves room for scepticism: it is conceivable, for example, that our physical beliefs are imposed by a malignant demon in such a way as to be self-endorsing in these ways. But at least there are no positive grounds for scepticism in the way there would be if these aspects of self-endorsement were absent or if we had some reason for thinking that our beliefs were not adequately grounded on past experience. The rational conclusion, I think, is to strike a balance between our ordinary convictions and the total agnosticism which the sceptic advocates. On the one hand, since we have no independent way of justifying the beliefs, it is unreasonable to hold them with an unqualified assurance: we must concede that they may be wrong – that there is room for doubt. On the other hand, unless there is some further reason for distrusting the beliefs (and the sceptic has not provided any), it is rational to retain them. This conclusion relies on a fundamental distinction between the rationality of acquiring beliefs and the rationality of retaining them. If the sceptic challenges this distinction, all I can say is that it reflects the way our minds actually work. For, whether we like it or not, our physical beliefs do survive the recognition that we have no independent way of justifying them. If such survival is irrational by the sceptic's standards, his standard of rationality is not one which we can achieve.

It is rational to retain our physical beliefs in the face of the sceptical challenge. But the sceptical challenge is not the only way in which these beliefs can be attacked. As we saw at the outset, it can also be argued that reductivism is incoherent. And if reductivism is incoherent, the refutation of realism amounts to a proof of nihilism: it establishes *a priori* that there is no physical world. Such an attack on our physical beliefs is more fundamental and more far-reaching than the sceptic's. It is also more central to our concern, since it depends on our argument for anti-realism. The sceptical argument, if it has any force, applies equally against the realist: it is not reductivism as such, but a belief in the existence of a physical world which the sceptic calls in question.

In an earlier chapter,[5] I spoke of reductive phenomenalism as that form of reductivism which is furthest from physical realism and closest to nihilism. Given that reductivism has to take this phenomenalistic form, it may be wondered whether the difference between it and nihilism is of much importance. Thus consider the position of someone who (a), accepting the incoherence of reductivism, denies the existence of a physical world, (b) recognizes the utility and naturalness of physical theory from the human viewpoint, and (c) accounts for this utility and naturalness in terms of the way in which, realistically construed, physical theory explains the constraints on human experience. On the face of it, there is only a marginal difference between this position (let us call it *phenomenalistic nihilism*) and reductive phenomenalism. The reductive phenomenalist takes human experience to be constrained in such a way as to make physical theory *true*. The phenomenalistic nihilist takes it to be constrained in such a way as to make physical theory *useful*. But why should we care whether it is truth or utility which physical theory achieves, if what underlies the achievement is the same in each case? The difference between the two positions seems even more tenuous when we remember that the phenomenalistic creation has to be retrospective. Even the phenomenalist must concede that, from a knowledge of the constraints alone, it is only the utility and naturalness of physical theory which can be discerned. It seems that the difference between the positions is one of perspective rather than of philosophical substance. The reductive phenomenalist looks at the role of the underlying reality from the viewpoint of physical theory. The phenomenalistic nihilist looks at the status of physical theory from the viewpoint of the underlying reality.

But, however close the two positions may seem, their difference *is* of crucial importance, because it has a crucial bearing on our epistemological situation. If we had some way of discovering the constraints on experience without recourse to physical knowledge, it would not matter much whether we thought of these constraints as sustaining the existence of a physical world or as merely ensuring the utility and naturalness of physical theory: our information would be the same, whether we interpreted it in reductivist or nihilist terms. But, as we have seen, our knowledge of the constraints depends on our knowledge of the physical world: there is hardly any information available about the course of human experience which does not depend, in one way or another, on taking our physical information for granted. Consequently, the cost of adopting nihilism would be not merely the rejection of our physical beliefs, but the elimination thereby of our main source of empirical knowledge. As nihilists, we would no longer have any reason to assert the utility and naturalness of physical theory, since, without recourse to our physical beliefs, we would have no reason to think that experience was constrained in a physically appropriate way. It might be objected that if it can be rational to retain our physical beliefs when there is no independent way of justifying them, then it can also be rational to retain our experiential beliefs when we discard the physical evidence on which they are grounded. Why should scepticism prevail in the second case, if not in the first? But it only takes a moment's reflection to see the absurdity of this objection. It is one thing to retain a system of non-inferential beliefs, which we already possess without a basis of independent evidence. It is something quite different and manifestly irrational to retain a hitherto inferential belief when the evidence from which it is inferred is discarded and no alternative evidence is put in its place. Once nihilism is accepted, there is no way of avoiding the most drastic form of scepticism, in which each subject forfeits all his empirical information apart from the knowledge of his current mental states and the relatively insignificant knowledge he possesses, through direct recall, of his former mental states. So the choice between reductivism and nihilism is not inconsequential *epistemologically*. Nor, indeed, is the real choice between reductive phenomenalism and *phenomenalistic* nihilism. For the very acceptance of nihilism would deprive us of any reason for accepting it in that quasi-phenomenalistic form.

Not only is the choice between reductivism and nihilism important epistemologically, but also, for that reason, we have a vested interest in preserving reductivism, if we can. But a vested interest does not, of course, constitute a philosophical justification. If there are arguments against the coherence of reductivism, they have to be taken seriously, however unpalatable their conclusion. We cannot just ignore the *a priori* arguments for nihilism on the grounds that the scepticism they generate is intolerable. Nor am I so pessimistic about human rationality as to think that we are psychologically incapable of accepting such an argument. I do not endorse Hume's famous dictum: 'It is in vain to ask, *Whether there be body or not*? That is a point which we must take for granted in all our reasonings.'[6]

As I said at the beginning, one way of arguing against the coherence of reductivism would be by claiming that our very concept of a physical world has a built-in commitment to realism – that whenever we say that things are thus and thus *physically*, we are saying that they are thus and thus *ultimately*, or, at least, excluding the possibility that ultimate reality is wholly non-physical. If such a claim were correct, reductivism would be incoherent. And nihilism would be the only tenable position, since we have already established, *a priori*, the falsity of realism. We should be forced to abandon all our physical beliefs, since these beliefs commit us to a metaphysical position (i.e. the ultimacy of the physical world) which we have already refuted. Such an argument for physical nihilism is analogous to the argument for moral nihilism of someone who maintains *both* that our ordinary moral thought commits us to recognizing objective values *and* that such objective values do not and cannot obtain.[7]

Let us call the claim that our concept of the physical has a built-in commitment to realism the *C-claim*. Now there is no denying that the C-claim has some intuitive plausibility. But it is important to see that its plausibility is, in a sense, presupposed by the very position (reductivism) whose coherence it denies. For, as we saw in chapter 3, reductivism would not (as it does) qualify as genuinely anti-realist if it were not developed in response to a *prima facie* case for nihilism. The point is that the mere exclusion of certain facts and entities from the sphere of the ultimate need not involve an anti-realist position towards what is excluded. Otherwise, we would be involved in an anti-realism towards aggregates simply by recognizing that their existence is logically sustained by the existence of their parts, and in an anti-realism towards weight-relations simply by recognizing that their obtaining is logically sustained by the weights of their *relata*. In order for an exclusion to count as genuinely anti-realist, it must preclude our accepting the reality of the excluded items at *face value* – preclude our accepting their reality in the form in which it is initially conceived. It is in this sense that reductivism counts as genuinely anti-realist towards the physical world. For reductivism, while preserving physical entities and facts, sets them in what is, relative to our initial conception of them, a radically different perspective.

It is in this sense too that it presupposes a *prima facie* case for nihilism. For it is developed in response to a *prima facie* conflict between the restrictions on the ultimate reality and the acceptance of a physical world. We may be able to eliminate the conflict, but we can only do so be revising (to suit the restrictions) our conception of what the existence of physical entities and the obtaining of physical facts involve. It follows that, even if false, the C-claim is bound to seem plausible in the framework of our initial intuitions. For reductivism would not be genuinely anti-realist unless it appeared, initially, to be incompatible with the ontological and factual commitments of our physical beliefs.

This ties in, of course, with the distinction between the two kinds of sustainment. It is just in those cases where a sustainment (or creation) thesis is anti-realist, i.e. one which conflicts with the perspective of our initial conception, that the postulated sustainment (creation) has to be retrospective, i.e. one which can only be established given a prior acceptance of the items sustained (created) – at least, this is so unless the perspective of our initial conception can be analysed away. The sustainment has to be retrospective, because, without a prior acceptance of the relevant items, there is no way of blocking the *prima facie* case for nihilism. The knowledge of the ultimate facts would not, on its own, oblige us to revise our initial conception of the entities and facts in question, and so would not, given the nature of that conception oblige us to accept their existence and obtaining. It is only where the entities and facts are independently assumed, that the restrictive account of the ultimate reality can lead us to revise our initial conception of them and accept that their existence or obtaining is nothing over and above the facts which the account specifies.

We can see, then, that the intuitive plausibility of the C-claim is something which the reductivist can explain, without having to accept. Of course, it does not follow from this that the claim is false: it may be that our concept of the physical is inherently realist and precludes a reductive account. It is just that, even if the concept is not inherently realist, anti-realism is bound to have a *prima facie* nihilistic force. And this is something we have to allow for in evaluating the claim.

Allowing for this, it seems to me that the C-claim is in fact false and that our concept of the physical does not preclude a reductive account. It seems to me that we can coherently suppose the physical world to be, retrospectively, the logical creation of an underlying non-physical reality, just as, prior to the rejection of realism, we could coherently suppose material continuants to be, retrospectively, the logical creation of the distribution and organization of a region-pervading quality. But I also think that this is not the real issue. For what really matters is not whether our actual concept of the physical embodies a commitment to realism, but whether, if it does, this commitment has any rationale. The reductivist is not going to be deterred if there is a commitment, but one which can be eliminated without disturbing the concept in other respects. He is not going to be deterred, for example, if what generates the commitment is merely that each physical proposition is formed by prefixing the realist operator 'It is ultimately the case that' to a core-proposition which can stand on its own. After all, if we can eliminate the commitment, we have every reason to do so, since (given the refutation of realism) it deprives physical concepts of even the possibility of application. Indeed, our reasons for wanting to eliminate it are even stronger than our earlier reasons for wanting to eliminate NMR.[8] In the earlier case, our aim was to make physical theory empirically testable. In the present case, our aim would be to make it coherent.

To establish his case, therefore, the nihilist must show not only that our concept of the physical has a built-in commitment to realism, but that this commitment is, as it were, *entrenched* – one that cannot be excised without damaging the concept in other respects. He must show that the commitment is not just a gratuitous addition, but something which is inextricably bound up with other aspects of the concept – something which we have to retain if we are to retain a concept of the *physical* in any recognizable form. I can see only one way in which he might try to do this, namely by deriving the commitment to realism from a commitment against phenomenalism. Thus he might argue that our concept of the physical is, and is irremediably, incompatible with reductive phenomenalism and so, there being no other viable form of reductivism, is irremediably committed to realism. This would be to turn the second of the three arguments I mentioned at the beginning of this chapter into the third. Our next task must be to examine this third argument in more detail.

15

THE TWO FRAMEWORKS

Put at its simplest, the argument I want to consider is that reductive phenomenalism does not allow the physical world the right kind of externality to human consciousness to qualify as a physical world in any decent sense. I shall call this the *externality-argument*. We have already shown that reductivism has to take a phenomenalistic form. So by challenging the coherence of phenomenalism, the externality-argument is, in effect, challenging the coherence of reductivism as such. Moreover, we have also established the incoherence of realism. So by challenging the coherence of reductivism, the externality-argument is, in effect, an *a priori* argument for nihilism.

The externality-argument can be formulated, in more detail, as follows:

It is a conceptual truth that the physical world, if there is one, is external to human minds. This conceptual truth is not something we can eliminate by revising our concept of the physical: the commitment to externality is too deeply entrenched for our concept to survive, in any recognizable form, without it. But the physical world is external to human minds, in the relevant sense, only if it could exist without them, i.e. only if its existence is logically independent of their existence. Now according to reductive phenomenalism, the physical world is the logical creation of, and hence wholly constituted by, the constraints on human experience. Hence, according to phenomenalism, the physical world cannot exist without the obtaining of such constraints. But each constraint is a causal limitation on the subsequent course of experience for a particular mind at a particular time. Obviously, such constraints cannot exist without the existence of human minds. Hence, phenomenalism denies the externality of the physical world and thus conflicts, and conflicts irremediably, with our concept of the physical.

On the face of it, this is a very plausible argument.

One way the phenomenalist could respond would be to concede the force of the argument, but modify his position in such a way that it no longer makes the existence of the physical world depend on experiential constraints of the envisaged sort. Thus he might invoke the notion of a higher-level causal field which exists independently of human minds and whose content is defined by the specific constraints it is disposed to yield, for minds at times, if minds of the appropriate sort exist. He could then construe the physical world as the logical creation of such a field, the encoding of the physical structure being achieved through the character of the constraints, whether actual or hypothetical, which the field has the potential to impose. This would be to retain the essentials of his original position without undermining the externality of the physical world. The phenomenalist would concede that the physical world could exist without the existence of human minds, while maintaining that its existence is wholly consti- tuted by the framework of natural necessity governing human experience.

Now there may be, I suppose, independent reasons for wanting to modify the phenomenalist position in this way. (This is a question I shall not pursue.) But it would be wrong to accept the modification *in response to* the externality-argument. For the argument rests on a confusion between two distinct ways in which the physical world may possess or lack the property of externa- lity – two distinct ways in which its existence may or may not depend on the existence of human minds. The distinction is, essentially, that between, on the one hand, what should be asserted *within* the framework of the physical theory whose truth is logically sustained, and, on the other, what should be asserted *about* the sustainment of the truth of such a theory. Once the distinction is appreciated, it will be evident that the kind of externality (mind-independence) which our concept of the physical requires is in no way incompatible with the kind of internality (mind-dependence) which reductive phenomenalism entails.

To see the distinction, it will help if we begin by focusing on a different, but related, problem concerning the status of psychophysical laws. In the broadest sense, psychophysical laws are any laws which causally link states of the physical world with states of human consciousness, in whichever direction the causation runs. But, as in earlier chapters, our concern here is with those psychophysical laws which link brain-states (as causes) with sense-experiences (as effects). Now it seems intuitively clear that, if there is a physical world, the obtaining of such psychophysical laws is not essential to its existence. Intuitively, it seems that the psychophysical laws are just a contingent addition to something (the space, matter, electromagnetic fields, physical laws, etc.) which could exist without them. Intuitively, it seems that the physical world could exist, with the same fundamental physical properties, but without any nomological links between brain-states (or any other physical states) and human experience. Of course, without such links, physical objects would be devoid of any secondary qualities, construed as Lockean powers, since physical objects only have powers to affect human experience via their powers to cause brain-states with experiential effects. But an object's possession of such powers, while essential to its perceptibility, does not seem to be essential to its existence. However, from the standpoint of reductive phenomenalism the situation seems quite different. According to the phenomenalist, the physical world is the logical creation of the constraints on human experience. The constraints encode a certain type of structure by being such that the ultimate realization of that structure would provide the simplest explanation of them (where simplicity requires, in particular, coming as close as possible to nomological uniformity and, subject to the pursuit of uniformity, avoiding unnecessary ontological or qualitative complexity). And the structure is physically (but non-ultimately) realized in virtue of its being encoded in this way. But obviously, the ultimate realization of this structure would not explain the constraints unless, in addition to an external component, the structure included laws linking the states of the component with human experience. So the creation of a physical world must always be part of the sustainment of a larger psychophysical reality consisting of a physical world *together with* certain psychophysical

241

laws. According to the phenomenalist, therefore, the obtaining of psychophysical laws is essential to the existence of the physical world. The physical world could not exist without such laws since *its* creation is necessarily conjoined with *their* sustainment.

On the face of it, then, there is a conflict between our initial intuitions and reductive phenomenalism over the status of psychophysical laws, just as there is, on the face of it, a conflict over externality. Our intuition is that the physical world could exist without such laws, while phenomenalism claims that it could not. But when we examine the situation more closely, we see that the conflict is only apparent and that a phenomenalist can, and indeed must, regard each claim as correct when properly interpreted.

Let us suppose that the structure encoded by the constraints is of the following form:

External world

(1) A 3-dimensional Euclidean space (the intrinsic nature of the points and distance-relations being unspecified).

(2) A stock of spherical continuants (of unspecified intrinsic nature) of the same size with a spatiotemporal arrangement of determinate type A.

(3) A set of arrangement-governing laws of determinate type N.

Link-laws: a set of laws of determinate type E assigning certain types of experiential effect, in human minds, to certain types of configuration of the spherical continuants.[1]

In other words, let us suppose that the topic-neutral theory which provides the simplest explanation of the constraints is that which postulates, as ingredients of the ultimate reality, an external world, as characterized by (1), (2) and (3), and link-laws (linking that world with human experience) of type E. Now it is obvious that, within the structure itself, the link-laws are only contingently attached to the external world. That is to say, in supposing the encoded structure to be of the specified form, we are, implicitly, supposing it to be thus:

External world

(1) ...
(2) ...
(3) ...

Link-laws *contingently attached to external world*: ...

We are implicitly supposing that the topic-neutral theory which provides the simplest explanation of the constraints is that which postulates, as ingredients of the ultimate reality, both an external world of the specified type and link-laws, of type E, *contingently attached to it*. Moreover, it is obvious that, within the structure itself, the external item has to be something which could exist without any link-laws at all. That is to say, in supposing the encoded structure to be of the specified form, we are, implicitly, supposing it to be thus:

$$
\left\{
\begin{array}{l}
\text{External world} \quad
\left.
\begin{array}{l}
(1)\ldots \\
(2)\ldots \\
(3)\ldots
\end{array}
\right\}
\left\{
\begin{array}{l}
\textit{with the capacity to exist,} \\
\textit{with this character, without} \\
\textit{any laws linking its states} \\
\textit{with human experience}
\end{array}
\right. \\
\\
\\
\text{Link-laws of type } E.
\end{array}
\right.
$$

We are implicitly supposing that the topic-neutral theory which provides the simplest explanation of the constraints is one which postulates both an external world, *capable of existing without link-laws*, and link-laws of type E. Now according to reductive phenomenalism, a structure is *physically* (but non-ultimately) realized by being encoded by the experiential constraints (i.e. by being that structure whose ultimate realization would provide the simplest explanation of the constraints). So, given our supposition, the phenomenalist must accept that the total physical reality sustained by the constraints is one within which the link-laws (= the psychophysical laws) are only contingently attached to the external component (= the physical world). Moreover, he must accept that it is one within which the external component (= the physical world) could exist without any link-laws (= psychophysical laws) at all.

At the same time, it is impossible for the constraints to be such that the structure they encode consists merely of an external component. For, without link-laws, the structure could not be one whose ultimate realization would explain the constraints, since it would have no causal relevance to human experience. So while the phenomenalist must concede that the physical reality sustained by the constraints is one within which the external component (= the physical world) could exist without any link-laws (= psychophysical laws), he must also insist that any sustainment of a physical reality has to be the sustainment of a reality in which link-laws are included. On the one hand, he admits that the contingency of psychophysical laws to the physical world is part of what the constraints sustain, and, on the other hand, maintains the impossibility of there being a creation of a physical world without the sustainment of psychophysical laws. If we speak of a proposition as being *physically* true iff, as a proposition of physical theory, its truth is logically sustained by the experiential constraints, and if, following the normal practice, we use the sumbol ' $\diamond$ ' to mean 'It is logically possible that', then we can schematically formulate the two claims which the phenomenalist must accept as follows:[2]

(a) It is physically true that ($\exists$ external world w) (ϕ (w) and $\diamond$ [ϕ (w) and $\sim$ ($\exists$ law-set L) (L links w-states with experiential states of human minds)])

(b) $\sim$ $\diamond$ it is physically true that ($\exists$ external world w) (ϕ (w) and $\sim$ ($\exists$ law-set L) [L links w-states with experiential states of human minds])

where ' ϕ ' holds place for some appropriate topic-neutral characterization such as (1), (2) and (3). The crucial point is the difference between (a) and (b) in the relative scopes of the two operators 'It is physically true that' and ' $\diamond$ ': (a) asserts the physical truth of a certain possibility, while (b) denies the possibility of a certain physical truth. It is this which renders the two claims compatible; it is physically true that there is an external world which needs no additional link-laws, but impossible for it to be physically true that there is an external world which has no additional link-laws.

We can see from this that there is no genuine conflict between reductive phenomenalism and our initial intuitions over the status of psychophysical laws. The claim that the physical world could exist without any psychophysical laws can be interpreted in two ways. On the one hand, it can be interpreted as a claim made within the framework of physical theory, and, thus interpreted, it becomes equivalent, in the phenomenalist's system, to (a). On the other hand, it can be interpreted as a philosophical claim made outside the framework of physical theory, and, thus interpreted, it becomes equivalent, in the phenomenalist's system, to what is denied by (b). Interpreted in the first way, the claim is one which the phenomenalist accepts, in accepting that the contingency of psychophysical laws to the physical world is part of what the constraints sustain. Interpreted in the second way, the claim is one which the phenomenalist rejects, in denying the possibility of there being a creation of a physical world without the sustainment of psychophysical laws. But, surely, in accepting the claim as interpreted in the first way, the phenomenalist satisfies, on this point, all that our intuitions demand. For the intuitive claim that the physical world could exist without psychophysical laws is a response to our understanding of the physical world in its own terms – a claim which we make, and are obliged to make, as first order physical theorists.

Let us now return to the issue of externality. The phenomenalist claims that the physical world is the logical creation of the constraints on human experience. This claim seems to conflict with the conceptual requirement of externality – the requirement that the physical world, if there is one, be something whose existence is logically independent of the existence of human minds. But is there really a conflict? As on the status of psychophysical laws, so on the question of externality, the phenomenalist will accept two contrasting, but compatible, claims. On the one hand, he will accept that what the constraints create is an external world – a world which, considered in its own terms, is independent of human minds. On the other hand, he will insist that what creates this external world are constraints on human experience – constraints which could not obtain without the existence of the minds on which they are imposed. Thus, on the one hand, accepting the physical truth of mind-independence, he asserts:

(c)   It is physically true that $(\exists w) (\phi (w)$ and $\Diamond$ [$\phi (w)$ and there are no human minds]).

On the other hand, claiming the mind-dependence of physical truth, he asserts:

(d) $\sim \Diamond$ (there are no human minds and it is physically true that $(\exists w) \phi (w)$).

He accepts it as physically true that there is a ϕ-world which is external to human minds, but denies the possibility of its being physically true that there is a ϕ world when there are no human minds. There is no inconsistency here.

We can now see how the phenomenalist can rebut the externality-argument. According to that argument, phenomenalism conflicts, and conflicts irremediably, with our concept of the physical, since phenomenalism construes the physical world as the logical creation of the constraints on human experience, while our concept requires it to be something whose existence is independent of human minds. But there are two ways of interpreting the claim that the physical world, if there is one, is independent of human minds. On the one hand, we can interpret it as a claim made within the framework of physical theory and hence as something which the phenomenalist accepts in asserting (c). On the other hand, we can interpret it as a claim of philosophical theory (concerning the metaphysical status of physical reality), namely what the phenomenalist denies in asserting (d). Now it is obvious that, as interpreted in the first way, the claim is a conceptual truth and one without which our concept of the physical could not survive in any recognizable form. For, obviously, this concept, as it features in physical theory (whether ordinary or scientific) is, and has to be, the concept of a realm which is external to and independent of human minds. But I can see no reason for taking the claim as a conceptual truth when interpreted in the second way. And even if, on this interpretation, it were a conceptual truth, it is one which, by conceptual revision, could and should be eliminated. There is simply no need for physical theory to embody a commitment – an incoherent commitment at that – to the metaphysical externality which the phenomenalist denies. Consequently, however the claim is interpreted, the externality-argument is misconceived. If the claim is interpreted in the first way, it is compatible with the phenomenalist's position. If it is interpreted in the second way, it is something which the phenomenalist can properly reject.

The crucial error in the externality-argument, therefore, is its failure to recognize the availability for the phenomenalist of the distinction between physical and meta-physical truth – between the physical facts sustained by the experiential constraints and the philosophical facts about such sustainment. The relationship between the physical world and human minds has to be characterized in quite different ways according to whether we are concerned with its physical or meta-physical aspects. Once these different aspects are distinguished, the externality-argument collapses.

The distinction between physical and meta-physical truth is one which the phenomenalist needs to exploit at another point. According to phenomenalism, the character of the physical world is wholly determined by the structure encoded by the constraints – the structure specified by that topic-neutral theory (of ultimate reality) which provides the simplest explanation of them. Now this theory, just because it is topic-neutral, leaves open a range of more specific alternatives concerning the intrinsic nature of that in which the structure is realized. Thus the theory we envisaged earlier, which postulates an external world (consisting of a space, space-occupying continuants and laws of arrangement) and link-laws of type E, does not specify the intrinsic nature of the postulated space, beyond a specification of its geometrical structure, nor the intrinsic nature of the postulated continuants, beyond their shape and size. So this theory will be compatible with a range of more specific theories which characterize the space and continuants more precisely. This seems to pose a problem for the phenomenalist. For logic demands that wherever a structure is realized, it is realized in some specific form. Yet phenomenalism requires that physical reality be no more specific than the topic-neutral structure encoded by the constraints.

To focus on a particular example, consider the question: 'Is physical space a sense-field?' By the law of the excluded middle, it either is or is not. But phenomenalism requires that, if it is, its being so is part of what the constraints sustain, and, if it is not, its not being so is part of what the constraints sustain. But neither alternative is thus sustained. For all that the constraints sustain is the physical realization of the structure they encode and the specification of this structure is neutral between the alternatives. So there seems to be a contradiction, in which logic requires that one of the alternatives obtains and phenomenalism excludes both.

Once again, the right response for the phenomenalist is to appeal to the distinction between physical and meta-physical truth. Given the law of the excluded middle, the phenomenalist must obviously accept that, considered in its own terms, physical space either has or lacks a sensory character. He must accept that the experiential constraints (assuming they sustain the existence of a space at all) sustain the existence of a space *as* something-which-is-a-sense-field-or-not. That is, he must accept:

(e) It is physically true that ($\exists$ external space s) (s is a sense-field or $\sim s$ is a sense-field)

At the same time, given the topic-neutrality of the encoded structure, he must also accept that neither the sensory nor the non-sensory character of physical space is part of what the constraints sustain. That is, he must accept both

(f) $\sim$ It is physically true that ($\exists$ external space s) (s is a sense-field)

and

(g) $\sim$ It is physically true that ($\exists$ external space s) ($\sim s$ is a sense-field).

Thus in requiring that physical space be no more specific than the topic-neutral structure encoded by the constraints, the phenomenalist is not denying the physical truth that space has a determinate intrinsic nature, but denying that there is a determinate physical truth about its intrinsic nature. He is not making a physical claim about the intrinsic paucity of space, but a meta-physical claim about the limits of physical truth. And this is how he resolves the problem quite generally, accepting the demands of logic within the scope of physical truth and the requirements of phenomenalism with respect to the sustainment of physical truth.

The point can be developed one stage further. So far we have been assuming, for the sake of simplicity, that the constraints encode a determinate structure, even though one which is topic-neutral. But this assumption may be false. We cannot exclude the possibility of there being alternative topic-neutral theories which provide equally simple explanations of the constraints. Thus we cannot exclude the possibility that there are two topic-neutral theories such that:

(1) The theories agree in postulating an external 3-dimensional Euclidean space and a stock of spherical continuants.
(2) The theories postulate the same laws (both laws of motion and link-laws with human experience), but differ slightly over the spatiotemporal arrangement of the continuants.
(3) Despite this difference, the two theories entail the same experiential constraints. (E.g. the differences in arrangement are confined to a period prior to the existence of human minds.)

(4) The theories provide equally simple explanations of the constraints they entail (e.g. they do equally well in achieving or approximating to nomological uniformity and in avoiding unnecessary ontological and qualitative complexity), and there is no other theory with equal or greater simplicity.

(5) The constraints they entail are ones which obtain.

In such a case, what the constraints encode is not a single structure, but the pair of structures, taken disjunctively, which the rival theories separately specify. This means that if one of the theories postulates an arrangement of type A_1 and the other an arrangement of type A_2, then it is physically true that either A_1 obtains or A_2 obtains, but neither physically true that A_1 obtains nor physically true that A_2 obtains. In particular, there will be at least one region-moment x of physical space-time such that, while it is physically true that x is either materially occupied or materially empty, it is neither physically true that it is occupied nor physically true that it is empty.

All in all, it seems to me that once we have distinguished the two assertive frameworks – the framework of ordinary physical theory and the framework in which we characterize the metaphysical status of physical truth – the coherence of reductive phenomenalism is secure. In particular, there is no conflict (none, at least, which is irremediable) between the claims of phenomenalism and our concept of a physical world. This does not, of course, establish that reductive phenomenalism is true. But this is not something which we could hope to establish by philosophical argument alone. For to establish the truth of reductive phenomenalism is, amongst other things, to establish the existence of a physical world. And there is no way of establishing the existence of a physical world *a priori*. The closest we can come, philosophically, to establishing the truth of reductive phenomenalism is to show that:

(a) Physical realism is untenable.
(b) Reductivism has to be phenomenalistic.
(c) Reductive phenomenalism is coherent.
(d) Scepticism can be resisted.

And, apart from one residual issue, which I shall consider in part V, all this we have done.

PART V

THE NATURE OF TIME

16

THE CONSTRUCTION OF INTER-SUBJECTIVE TIME

Reductive phenomenalism has to recognize a form of time which is logically independent of the physical world. For the phenomenalist takes the physical world to be the logical creation of the constraints on human experience, and each constraint is a causal limitation on the subsequent course of experience for a particular mind at a particular time. Obviously, this requires that human experiences have temporal locations independently of the physical world which the constraints on their occurrence create, whether or not this pre-physical time is also the time in which physical events are located. Moreover, it seems that what the phenomenalist needs is a form of time which, as well as being pre-physical, is *inter-subjective* – something which temporally relates experiences in different minds as well as those in the same mind. For even if we could assign a separate time-dimension to each mind and then construe each constraint as controlling the course of experience in one such dimension, we could hardly think of the constraints on different minds as combining to create a common physical world, unless we could, independently of the creation, inter-relate these separate subjective dimensions in a common temporal framework.

But can time be detached from the physical world in this way? In particular, can it be detached as something inter-subjective? If it can, is it something ultimate or something created by an underlying reality of pre-temporal facts? And, whether ultimate or created, how does this pre-physical time relate to the temporal location of physical events? It is clear that the phenomenalist owes us some further account of the nature of time and its place in his theory. It is such an account that I shall try to provide in these final chapters. My account will come in three parts. In the first part, I shall try to define a system of temporal concepts adequate for the specification of inter-subjective time in a pre-physical form. I shall sometimes speak of this definitional part as the 'construction' of inter-subjective time. In the second, I shall consider the ways in which we might take inter-subjective time, thus defined, to be ultimately constituted. In other words, I shall consider the sorts of ultimate reality we might postulate to give the system of temporal concepts, as we have defined it, application. In the third, I shall consider the nature of physical time – time as it forms part of the framework of the physical world. Part one, the construction of inter-subjective time, will take up the rest of this chapter. Parts two and three will come in the next.

We have mentioned the distinction between *inter-subjective* time (a single time-dimension for all minds) and *subjective* time (a separate time-dimension for each mind). But before we can deal properly with this distinction, there is another and more fundamental one to be drawn. This more fundamental distinction is between time as something which features in the *content* of sense-experience and time as something in which sense-experience is *located*. I shall call these two kinds of time, respectively, *phenomenal* and *mental*. As we have seen (in chapter 6), a sense-experience (sensation) is no more nor less than the realization of the total sense-quale, whether a quality or a quality-pattern, which it presents. So phenomenal time is time as it forms, along with other qualia, an element of what is experientially realized – an element of the total quality-pattern of which a sensation is the realization. In contrast, mental time is that in which sensations (the qualia-realizations) are themselves ordered and dated. Thus if we ask, 'Of what temporal pattern is sensation S a realization?' we are asking a question about phenomenal time; while if we ask, 'Did sensation S_1 occur before sensation S_2?' we are asking a question about mental time. Subjective and inter-subjective time are different forms of mental time. It is a pre-physical version of inter-subjective mental time which the phenomenalist needs and which I shall try to construct. In doing so, I shall use phenomenal time as the basis.

The existence of mental time, however it is to be construed, is uncontroversial. We have to accept that human sensations are located in time, whether this time is tied to or independent of the physical world, and whether it is subjective or inter-subjective. But why should we accept the existence of phenomenal time? Why should we accept that some sensations, as well as having temporal location, are realizations of temporal patterns? The reasons are partly empirical and partly conceptual.

In the first place, duration and change through time *seem* to be presented to us with the same phenomenal immediacy as homogeneity and variation of colour through space. Just as I directly see the extension of a colour-patch or the juxtaposition of two differently coloured patches, so I also seem to see, as directly, the rest or motion of a colour-patch relative to the surrounding pattern, and to hear, as directly, periods and sequences of sound. Thus when a bird flies past my window, in full view, the movement of the bird-shaped patch seems to be as much a visual datum – part of the content of my visual experience – as its colour and shape. And when I listen to a tune, the duration and succession of notes seem to be as much an auditory datum – part of the content of my auditory experience – as their pitch and loudness. The natural conclusion to draw from this is that, in such cases, things are as they seem, i.e. that time-relations form part of the presented pattern – part of what the sensations realize. It might be objected that what seems like the sensing of a temporal pattern is really the recollection of a mental succession: I seem to see the movement of the bird because, at each time (i.e. moment of mental time) when I see its current position, I remember what positions I successively saw it occupy over the preceding (mental) period. But this objection fails. There is a clear difference between the kinds of experience I have when, on the one hand, I witness the movement of a bird through the series of points from P_1 to P_2, and when, on the other, seeing it at P_2, I remember that, some twelve hours earlier, I successively saw it occupy the successive points in the same series. This difference cannot be eliminated or diminished merely by reducing the time-interval from twelve hours to twelve minutes or to one minute or to one second or to a fraction of a second. Of course, it is diminished, though not eliminated, if we suppose the remembering to be accompanied by an image of the previous movement – an image whose content includes a temporal succession of bird-patch positions. But such a suggestion requires the acceptance of phenomenal time. For if motion can be imaged, it can also be sensed. And if motion can be sensed, it would be perverse to deny that it *is* sensed on those occasions when it seems to be.

However, our reasons for accepting phenomenal time are not solely empirical. For at least in the case of the auditory realm, we cannot even conceive of there being a complete sensation (a sensation which could stand on its own[1]) whose content lacked a temporal element. Just as it is inconceivable that there should be a sensation of colour which was not the sensation of a colour-pervaded region, so, equally, it is inconceivable that there should be a sensation of sound which was not the sensation of a sound-filled period.[2] Phenomenal time is the essential medium for the realization of sound-qualia, as phenomenal space is the essential medium for the realization of colour-qualia. This claim is not to be confused with another, namely that any auditory sensation must be or be part of a *mental* period of continuous auditory awareness. This latter claim, indeed, might be disputed: it is at least arguable that a timeless being could have auditory experience. What I am claiming, and what semes to me to be indisputable, is that any complete auditory sensation, whether or not it is extended in mental time, must be the sensation of a phenomenal period. A mere pitch-loudness, abstracted from a time-field, cannot form a complete auditory datum, just as a mere colour, abstracted from a space-field, cannot form a complete visual datum. I am not sure whether phenomenal time is, in the same way, an *essential* ingredient of the other (non-auditory) sense-realms. But if it is essential to the auditory realm, it is at least available to the other realms. And granted its availability, we have no reason to doubt its presence in these other realms, given the empirical evidence in its favour.

The distinction between phenomenal and mental time raises an intriguing question. The two forms of time must have something in common which makes them species of the same genus – something which makes it appropriate to classify both as forms of *time*. This common factor must consist in more than just the formal structure of a time-dimension (in the fact, say, that time is 1-dimensional and continuous), since this does not capture the distinctively temporal aspect: it does not distinguish a time-dimension from, for example, the dimension of phenomenal pitch or from a line in the visual field. On the other hand, it must consist in something less than a sharing of exactly the same modes of temporal arrangement, since, as sense-qualia, modes of phenomenal time-arrangement are not realized outside the content of sensation: mental beforeness is not just phenomenal beforeness transferred to the domain of sensations. In what, then, does the common factor consist? What justifies our use of the same temporal terms, such as 'before' and 'after', 'earlier than' and 'later than' to signify both relations within the content of sensations and relations between sensations themselves? The answer, whatever it is, must lie in the way in which phenomenal time-concepts and mental time-concepts are analytically connected. It must lie in either (a) the way in which the mental time-concepts are analysable (partly) in terms of the phenomenal, or (b) the way in which the phenomenal time-concepts are analysable (partly) in terms of the mental, or (c) the way in which both are analysable, collaterally, in terms of something else. Of these alternatives, (b) and (c) are excluded, because phenomenal time-concepts cannot be further analysed (except in terms of each other): like concepts of phenomenal pitch and colour, they can be defined only ostensively, through a sensation or image of that which exemplifies them. (Someone incapable of either sensing or imaging temporal patterns could form no transparent conception of phenomenal time, just as someone incapable of either sensing or imaging colour-arrays could form no transparent conception of phenomenal colour.) The answer must therefore lie in alternative (a). This point determines the whole strategy of my subsequent account. My construction of inter-subjective time is, in effect, a detailed elaboration of the way in which mental time-concepts are analysable in terms of phenomenal time-concepts together with certain concepts of a non-temporal kind. And, as such, it shows how mental time, in its various forms, derives its temporal character from phenomenal time.

We must begin by looking more closely at the way in which phenomenal time is related to the mental succession of sensations in a stream of experience. Let us focus on the example of someone listening to a tune – say, for simplicity, the scale of middle C: C_1 – silence – D – silence ... silence – B – silence – C_2. His stream of auditory experience will comprise a series (Σ_1), in mental time, of total auditory sensations (an auditory sensation being *total* iff there is no larger auditory sensation of which it is a part), and each of these sensations will be a sensation of a temporal pattern – the realization of a time-field in which periods of sound and silence are arranged. For simplicity, let us assume that, throughout the series, the phenomenal periods of sound and silence are of a constant size (1 ϕ-unit), except where shortened by the boundaries of the time-field, and that the time-field itself is of constant size, comprising exactly 3 ϕ-units. Then, by choosing an appropriately corresponding unit (μ) of mental time, we can select from Σ_1 a second and less tightly packed series (Σ_2) of sensations spaced at μ-intervals, thus: [3]

Mental time	Σ_2	*Phenomenal time-pattern*
t_1	S_1	2 ϕ-units of silence before 1 ϕ-unit of C_1
$t_2 (= t_1 + \mu)$	S_2	1 ϕ-unit of silence before 1 ϕ-unit of C_1 before 1 ϕ-unit of silence
$t_3 (= t_2 + \mu)$	S_3	1 ϕ-unit of C_1 before 1 ϕ-unit of silence before 1 ϕ-unit of D
.	.	
.	.	
.	.	
t_{15}	S_{15}	1 ϕ-unit of B before 1 ϕ-unit of silence before 1 ϕ-unit of C_2
t_{16}	S_{16}	1 ϕ-unit of silence before 1 ϕ-unit of C_2 before 1 ϕ-unit of silence
t_{17}	S_{17}	1 ϕ-unit of C_2 before 2 ϕ-units of silence

Notice that, in Σ_2, the time-patterns realized by successive sensations overlap, in that some last portion of the pattern realized by the earlier sensation is the same as some first portion of the pattern realized by the later one. Thus the last two units of the time-field of S_1 are filled by the same pattern (a period of silence before a period of C_1) as the first two units of the time-field of S_2, and the last two units of the time-field of S_2 are filled by the same pattern (a period of C_1 before a period of silence) as the first two units of the time-field of S_3. And so on through the series. Now, on the face of it, this is puzzling. For it seems to imply that, for each note N, there are three separate realizations of a ϕ-period of N – one for each of the three positions in the time-field which, in successive Σ_2-sensations, the period occupies. Thus it seems to imply that the subject has, on successive occasions in mental time, three distinct sensations of a ϕ-period of C_1, one as part of S_1, a second as part of S_2 and a third as part of S_3. Indeed, taking into account all the other Σ_1-sensations between S_1 and S_2 and between S_2 and S_3, it seems to imply that he has many more than three sensations of a

ϕ-period of C_1 – infinitely many, if Σ_1 is continuous. This result is puzzling because it does not fit the character of our experience. When I listen to a scale, I seem to hear the succession of notes, but I do not hear each note more than once, except in so far as the note-period can be subdivided.

How are we to account for the apparent contradiction? The answer is that where the temporal patterns realized by successive Σ_2-sensations overlap, the sensations themselves overlap in a corresponding way. Thus while S_1, S_2 and S_3 are distinct, S_1 and S_2 contain the same sensation of *a ϕ-period of silence before a ϕ-period of C_1*, S_2 and S_3 contain the same sensation of *a ϕ-period of C_1 before a ϕ-period of silence*, and all three contain the same sensation of *a ϕ-period of C_1*. In line with this, each sensation extends through a period of mental time proportional to the phenomenal period which it realizes. Thus the succession of mental times $t_1 \ldots t_{17}$ turns out to be a succession of overlapping mental periods, each period covering a total span of auditory awareness. Obviously, the situation will be analogous in other sense-realms. In each realm, a stream of sense-experience will be constituted by a series of overlapping sensations, each of these sensations being the realization of a temporal pattern and each extending through a mental period proportional to the time-field in this pattern. These conclusions may seem surprising. For we might assume, prior to a thorough investigation, that the relation of being parts of the same sensation is transitive, so that if there is a single sensation which contains both x and y and a single sensation which contains both y and z, then there is a single sensation which contains both x and z. If this were so, then successive total sensations could not contain a common component, since the transitivity would then combine the supposedly total sensations into a single larger sensation. The character of our experience requires us to abandon the assumption of transitivity. The same sensation can be a component of two distinct total sensations. It can be united, within a single span of sense-awareness, with a sensation x and also united, within a single span of sense-awareness, with a sensation z, even though x and z are not themselves so united.

We are now in a position to take the first step in our constructive project. For we can now define, solely in terms of phenomenal time and the overlapping of sensations, the concepts of temporal order and distance in *streamal* time, i.e. in mental time as it applies, exclusively, to sensations in the same stream of experience. As a preliminary, we should note that since phenomenal time cuts across the different sense-realms, so that sensations in different realms may share the same time-field, sensations in different realms may be, in the relevant sense, components of a single sensation. Thus there may be, in a certain mental period, a single visuo-auditory sensation of a temporal pattern of colour-arrays and sounds. It follows that what we have been calling a *total auditory sensation* (one which is not a component of a larger *auditory* sensation) need not be a *total sensation* (one which is not a component of a larger *sensation*). A total sensation can, and often will, include components from different realms.

Let us say that *x O-precedes y* iff, for some sensation *z*:

(1)   *x* and *y* are total sensations and *z* is a component of both *x* and *y*.

(2)   *x* and *y* are realizations of temporal patterns.

(3)   *z* is the realization of some phenomenally last portion of the *x*-pattern and is the realization of it *qua* last portion of this pattern.

(4)   *z* is the realization of some phenomenally first portion of the *y*-pattern and is the realization of it *qua* first portion of this pattern.[4]

O-precedence is the relation of overlapping precedence – the relation which holds, within a stream of experience, between an earlier total sensation and a later total sensation which overlaps it. Let us further say that *x Σ-precedes y* iff there is a series of total sensations, of which *x* is the first member and *y* the last, such that each member, other than *y*, O-precedes its successor.[5] In other words, Σ-precedence is the *ancestral* of O-precedence – what stands to O-precedence in the way that *being an ancestor of* stands to *being a parent of*. Σ-precedence is the relation of streamal precedence – the relation which holds between earlier and later total sensations in the same stream. This defines the streamal time-order. Temporal distance is then defined by two further principles. Firstly, the extent of any sensation in streamal time is measured by the extent (in phenomenal time) of the time-field it realizes. Secondly, if *x* O-precedes *y* and *z* is the common component sensation, in which *x* and *y* overlap, then the temporal extent of *x* + *y* is the sum of the temporal extents of *x* and *y* less the temporal extent of *z*.

These two principles determine the temporal extent of any stream or stream-phase. Thus given any stream or stream-phase A, with S and S' as, respectively, its earliest and latest total sensations, we select from A a series of successively O-precedent sensations running from S to S'. To measure the temporal extent of A we then add the extents of the members of the series and subtract, for each pair of successive members, the extent of their overlap.

A stream of experience is any largest collection of total sensations such that the members of each pair of sensations are linked, one way or the other, by the relation of Σ-precedence. Typically, a single human mind contains many streams, separated by periods of unconsciousness, or, at least, periods in which there is no sense-awareness. We have shown how temporal order and temporal distance apply within a stream. The next step must be to show how they apply within a whole mind – to show how, within a single mind, the different streams, together with the non-sensory interludes, are located in a single time-dimension. Thus in what sense are my current sensations temporally related to those I had yesterday, given the intervening period of sleep?

Suppose A and B are streams and (however this is to be construed) that A is earlier than B. If A and B belong to the same mind (if they are, as I shall say, *consubjective*), then they have, in a certain sense, the potential for being co-streamal: their consubjectivity requires that, with B held constant, a sufficient continuation of A would join up with beginning of B, making A and B phases of a single stream. On the other hand, if A and B belong to different minds (if they are *dissubjective*), they do not have this potential. Indeed, their dissubjectivity requires that, with B held constant, no continuation of A, however protracted, would make A and B phases of a single stream. Now this point is the key to the construction of subjective time (i.e. mental time as it applies, exclusively, to sensations in the same mind). For given two consubjective streams, their temporal order and the temporal distance between them can be defined in terms of the hypothetical intervening stream-phase required to join them: the earlier stream is that one of which this intervening phase is a continuation and the distance between them is the extent of this phase in streamal time. To be precise, let us say that X is a *continuation* of y iff x and y are aggregates of total sensations such that (1) every total sensation in x Σ-precedes every total sensation in y and (2) every sensation which some x-sensation Σ-precedes and which Σ-precedes some y-sensation is a constituent of either x or y. In other words, x is a continuation of y iff x and y are adjacent phases of the same stream, with x earlier than y. The crucial definition is then this:

> Stream x *subjectively precedes* stream y *by extent* e iff, for some e', it is nomologically ensured that if y were to remain the same and x were to have a continuation z, with streamal extent e', then y would be a continuation of z and e would be the streamal extent of that portion of z which neither the last total sensation in x nor the first total sensation in y overlapped.

Or put more precisely:

> Stream x *subjectively precedes* stream y *by extent* e iff there is an e' such that, for any possible world w, if w has the same ultimate laws as the actual world and w contains x and y, then if, in w, x has a continuation with streamal extent e', then, in w, there is a stream-phase z, with extent e', such that z is a continuation of x, y is a continuation of z and e is the streamal extent of that portion of z which neither the last total sensation in x nor the first total sensation in y overlaps.

At the cost of marginally overestimating the extent, we could conveniently simplify the definition to read: stream x subjectively precedes stream y by extent e iff it is nomologically ensured that, if y were to remain the same and x were to have a continuation z, with streamal extent e, then y would be a continuation of z (i.e. iff, for any possible world w, if w has the same ultimate laws as the actual world and w contains x and y, then if, in w, x has a continuation with streamal extent e, then, in w, there is a stream-phase z, with extent e, such that z is a continuation of x and y is a continuation of z).

Combined with our construction of streamal time, this immediately yields the definitions of both order and distance in subjective time. Thus a sensation S_1 is *subjectively earlier than* a sensation S_2 iff either (a) S_1 is streamally earlier than S_2 or (b) for some stream x, some stream y and some extent e, S_1 is a constituent of x and S_2 is a constituent of y and x subjectively precedes y by e. And if S_1, in stream x, is subjectively earlier than S_2, in stream y, then (a) if $x = y$, the subjective distance from S_1 to S_2 (i.e. if S_1 and S_2 are temporally extended, from the beginning of S_1 to the end of S_2) is the extent of the stream-phase from S_1 to S_2, and (b) if $x \neq y$, the subjective distance from S_1 to S_2 is the sum of (1) the extent of the stream-phase from S_1 to the end of x, (2) the extent of the stream-phase from the beginning of y to S_2 and (3) the extent by which x subjectively precedes y. It is interesting to note, *en passant*, that these definitions of subjective order and distance do not employ the concept of consubjectivity. There would be no circularity in defining consubjectivity in terms of subjective time, thus: two streams are consubjective iff, for some e, one of them subjectively precedes the other by extent e, and two sensations are consubjective iff they are constituents either of the same stream or of consubjective streams. Whether such definitions are philosophically appropriate is another matter. We may have independent reasons for taking the concept of a subject as fundamental and for defining consubjectivity in terms of it. I shall not go into this issue here.[6]

We have defined streamal time in terms of phenomenal time and the overlapping of sensations and we have defined subjective time in terms of streamal time and natural law. These results, however limited, are in line with our constructive aims. In the first place, the definitions show how, in its subjective form, mental time derives its temporal character from phenomenal time, which is conceptually fundamental. Secondly, thus defined, subjective time seems to be something which could, given an appropriate ultimate reality, obtain pre-physically and thus contribute, as the phenomenalist requires, to the creation of the physical world. On this second point, however, we must leave the final verdict till the next chapter. In our present agenda, the next task must be to take our constructive project into its final stage: the construction of inter-subjective (IS) time. In what sense can dissubjective sensations be temporally related? In what sense can different minds share a common time-dimension?

My basic strategy will be to define the concepts of inter-subjective time (i.e. the concepts of IS-temporal order and IS-temporal distance) in terms of the concepts of subjective time and inter-subjective causation. Such a strategy is available, because the concept of inter-subjective causation does not presuppose the concept of inter-subjective time: we can grasp what it is for an event in the subjective time of one mind to cause (or contribute to the causation of) an event in the subjective time of another mind, without first assigning the two events to a common time-dimension.

So it is possible, without circularity, to make use of the concept of IS-causation in the construction of IS-time. Moreover, this strategy promises to be in line with the phenomenalistic enterprise. For a framework of IS-causation seems to be something which the phenomenalist could postulate at the pre-physical level, and it seems to be just what is required to give human minds that communal organization needed for the creation of a common physical world.

The strategy will be developed in accordance with three fundamental principles, which concern the relationship between IS-time and the elements (subjective time-order, subjective distance and inter-subjective causation) out of which it is to be constructed. The first principle (*P1*) is that, within a single mind, the IS time-order necessarily coincides with the subjective time-order. That is to say, we are to take it as a conceptual truth that, given a framework of IS-time, if S_1 and S_2 are consubjective sensations, located in that framework, then S_1 is IS-earlier than S_2 iff S_1 is subjectively earlier than S_2. The second principle (*P2*) is that, within a single mind, IS time-distances are necessarily proportional to subjective time-distances. That is to say, we are to take it as a conceptual truth that, given a framework of IS-time, if S_1, S_2, S_3 and S_4 are consubjective sensations, located in that framework, then the IS-distances between S_1 and S_2 and between S_3 and S_4 are equal iff the subjective distances between them are also equal. *P2* does not, it should be noted, require that where the subjective distances in *different* minds are equal (unequal) the IS-distances are also equal (unequal). It leaves open the possibility that the same unit of IS-distance may coincide with different units of subjective distance in different minds. The third principle (*P3*) is that IS-causation necessarily runs forwards (from earlier to later) in IS-time. That is to say, we are to take it as a conceptual truth that, given a framework of IS-time, if x and y are events in different minds, located in that framework, and if x causes, or contributes to the causing of, y, then x is IS-earlier than y. These three principles constitute the basic guidelines for our construction. We are to define the concepts of inter-subjective time in such a way that these principles hold.

As we have constructed it, subjective time consists in certain relations of order and distance between consubjective sensations. The ontology is an ontology of mental events and subjective time is constituted by certain facts about them. However, for the purposes of constructing IS-time, it will be convenient to assign to each mind a subjective *time-dimension* and to introduce an ontology of subjective moments and periods drawn from such dimensions. These dimensions, of course, are the logical creation of, and hence nothing over and above, the temporal facts about sensations. Each dimension exists solely in virtue of the fact that, in the relevant mind, the sensations are arranged in a certain temporal order and at certain temporal distances, and that the positions in this arrangement leave room for indefinitely many other positions which might have been occupied by other (hypothetical) sensations in the same mind. Moreover, the identity of each subjective moment is fixed by the identity of the sensation (or momentary sensation-slice) which occurs at it or by its temporal relations with other moments, on the same dimension, whose identities are fixed by the sensations which occur at them.

Each human mind has (presumably) only a finite span of sense-experience, bounded by an earliest and a latest sensation. But I shall take its subjective time-dimension to be infinitely extended in both directions. I can do this because the temporal arrangement of sensations leaves room for positions before the earliest sensation and after the latest, just as it leaves room for other positions in between. If we can mark out non-sensory periods *between* streams by envisaging their hypothetical connection by some intervening stream-phase, then, in the same way, we can mark out a non-sensory period before the first stream by envisaging a hypothetical earlier phase and mark out a non-sensory period after the last stream by envisaging a hypothetical later phase. And there is no limit on the possible extent of these additional phases.

Although the subjective dimensions are created by the temporal relations between *sensations*, once we have the dimensions, we can use them to provide temporal locations for mental events of other kinds. In particular, we can speak of an act of volition V as located at a subjective moment t in virtue of the fact that if there is, or were, a sensation at t, V is, or would be, consciously conjoined with it. This is important for our constructive project. If we are to construct inter-subjective time out of subjective time and inter-subjective causation, we have to envisage causal lines running from an event in one mind to an event in another. And while we can plausibly think of such lines as terminating in a sensory effect, it is much less plausible to think of them as originating from a sensory cause. It is much more plausible to take the causing event to be a volition. It is not by having sensations, but by *doing* something that I have a causal influence on other minds, even if my sensations (or the beliefs I acquire from them) help to provide a reason for my action. Given this, the key concept in my construction of inter-subjective time will be what I shall call *volitional inter-subjective causal priority*, or for short, *V-priority*. V-priority is a relation which holds between moments (points) on different subjective dimensions. Using '*x[m]*' as short for 'moment *x* on the subjective dimension of mind *m*', it can be defined in two steps. Thus let us say that *x[m]* is *directly V-prior to y[m']* iff *m* and *m'* are different minds and *m* is in a position to causally affect, by an act of volition at *x*, the sensory state of *m'* at *y*. Then *x* is *V-prior to y* iff, for some *x'* and *y'*, (1) *x* is either identical with or subjectively earlier than *x'*, (2) *y* is either identical with or subjectively later than *y'* and (3) *x'* is directly V-prior to *y'*. In other words, *x[m]* is V-prior to *y[m']* iff *m* and *m'* are different minds and *m* is in a position to causally affect, by an act of volition at or *m*-later than *x*, the sensory state of *m'* at or *m'*-earlier than *y*.

Where two minds share a common framework of IS-time, let us speak of them as *IST-related*. This relation, of course, is one which we will have to define, in due course, as part of the construction of IS-time. Now we know from *P1* and *P3* that if *m* and *m'* are IST-related and if *x[m]* is V-prior to *y[m']*, then *x* is IS-earlier than *y*. (For we know from *P1* that, within a single mind, the IS time-order coincides with the subjective time order, and we know from *P3* that IS-causation has to run forwards in IS-time.) Given this, we may be tempted to adopt the following very simple definition of temporal priority in IS-time (with variables ranging over subjective moments):

D: *x* is *IS-earlier than y* iff *x* is either subjectively earlier than or V-prior to *y*.

However, there are two faults in *D*. In the first place (*Fault A*), the *definiens* does not entail the *definiendum*. For if *x* and *y* are moments on different subjective dimensions, *x* and *y* will not stand in any IS time-relation unless the two dimensions are, as a whole, inter-subjectively related, and this requires more than just that one moment on one of them be directly V-prior to one moment on the other. It requires that the two dimensions be, in some appropriate way, systematically linked by relations of actual and potential causation. Secondly (*Fault B*), the *definiendum* does not entail the *definiens*. For the fact that $x[m]$ is IS-earlier than $y[m']$, where $m \neq m'$, does not ensure that x is V-prior to y: it does not ensure m is in a position to affect, by an act of volition at or m-later than x, the sensory state of m' at or m'-earlier than y. For the time being, I shall focus exclusively on *Fault B*.

Suppose that m_1 and m_2 are different minds and that $a[m_1]$ is IS-earlier than $b[m_2]$. There are two ways in which a may fail to be V-prior to b:

(1) It may be that the IS-interval between a and b (the IS-temporal distance between them) is less than the minimum required by the laws of nature, for a causal line from a volition in one mind to a sensation in another.[7] Thus (for convenience) looking at things in physical terms, imagine the situation in which my body is next to yours, in which you are awake and alert and in which my muscular and your sensory systems are in perfect order. The circumstances are ideal for a swift causal communication from my volitions to your sensations. None the less, there is a minimum extent E of IS-time such that no volitional act of mine at IS-time t can affect your sensory state before $t + E$. It may be, of course, that with some form of surgical intervention (e.g. the insertion of super-conductive wires running from my brain to yours), this minimum could be reduced. But even so, there is likely to be some absolute minimum, fixed by the very laws of IS-causation, such that no causal line from a volition in one mind to a sensation in another could be temporally shorter. And if there is such a minimum – let us call it the *ISC-minimum* – and if the IS-interval between a and b is less than it, then a will, for that reason, fail to be V-prior to b. In such a case I shall describe the failure as *nomological*.

(2) It may be that, while the IS-interval between a and b is not less than the ISC-minimum (if there is one), the other circumstances are, in one way or another, unfavourable. Here there is a multiplicity of different cases. To mention some of the more obvious ones: it may be that (i) m_1 no longer exists at a or has yet to come into existence at some point too late for it to be

sufficiently IS-earlier than b, or (ii) m_2 does not yet exist at b or has gone out of existence at some point too early for it to be sufficiently IS-later than a;[8] or looking at things in physical terms, it may be that (iii) m_1 exists at a but is, and will be for some time, disembodied or physically paralysed, or (iv) m_2 exists at b but is, and has been for some time, disembodied or physically anaesthetized, or (v) over the relevant IS-period, the spatial distance between the bodies of m_1 and m_2 is too great to allow the transmission of a signal in the time available. The differences between these cases (and all the others I have not mentioned) need not concern us. What matters is the common factor, namely that in each of these cases we can, retaining the same laws and the same IS-time relation between a and b, envisage different circumstances in which a would be V-prior to b. For example, if m_1 no longer exists at a, we can envisage circumstances in which it continues up to and beyond a; or if m_2 is anaesthetized over a period up to and including b, we can envisage circumstances in which it is not; or if the bodies of m_1 and m_2 are, over the relevant IS-period, spatially too remote, we can, by adjusting their previous histories, envisage circumstances in which they are sufficiently close. In all these cases I shall describe the failure of a to be V-prior to b as *circumstantial*. This contrasts with cases of type (1), where the failure is nomological. For where the failure is nomological, the IS-interval between a and b is less than the ISC-minimum – the minimum fixed by the laws of IS-causation – so that there could not be circumstances in which, with the same interval and subject to the same laws, a was V-prior to b.

This distinction between the nomological and circumstantial failures is an elaboration of *Fault B* of definition D. In effect, *Fault B* now divides into two faults: (1) $x[m]$ may be IS-earlier than $y[m']$, where $m \neq m'$, but fail, *nomologically*, to be V-prior to y; (2) $x[m]$ may be IS-earlier than $y[m']$, where $m \neq m'$, but fail, *circumstantially*, to be V-prior to y. To correct these faults, we have to find some way of capturing the temporal priority in terms of IS-causation when the V-priority is blocked in either of these ways.

It may seem that we can immediately deal with the case of circumstantial failure by introducing the weaker relation of *potential*

V-priority, defined thus: x is *potentially V-prior* (PV-prior) *to y* iff it is nomologically possible for x to be V-prior to y, i.e. iff there is a possible world w, with the same laws as the actual world, and x is V-prior to y in w. The idea would be that, where the failure is merely circumstantial, the temporal priority of x to y shows up in the fact that, to make x V-prior to y, we only have to transfer the moments to a world, with the same laws, in which the circumstances are more favourable. But, while we are moving in the right direction, PV-priority, as defined, is too weak for our purposes. For we have no guarantee that it is asymmetric. The laws may be sufficiently permissive to allow x to be V-prior to y in one possible world and y to be V-prior to x in another. And if this were so, PV-priority would give no indication of temporal order. What we need is the stronger relation of *rigid* PV-priority, defined thus: x is *rigidly PV-prior* (RPV-prior) *to y* iff x is PV-prior to y and y is not PV-prior to x. RPV-priority has the asymmetry built into it. Of course, RPV-priority will only be of use to us if we impose a certain restriction on the nature of IS-time, namely that the IS-time relation between any two subjective moments holds constant through all nomologically possible worlds (worlds with the same laws as the actual world) in which these moments exist. For we cannot hope to keep the relations of PV-priority rigid if we allow the temporal order of the *relata* to vary from world to world. But I do not see this restriction as problematic. It seems to me quite natural to construct IS-time in such a way that IS-time relations are logically tied to the identities of the subjective moments they relate (thus ultimately to the identities of, and subjective time-relations between, the sensations in the relevant minds) and the ultimate laws of nature.[9] (Incidentally, an analogous restriction on the nature of subjective time was implicit in the definition of what it is for one stream to subjectively precede another by a certain extent. For, thus defined, the subjective order of two streams and the subjective distance between them hold constant through all nomologically possible worlds in which the streams exist.)

Given this restriction, the relation of RPV-priority solves the problem of circumstantial failure. For where x fails, *circumstantially*, to be V-prior to y, the temporal priority of x to y shows up in its RPV-priority – in the fact that it is nomologically possible for x to be V-prior to y but not nomologically possible for y to be V-prior to x. But RPV-priority does not provide an immediate solution to the problem of nomological failure. For where x fails, *nomologically*, to be V-prior to y, it also fails to be RPV-prior to y, since, with the IS-interval between them holding constant through all nomologically possible worlds, there is no world, with the same laws as the actual world, in which x is V-prior to y.

To deal with the case of nomological failure, where the IS-interval is less than the ISC-minimum, we need to alter, slightly, our constructive direction. Instead of seeking an immediate definition of temporal priority in terms of inter-subjective causation, we must first look for a definition of simultaneity and let the definition of temporal priority emerge from this. To this end, I shall now introduce a further relation, which I call *coincidence*. This relation is defined in four steps. Firstly, let us say that $x[m]$ and $y[m']$ are *causally isolated* iff $m \neq m'$ and x is not PV-prior to y and y is not PV-prior to x. Secondly, let us say that $x[m]$ is *the anterior m-boundary for y* iff (a) every moment which is subjectively earlier than x is RPV-prior to y, and (b) y is either causally isolated from or RPV-prior to each moment which is subjectively later than x. Thirdly, let us say that $x[m]$ is *the posterior m-boundary for y* iff (a) y is RPV-prior to every moment which is subjectively later than x, and (b) any moment which is subjectively earlier than x is either causally isolated from or RPV-prior to y. Then:

$x[m]$ and $y[m']$ *coincide* iff x and y are causally isolated and either (a) x is both the anterior and the posterior m-boundary for y and y is both the anterior and the posterior m'-boundary for x, or (b) x is, in m-time, midway between the anterior and posterior m-boundaries for y, and y is, in m'-time, midway between the anterior and posterior m'-boundaries for x.

The point of this definition is that, using *P2*, we can establish that if m and m' are IST-related (i.e. are different minds which share a common framework of IS-time), then $x[m]$ and $y[m']$ are simultaneous iff they coincide. There are two cases to be considered: (1) where there is an ISC-minimum (a minimum IS-interval nomologically required for a causal line from a volition in one mind to a sensation in another), and (2) where there is not. Case (2) is straightforward: $x[m]$ and $y[m']$ are simultaneous iff they are causally isolated, with each as the anterior and posterior boundary for the other. Case (1) is more complex. Let d be the ISC-minimum. Then if $x[m]$ occurs at the IS-time t and $y[m']$ occurs at the IS-time

t', then the anterior and posterior m'-boundaries for x occur, respectively, at $t - d$ and $t + d$, and the anterior and posterior m-boundaries for y occur, respectively, at $t' - d$ and $t' + d$. But we know from *P2* that, within a single mind, equal IS-distances are correlated with equal subjective distances. It follows that $x[m]$ and $y[m']$ are simultaneous (i.e. $t = t'$) just in case each is, in its own subjective dimension, midway between the anterior and posterior boundaries for the other. Thus, whether or not there is an ISC-minimum, $x[m]$ and $y[m']$ are simultaneous iff they coincide. Given the relations of simultaneity between m-moments and m'-moments, temporal order is then determined, in accordance with *P1*, by the subjective order in each mind. Thus $x[m]$ is earlier than $y[m']$ iff x is subjectively earlier than the m-moment which is simultaneous with y, and $x[m]$ is later than $y[m']$ iff y is subjectively earlier than the m'-moment which is simultaneous with x.

However, we do not yet have a definition of simultaneity. For the proof that $x[m]$ and $y[m']$ are simultaneous iff they coincide rested on the prior assumption that m and m' are IST-related. We cannot define simultaneity as coincidence (or, strictly, as the disjunction of coincidence and identity), since for $x[m]$ and $y[m']$ to be simultaneous, where $m \neq m'$, it is necessary that *each* m-moment stand in some IS time-relation to *each* m'-moment, and a single relationship of coincidence does not ensure that this is so. This brings us back to the problem revealed in *Fault A* of *D* – the problem of formulating our definitions in a way that makes the IS time-relation between two subjective moments depend on the way in which the dimensions to which they belong are, as a whole, inter-subjectively related. To solve this problem, we have to start by defining what it is for two minds to be IST-related and then, as it were, build such relatedness into our definitions of simultaneity and temporal order for moments.

Given the relation of coincidence, the solution is now quite simple. Bearing in mind *P1* and *P2*, we can say that two minds, m and m', are *IST-related* iff:

(1) Each $x[m]$ coincides with some $y[m']$ and each $y[m']$ coincides with some $x[m]$

(2) If $x_1[m]$ and $y_1[m']$ coincide and $x_2[m]$ and $y_2[m']$ coincide, then x_1 is subjectively earlier than x_2 iff y_1 is subjectively earlier than y_2.

(3) If $x_1[m]$, $x_2[m]$, $x_3[m]$ and $x_4[m]$ coincide, respectively, with $y_1[m']$, $y_2[m']$, $y_3[m']$ and $y_4[m']$, then there are equal subjective distances between x_1 and x_2 and between x_3 and x_4 iff there are equal subjective distances between y_1 and y_2 and between y_3 and y_4.

Strictly speaking, condition (2) is redundant, since its truth is guaranteed by the definition of coincidence. But it is helpful to set it out, along with the other conditions, as part of what systematically relates the two subjective dimensions and gives the two minds a common framework of IS-time. The definition of simultaneity and order now follows immediately:

$x[m]$ and $y[m']$ are *IS-simultaneous* iff either (a) $x = y$ or (b) m and m' are IST-related and x and y coincide.
x is *IS-earlier than y* iff $\exists z$ (y and z are IS-simultaneous and x is subjectively earlier than z).
x is *IS-later than y* iff y is IS-earlier than x.

Given the relation of IS-simultaneity, we can also say what it is for a group of two or more minds to share a common framework of IS-time. Thus let us say that a group α of minds forms an *IST-community* iff (a) every two minds in α are IST-related, and (b), within α, the relation of IS-simultaneity is transitive (i.e. if x and y are IS-simultaneous and y and z are IS-simultaneous, then x and z are IS-simultaneous). Then a group of minds share a common framework of time iff they form an IST-community.

Our construction of inter-subjective time is almost complete. The only remaining task is to define the concept of IS-temporal distance. Let us say that $x[m]$ is an α-*moment* iff α is an IST-community and m is a member of α. And let us say that d is *the m-projection for* $\langle x,y \rangle$ in α iff x and y are α-moments, m is a member of α and d is the subjective distance between the $x'[m]$ which is IS-simultaneous with x and the $y'[m]$ which is IS-simultaneous with y. Then the m-projection for $\langle x,y \rangle$ in α is the measure of the IS-distance between x and y *from the viewpoint of* (or *relative to*) m. It is the measure of the IS-distance, *with m as the frame of reference*. Now there is no guarantee that if $x_1[m]$ is IS-simultaneous with $y_1[m']$ and $x_2[m]$ is IS-simultaneous with $y_2[m']$, then the subjective distance between x_1 and x_2 is the same as the subjective distance between y_1 and y_2. And, consequently, there is no guarantee that, for each pair of α-moments x and y and each pair of α-minds m and m', the m-projection for $\langle x,y \rangle$ is the same as the m'-projection for $\langle x,y \rangle$. In other words, the same IS-distance may have different measures from the viewpoints of different minds – different measures in different frames of reference. Moreover, there is nothing to make one viewpoint superior to another – nothing to give one frame of reference a privileged status. So we must think of objective IS-distance as simply whatever holds constant, and necessarily holds constant, through the different projections. But we can see, from our definition of IST-relatedness and our definition of IS-simultaneity, that what has to hold constant is the ratio of one IS-distance to another, as measured by each projection. Thus let us say that r is the *m-ratio for* $\langle x, y, w, z \rangle$ in α iff, if d is the m-projection for $\langle x, y \rangle$ in α and d' is the m-projection for $\langle w,z \rangle$ in α, then r is the ratio of d and d' (i.e. d/d'). Then our definitions ensure that, for any α-moments x, y, w and z and α-minds m and m', the m-ratio for $\langle x, y, w, z \rangle$ and the m'-ratio for $\langle x, y, w, z \rangle$ are the same. For our definitions ensure, in accordance with *P2*, that if $x_1[m]$, $x_2[m]$, $x_3[m]$ and $x_4[m]$ are, respectively, IS-simultaneous with $y_1[m']$, $y_2[m']$, $y_3[m']$ and $y_4[m']$, then there are equal subjective distances between x_1 and x_2 and between x_3 and x_4 iff there are equal subjective distances between y_1 and y_2 and between y_3 and y_4. Hence, given an IST-community α and two α-moments x and y, we cannot speak of the *absolute* IS-distance between x and y. We can only speak either (1) of the IS-distance between x and y *relative to some* α-*mind m* (= the m-projection for $\langle x, y \rangle$ in α) or (2) of the IS-distance between x and y *relative to the IS-distance between two other* α-*moments w and z* (=, for each α-mind m, the m-ratio for $\langle x, y, w, z \rangle$ in α). Either way, IS-distance turns out to be something *relative*, whether relative to the viewpoint of a mind or relative to other distances. And either way it is definable in terms of subjective distance and IS-simultaneity in the specified way.

17

THE UNDERLYING REALITY

To provide a framework for the constraints on human experience, the phenomenalist, as we have said, has to recognize a form of mental time which is logically independent of the physical world. Moreover, if the constraints on different human minds are to combine in the creation of a common physical world, this pre-physical time must also be inter-subjective – a time which relates experiences in different minds, as well as those in the same mind. Now the kind of inter-subjective time which I have constructed seems to be just what the phenomenalist needs. For being defined solely in terms of phenomenal time, the overlapping of sensations, natural law and inter-subjective causation, it seems to be something which, with a suitable ultimate reality, could obtain independently of the physical world and provide an appropriate framework for the constraints.

However, there is something here which we need to examine more closely. At three points in the construction of IS-time I have exploited the notion of *potentiality* – of what, compatibly with the laws of nature, *could* be the case, or of what, in virtue of the laws of nature, *would* be the case in certain hypothetical circumstances. Thus firstly, in the construction of subjective time, I appealed to the fact that consubjective streams have a potential, by a sufficient extension of the earlier one, to form phases of a single stream. The crucial definition (in its conveniently simplified form) was: stream x subjectively precedes stream y by extent e iff it is nomologically ensured that, if y *were to* remain the same and x *were to* have a continuation z, with streamal extent e, then y *would* be a continuation of z. Secondly, in the move from subjective to inter-subjective time, the key concept of V-priority was defined in terms of the potential of one mind to affect the sensory state of another: $x[m]$ is V-prior to $y[m']$ just in case m and m' are different minds and *m is in a position* to causally affect, by an act of volition at or m-later than x, the sensory state of m' at or m'-earlier than y. And to say that *m is in a position* to do this is to say that there is a moment x' in m-time, no earlier than x, and a type T of volition such that, given the laws of nature and the prevailing circumstances, (1) *m could* perform a T-volition at x' and (2) a T-volition at x', if performed, *would* causally affect the sensory state of m' at or m'-earlier than y. Thirdly, to deal with the problem of circumstantial failure (where the relation of V-priority is blocked by unfavourable circumstances), I introduced the concept of rigid *potential* V-priority (RPV-priority), where x is potentially V-prior (PV-prior) to y iff it is *nomologically possible* for x to be V-prior to y (i.e. there is a nomologically possible world in which x is V-prior to y), and where x is RPV-prior to y iff x is PV-prior to y and y is not PV-prior to x. RPV-priority was then taken as the criterion of temporal priority in those cases where the IS-interval is not below the ISC-minimum.

A conspicuous feature of these three types of potentiality is that, for each type, each instance of that type is concerned with a specific pair of particulars – in the case of the first type, with a specific pair of streams, and, in the case of the second and third types, with a specific pair of subjective moments. Now, in the case of each type, it is very plausible to suppose that the specific instances can be explained in terms of the general properties of the pairs of particulars they concern and some correspondingly general framework of law. Thus, in the case of the first type, it is very plausible to suppose that if, in the sense defined, stream A subjectively precedes stream B by extent e, then there is a general relation R such that (1) A is R-related to B, and is so in every possible world in which A and B exist, and (2) the laws ensure that, for any stream-phases x, y and z, if x is R-related to y and z is a continuation of x and z is of extent e, then y is a continuation of z. (Indeed, it is very plausible to suppose that, still more generally, there is an uncountable set α of general relations, a natural way W of ordering α-relations, and a 1-1 function f from α-relations to streamal extents such that (1) for any α-relations R_1 and R_2, R_1

W-precedes R_2 iff $f(R_1)$ is less than $f(R_2)$, and (2) the laws ensure that, for any stream-phases x, y and z and any α-relation R, if x is R-related to y and z is a continuation of x and z is of extent $f(R)$, then y is a continuation of z.) The alternative would be to suppose that there is an ultimate law concerning A and B – the law that, for any stream-phase z, if B exists and z is a continuation of A and z is of extent e, then B is a continuation of z. And it is very implausible – perhaps not even coherent – to think that the ultimate laws have an irreducible reference to particular streams in this way. Likewise, in the case of the other types, it is very plausible to suppose that each instance of potentiality, for a particular pair of subjective moments, is to be explained in terms of certain general properties of that pair and certain general laws to which these properties are relevant. The alternative would be to suppose, very implausibly, that there are ultimate laws with an irreducible reference to particular moments or, rather, to the particular sensations from which these moments derive their identity.

The trouble is, however, that when we come to consider how we might thus explain the instances of potentiality, it is hard to think of general properties of an appropriate sort. Indeed, our initial intuitions take us in what is, from the standpoint of the construction, quite the wrong direction. For our initial inclination is to explain the potentialities in terms of the ordinary framework of time which, prior to philosophical reflection, we take for granted. Thus suppose A is the stream of sensations I had before falling asleep last night and B is the stream which began when I woke up this morning, 7 hours later. There is a certain streamal extent E, measured in units of phenomenal time, such that A subjectively precedes B by E in the sense defined, i.e. it is nomologically ensured that if B were to remain the same and A were to have a continuation C with extent E, then B would be a continuation of C. Now our first inclination is to explain this relationship of subjective precedence in the following way:

(1) A and B are consubjective, i.e. they belong to the same mind.
(2) B began 7 hours after A ended (in ordinary time).
(3) There is a function f from streamal extents to ordinary time-extents such that (a) the laws ensure that, for any e, a stream-phase of streamal extent e has an ordinary temporal extent of $f(e)$; and (b) $f(E) = 7$ hours.

(4)   It is logically necessary that any sensations which are both consubjective and (in ordinary time) simultaneous are parts of the same total sensation.

Thus given (3), it is nomologically ensured that any continuation of *A* with streamal extent *E* takes 7 hours. Given this and (2), it is nomologically ensured that if *B* were to remain the same and *A* were to have a continuation *C* with extent *E*, then the end of *C* would be simultaneous with the beginning of *B*. Given this, (1) and (4), it is nomologically ensured that if *B* were to remain the same and *A* were to have a continuation *C* with extent *E*, *B* would be a continuation of *C*. Such an explanation grounds the subjective precedence of *A* to *B*, by extent *E*, partly on the relation between *A* and *B* in ordinary time. In the same way, our initial inclination is to invoke the ordinary framework of time in explaining instances of V and RPV priority. Thus if *m* is in a position to affect, by an act of volition at *a*[*m*], the sensory state of *m'* at *b*[*m'*], we are inclined to account for this partly in terms of the ordinary temporal relation between *a* and *b* – the fact that *a* is earlier than *b* and separated from it by what is, given the laws and circumstances, a sufficient temporal interval. We are also, of course, inclined to think of the relevant laws and circumstances mainly in physical terms.

Now, obviously, we cannot, compatibly with our constructive project, invoke the ordinary framework of time in this way. For this ordinary framework is either what we have tried to construct on the basis of the potentialities, or else it is something which our constructed time and the related constraints on experience create as part of the structure of the physical world. Either way we cannot, without circularity, ground the potentialities on relations in this framework. It is implausible to leave the potentialities ungrounded, but it is incoherent to ground them on the very properties which we need them to define or sustain.

The final challenge, then, is to provide, without circularity, a description of a possible ultimate reality sufficient to yield, for human minds, a framework of inter-subjective time of the constructed kind, and to yield it in a way that plausibly explains the potentialities involved in terms of more general properties and laws. Of course, we do not have to show that the description is true – that ultimate reality is as described. For there may be

277

alternative descriptions which meet the requirements (indeed, if there is one, there are bound to be others on the same general lines). It is enough to show, by one example, how there could be an ultimate reality which secured a framework of IS-time in the requisite way.

Can the challenge be met? One important point, which promises to be of help in meeting it, is that we have one form of mental time, namely streamal time, which has been defined solely in terms of phenomenal time and the overlapping of sensations, without recourse to any notions of potentiality or natural necessity. This promises to be of help in two ways. Firstly, it means that at least part of what makes up mental time on the human side can be built into the ultimate reality without problem. Secondly, and more importantly, it means that we can retain a time-dimension in the external component – that component of ultimate reality which lies outside human minds and by which, apart from the influence of human volition itself, the constraints on human experience are imposed. For, as before, we can suppose this component (or the relevant portion of it) to consist of a stream of experience, with its own internal mental time. The advantage of this is that, given the causal links between events in the external component and events in human minds, the streamal time of the component may form the basis for a temporal framework in which the human events are located. Thus, by imposing an appropriate structure and organization on this external stream, we may be able to envisage laws controlling the causal links between events in this stream and human events in such a way as to yield the potentialities required for subjective and inter-subjective time on the human side.

Pursuing this strategy, let us suppose that ultimate reality consists of the following elements:

(1)   A set H of minds (intuitively, the set of human minds).

(2)   A stream of experience M, outside H-minds.

(3)   A set of laws, including:

    (a)   A subset α controlling events in M (but leaving room for the influence of H-volitions on M-events).

    (b)   A subset β concerning the causation of H-sensations by M-events.

    (c)   A subset γ concerning the causation of M-events by H-volitions.

Let us further suppose (to make the example as straightforward as we can) that M is structured and organized on the lines of a physical world, with α corresponding to physical laws and with β and γ corresponding to psychophysical laws (in the case of β, laws concerning the causation of sensations by brain-events, and in the case of γ, laws concerning the causation of brain-events by volitions). Thus

(1) For some 3-dimensional sense-field F and sense-qualities Q_1 and Q_2, M consists of a continuous series of total sensations, ordered by Σ-precedence, such that each of these sensations is a realization of a phenomenal time-pattern of F-arrays of Q_1 and Q_2. Let us use 'T' to designate streamal M-time.

(2) α controls the F-T arrangement of Q_1 and Q_2 in such a way as, for some F-distance d, to ensure that (i) for each T-time t, the F-t arrangement is an array of Q_1-spheres, of radius d, against a uniform Q_2-background, and (ii) all changes over T in the F-arrangement of Q_1-spheres are F-T continuous. Given this, it will be convenient, in what follows, to speak as if each F-T continuous series of Q_1-spheres were the path of a continuant – of a mobile sphere which occupies F and persists through T. I shall call these mobilia 'Q_1-continuants'. (This talk of Q_1-*continuants* is, it should be noted, only a *façon de parler*, devoid of genuine ontological commitment. For, given my earlier point about retrospective sustainment,[1] we could only accept a *derivative ontology* of Q_1-continuants if we had independent knowledge of their existence.)

(3) Under the control of α, Q_1-continuants are arranged and organized in F-T in a quasi-physical way – the way that, according to scientific theory, atoms are arranged and organized in physical space-time. (Admittedly, we here have to assume a scientific theory of a rather simplified kind, which holds all atoms to be of exactly the same size and type. To achieve isomorphism with a more realistic theory, we should have to build more variation into M. This would be possible, but philosophically cumbersome.) Thus arranged and organized, Q_1-continuants, like their atomic counterparts, often form elements of more complex

systems. Let us, then, use the term 'B-system' to signify that type of system whose physical counterpart is the human brain. Each B-system is a complex continuant which persists, through T-time, by the preservation of a brain-like structure and organization. It need not be composed of exactly the same Q_1-continuants at all times (just as a brain need not be composed of exactly the same atoms at all times), though, to preserve its identity, any changes in its composition must be gradual. There are exactly as many B-systems as there are H-minds.

(4) There are two classes E and V of possible states of B-systems at T-times (each state being simply a mode of F-configuration of the component Q_1-continuants) such that β is exclusively concerned with the causation of H-sensations by E-states (strictly, E-state-realizations) and γ is exclusively concerned with the causation of V-states (strictly, V-state-realizations) by H-volitions. It is not required here that E and V exhaust the possible states of B-systems nor that their members be entirely distinct.

Given this basic framework, the project is to impose specific conditions on β and γ so as to yield the required potentialities. Amongst other things, this will involve getting each H-mind causally attached to a unique and distinct B-system (on the model of human minds and human brains) so that the E-states of that system (and no other) directly control the sensations of that mind (and no other) and the volitions of that mind (and no other) directly control the V-states of that system (and no other). Inevitably, the details will be rather complicated.

Each total H-sensation is, we may assume, temporally extended in streamal time. I shall use the term 'sensation-slice' to signify a streamal cross-section of a total sensation – a cross-section located at a stream-moment and having no streamal extent. Each total H-sensation and hence each H-stream is then composed of uncountably many sensation-slices. (I am working on the assumption that streamal time is always continuous.) For any E-state ϕ, B-system S and T-time t, if S is in ϕ at t, I shall speak of the realization of ϕ by S at t (i.e. S's being in ϕ at t) as an *instance* of ϕ. I shall also use the term 'E-instance' to apply to any instance of any E-state and the term 'E-phase' to apply to any T-continuous series of *E*-instances in the same B-system. And I shall speak of *x* as an *E-continuation of y* when *x* and *y* are contiguous portions of a single *E*-phase and *x* is *T*-later than *y*.

Given this terminology, the conditions to be imposed on β are as follows:

(1) For each *E*-state φ there is a slice-type ψ such that β ensures that any instance of φ directly causes, in some *H*-mind, a sensation-slice of type ψ. (The causation is *direct* in the sense that there is no intermediary event which causally links the *E*-instance with the resulting sensation-slice.)

(2) β ensures that each *E*-instance directly causes only one *H*-sensation-slice, and that no *H*-sensation-slice occurs except as the direct effect of a unique *E*-instance in accordance with (1).

(3) β ensures that for each *E*-phase *X*, there is a stream or stream-phase *A*, in some *H*-mind, such that each *E*-instance in *X* directly causes a sensation-slice in *A* and each sensation-slice in *A* is the direct effect of an *E*-instance in *X*, and such that the streamal order of these slices corresponds to the *T*-order of their causes.

(4) β ensures that no *H*-stream occurs except as causally generated by an *E*-phase in accordance with (3).

(5) β ensures that two *H*-streams are consubjective (are in the same *H*-mind) iff the *E*-phases which generate them are co-systematic (are phases of the same B-system).

(6) β ensures that two consubjective *H*-stream-phases have the same streamal extent iff the co-systematic *E*-phases which generate them have the same *T*-extent.

We shall now see how, given the satisfaction of these conditions, β yields the potentialities required to arrange the sensations in each *H*-mind in subjective time.

We know from our definition, in its simplified form, that stream *x* subjectively precedes stream *y* by extent *e* iff it is nomologically ensured that, if *y* were to remain the same and *x* were to have a continuation *z*, with streamal extent *e*, then *y* would be a continuation of *z*, i.e. iff in any nomologically possible world in which *y* exists and *x* has a continuation with extent *e*, there is a stream-phase *z*, with extent *e*, such that *z* is a continuation of *x* and *y* is a continuation of *z*. Before we can evaluate how the conditions on β affect the obtaining of subjective precedence, thus defined, we need to know, to some extent, what is required for the preservation of the *same* H-stream across different possible worlds: given a stream x in the actual world, we need to know what aspects of the actual world have to be retained in any possible world in which x exists, and what aspects can be changed. Now obviously, given any stream, two factors which are essential to its identity are (a) its intrinsic character, as composed of certain types of sensation streamally arranged in a certain way, and (b) the identity of the H-mind in which it occurs. We cannot envisage the same stream in a possible world in which these factors are changed. But, equally, it is clear that these are not the only essential factors. If they were, then given two streams of the same intrinsic character and in the same H-mind, we could envisage a possible world which was just like the actual world except that the causal positions of the two streams, with respect to M, were interchanged. Thus, given two consubjective streams A and B of the same intrinsic character, and given the two co-systematic E-phases X_1 and X_2 which respectively generate them, we could envisage a world W which was just like the actual world except that A was generated by X_2 and B by X_1. But this is not possible, since, given their coincidence in intrinsic character and mind, we have no way of re-identifying A and B in W except in terms of the E-phases which generate them: if A' and B' are the two W-streams, the very fact that A' is generated by X_1 and B' by X_2 forces us to identify A with A' and B with B'. Consequently, we must add as a third factor essential to the identity of an H-stream: (c) the identity of the E-phase by which the stream is generated. Now the identity of an E-phase depends on the identity of the B-system in which it occurs, the period of T-time through which it extends and the series of E-states which, over this period, it successively instantiates. So, to envisage the same stream in a different world, we have to retain its generation by the same B-system's passing through the same series of E-states over the same T-period.

Given this, let us now consider the effect of the six β-conditions on subjective precedence. Suppose m is an H-mind and A and B are streams in m. We know from condition (4) that A and B are generated by E-phases in accordance with (3), and we know from condition (5) that these E-phases are co-systematic. Let us call these two E-phases, respectively, X_1 and X_2 and the B-system in which they occur S, and let us suppose that X_1 is T-earlier than X_2 and separated from it by the T-distance d. Now we know that in any possible world in which A exists it is generated by X_1. So, given (4) and (5), β ensures that, whatever the circumstances, any continuation of A would be generated by an E-continuation of X_1. We also know from (6) that, for each B-system x, there is a way of 1-1 correlating T-extents with streamal extents such that, if e_1 is correlated with e_2, β ensures that any E-phase in x of extent e_1 generates a stream or stream-phase of extent e_2 and that any E-phase in x which generates a stream or stream-phase of extent e_2 is of extent e_1. Let e be the streamal extent with which d is thus correlated in respect of S. Then β ensures that, whatever the circumstances, any continuation of A with extent e would be generated by an E-continuation of X_1 with extent d. But in any possible world in which B exists, it is generated by X_2, and in any possible world in which X_1 and X_2 exist, they retain their original locations in T-time. So, since d is the T-distance between X_1 and X_2, β ensures that, with the existence of B retained, any continuation of A, with extent e, would be generated by an E-phase X, with extent d, such that X was an E-continuation of X_1 and X_2 was an E-continuation of X. Hence, by (2) and (3), β ensures that, if B were to remain and A were to have a continuation C with extent e, B would be a continuation of C. That is to say, in any possible world which is compatible with β and in which B exists and A has a continuation with extent e, there is a stream-phase C, with extent e, such that C is a continuation of A and B is a continuation of C. Thus A subjectively precedes B by extent e in the sense defined. It follows that, as characterized, M and β suffice to yield, for each H-mind, a framework of subjective time in the form we have constructed.

Before moving on, we must pause to consider a possible objection. We are supposing β to satisfy conditions (1) - (6). But this can be interpreted in two ways. On the one hand, it might mean that β-laws have the very form which these conditions express, so that we can replace 'β ensures that' by 'It is a law that' throughout (1) – (6) to obtain a specification of β itself. On the other hand, it might mean that the β-laws have a different form, yet to be specified, and that (1) – (6) are merely consequences of this further specification. The objection is that neither of these interpretations leaves us with a satisfactory account. If we accept the first, we have to take the causation of *H*-sensations by *E*-instances as part of the subject-matter of the laws – as part of what the laws, canonically specified, are about. And it might be held that, given the ultimacy of β, this is incoherent, since it is only as the logical product of laws and non-causal conditions that causal relations obtain: the ultimate laws cannot be laws about causation, since we need the ultimate laws to form part of that by which the causal facts are sustained. On the other hand, if we accept the second interpretation, we have yet to specify β. And it is far from clear how this can be done, in such a way as to yield (1) – (6) as consequences, if we cannot allow causation to form part of what the laws concern. The problem is that, without any common framework of time relating *M*-events to *H*-sensations, it is hard to see how the laws could ensure unique causal pairings – ensure that each *E*-instance is the cause of a particular sensation-slice and that each sensation-slice is the effect of a particular *E*-instance.

However, the objection to including causation in the subject-matter of the ultimate laws is misconceived. For, as I have argued elsewhere, there is no conceptual requirement that causal relations be the logical product of laws and non-causal conditions.[2] To take an example (only fictitious) from the physical realm, suppose that for a certain kind *K* of metal, it is a law of nature that, when any spherical *K*-lump reaches a specified temperature, a flash occurs half a second later somewhere (unspecified) in the region of points no further from the centre of the sphere than twice its diameter. Suppose further that there is no stronger law which fixes the position of the flash more precisely – that, at the moment when the critical temperature is reached, all positions within the specified region are equiprobable. Now imagine that two large *K*-spheres, a few inches apart, simultaneously reach the critical temperature and, half a second later, two flashes occur, both within the specified region for each sphere. It is coherent and indeed plausible to suppose that each flash is the effect of just one of the sphere temperatures and that each sphere temperature is the cause of just one of the flashes. At the same time, the causal pairings are not determined by the law and the non-causal conditions, since each flash falls within the specified region for each sphere. So this would be a case in which (assuming, for the sake of argument, physical realism) the causal relations were ultimate. Consequently, we could legitimately reformulate the relevant law so as to make it causation-concerning. We could suppose it to be a law (and granted physical realism, an ultimate law) that any event of a K-sphere's reaching the specified temperature *causes* a flash-event (and causes only one flash-event) half a second later somewhere (unspecified) in the relevant region for that sphere. (Such a law would not, of course, enable us to discern the causal pairings in the case envisaged, though it would ensure that the pairings obtained.) In the same way, we can coherently suppose that the β-laws are explicitly causal and have the form expressed in (1) – (6). Thus corresponding to condition (1), we can suppose that, for each E-state ϕ, there is a slice-type ψ such that it is an ultimate law that any instance of ϕ directly causes, in some H-mind, a sensation-slice of type ψ. And so on, throughout all the conditions. Incidentally, in claiming that causal relations may be ultimate, I am not thereby denying that they must be law-governed. Even if causation is not reducible to law, it may be logically necessary that, for any events x and y, if x is the (efficient) cause of y, then it is a law that any event of the x-type causes some event of the y-type.

We have seen how, as characterized by (1) – (6), β secures a subjective time-dimension for each H-mind. But as well as securing these dimensions, it also provides a unique way of 1-1 correlating the points on each with the points on T. Thus given an H-mind m and the B-system S with which it is causally linked, we can *directly* correlate an m-time x with a T-time t iff a sensation-slice of m at x is the direct effect of an E-instance in S at t. We can then correlate the remaining m-times with T-times in that unique way which, given the framework of the direct correlations, preserves order and relative distance. Thus if A and B are two m-streams separated by a non-sensory interlude I, and if X_1 and X_2 are the two E-phases of S which respectively generate A and B and which are separated by the T-period P, we correlate I-times and P-times in such a way that the m-order of the I-times coincides with the T-order of the P-times and equal distances in I coincide with equal distances in P. The significance of this method of correlation is twofold. Firstly, it imposes a structure on the possible lines of causation from M to H-sensations, in that, given the character of β, it is nomologically ensured that each such line terminates in the direct causation of a sensation-slice at a subjective time by an E-instance at the correlated T-time. Secondly, in terms of it, we can envisage a form for the γ-laws which is suitable, in conjunction with α, for the genesis of inter-subjective time through the genesis of certain potentialities for inter-subjective causation.

γ, as we have said, is a set of laws concerning the causation of M-events by H-volitions – more specifically, laws concerning the way in which H-volitions affect the realization of V-states in B-systems. Let us use the term 'V-instance' to mean 'instance of a V-state', as we have used 'E-instance' to mean 'instance of an E-state'. If we continue to model the relationship between H-mind and B-system on the relationship between human mind and human brain, there are two conditions which it is natural to impose on γ. Firstly, it is natural to insist that, for each H-mind m, m-volitions can only directly affect the states of that unique B-system on which m-sensations directly depend. This gives each H-mind a double causal attachment to a unique B-system and each B-system a double causal attachment to a unique H-mind – attachments which involve both the causation of H-sensations by E-instances and the causation of V-instances by H-volitions. Secondly, it is natural to insist, at least as a simplifying approximation, that there is a constant T-extent e such that, for any T-time t, any H-mind m and any m-time x, if x and t are correlated (in the way specified above), then the direct effect of any m-volition at x has to occur at $t + e$, i.e. at that T-time which is later than t by extent e. (Speaking loosely, we might say that e is the sum of the time taken for the realization of an E-state to directly cause an H-sensation-slice and the time taken for an H-volition to directly cause the realization of a V-state. This, of course, is not strictly true since H-events are not located in T.) Under these conditions, and with the constant e as the unit of T-time, γ-laws will turn out to have the following form:[3]

> It is a law that $\forall m\ \forall x\ \forall v\ \forall t\ \forall S$ ([m is an H-mind and v is a volition of m at m-time x and v is of type ψ and S is that B-system on which m-sensations directly depend and t is the T-time with which x is correlated and S is in state ϕ_1 at t and the M-environment of S at t is of kind K] ⊃ S is in V-state ϕ_2 at $t +$ 1).

Thus by such laws, given a B-system S and the associated H-mind m, and given a T-time t and the correlated m-time x, the character of m's volition at x, in conjunction with the state of S at t and any other relevant M-conditions at t (conditions which might affect the subsequent states of S up to $t + 1$), may causally determine the V-state of S at $t + 1$.

It is not difficult to see how, together with an appropriate α (controlling processes within M), such laws would generate the potentialities required for IS-time. In the first place, we can see how an H-mind m_1 might be in a position to affect, by an act of volition at $x[m_1]$, the sensory state of another H-mind m_2 at $y[m_2]$. For things might be such that, if S_1 and S_2 are, respectively, the B-systems to which m_1 and m_2 are causally attached and if t_1 and t_2 are, respectively, the T-correlates of x and y, with t_1 T-earlier than t_2 then:

(1) There is a type ψ of volition in the repertoire of m_1 such that, given the state of S_1 at t_1 and the other relevant M-conditions at t_1, a ψ-volition by m_1 at x would, in accordance with γ, be causally sufficient for the realization of some V-state ϕ_1 in S_1 at $t_1 + 1$.

(2) In the relevant M-conditions, S_1's being in state ϕ_1 at $t_1 + 1$ would, in accordance with α, be causally sufficient for a chain of events in M terminating in the realization of an E-state ϕ_2 in S_2 at t_2.

(3) S_2's being in state ϕ_2 at t_2 would, in accordance with β, be causally sufficient for the occurrence of a certain type of sensation-slice at y.

Given this, we can also see how one subjective moment can be V-prior to another. For, given two H-minds m_1 and m_2, $x[m_1]$ is V-prior to $y[m_2]$ just in case m_1 is in a position to affect, by a volition at or m_1-later than x, the sensory state of m_2 at or m_2-earlier than y. Finally, we can see how, with an appropriate α, there could be a T-distance d (representing, in T-time, the ISC-minimum) such that, for any two H-minds m_1 and m_2, $x[m_1]$ is potentially V-prior (PV-prior) to $y[m_2]$ whenever the T-correlate of x is T-earlier than the T-correlate of y and the T-distance between these correlates is not less than d. For, given an appropriate α, if S_1 and S_2 are the B-systems to which, respectively, m_1 and m_2 are causally attached and if t_1 and t_2 are the T-correlates of $x[m_1]$ and $y[m_2]$, then, provided t_1 is sufficiently earlier than t_2, we can envisage a nomologically possible world (a world with the same laws as the actual world) in which the M-circumstances of S_1 and S_2 are such that a suitable m_1-volition at (or m_1-later than) x would causally affect the sensory state of m_2 at (or m_2-earlier than) y. Moreover, depending, as it does, on the temporal relation between the T-correlates, the relation of PV-priority is *rigid* (RVP-priority) in the sense defined, i.e. wherever x is PV-prior to y, y is not PV-prior to x. For just as the identity of an H-sensation-slice partly depends on the identity of the E-instance which directly causes it, so the identity of an H-subjective moment partly depends on the identity of the T-time with which it is correlated, so that each moment has the same T-correlate in every possible world in which it exists. Thus, since the laws (α, β, and γ) require inter-subjective causation to run forwards in T-time, we know that if there is a nomologically possible world in which $x[m_1]$ is V-prior to $y[m_2]$, then there is no nomologically possible world in which $y[m_2]$ is V-prior to $x[m_1]$.[4]

In short, given the subjective dimensions supplied by β and given appropriate laws (α) controlling processes in M, γ yields a network of links of PV and RPV priority sufficient for a framework of IS-time as defined by our earlier construction. The framework which emerges is one in which the IS-arrangement of subjective moments exactly matches, in respect of order and relative distance, the T-arrangement of their correlates. And the framework is generated in a way which explains the potentialities involved in terms of general properties and laws.[5] Taking H-minds as human minds, we have met the challenge originally posed. And in so doing, we have shown how the phenomenalist can legitimately retain a form of inter-subjective mental time which is logically independent of the physical world.

There is still, however, one final question to be resolved. It is true that the phenomenalist needs inter-subjective time in a pre-physical form and that the kind of time I have constructed meets this need. But he also has to recognize a time-dimension in the physical world itself – a time-dimension for physical events and physical processes. This physical dimension cannot be identified with the IS-time we have constructed, since this constructed time is exclusively mental. Our definitions allow no sense to (for example) the claims that one physical event is IS-earlier than another or that the IS-distance between physical events x and y is twice the IS-distance between physical events x' and y'. Physical time must be something which emerges at the physical level: it must be part of what the constraints on experience, in the framework of IS-time, create. The question is: how does it emerge at the physical level?

And how does it emerge as a dimension which is distinctively *temporal*?

Let θ be the theory of ultimate reality I have sketched above as a possible explanation of the genesis of IS-time – the theory which postulates the external stream *M* and the sets of laws α, β and γ. And let θ′ be what results from θ by eliminating its topic-specificity (strictly, speaking, its topic-specificity with respect to the external reality), while retaining its essential explanatory structure. Thus where θ postulates an external stream, with two sense-qualities distributed over a 3-dimensional sense-field (*F*) at each moment of streamal time (*T*), θ′ merely postulates an external 4-dimensional continuum *C* (of unspecified intrinsic nature, but corresponding to *F-T* in θ) and a pair of intrinsic properties (not specified as sense-qualities) distributed over the points of this continuum. In all other respects the two theories coincide, with θ′ postulating the same distribution and organization of properties in *C* as θ postulates for sense-qualities in *F-T*, and with θ′ postulating the same nomological links between human minds and *C* as θ postulates between human minds and *M*.

Now suppose *T*′ is that dimension in *C* which corresponds to *T* in *M*. Unlike *T*, *T*′ is not characterized as intrinsically temporal: its intrinsic nature is not, beyond its formal properties, specified at all. None the less, there are two respects in which, in the context of θ′, it assumes a distinctively temporal *role* – or, as we might put it, retains the distinctively temporal role of *T* in θ. Firstly, corresponding to the direction *streamally earlier → streamally later* in *T*, there is a *T*′ direction (*D*) such that causality in *C* always, and of natural necessity, runs in that direction. This causal directionality is not characteristic of any of the other three dimensions in *C*. Secondly, direction and distance in human time, in its various forms, is correlated with and grounded on direction and distance in *T*′. Thus, using ‘*E*′-instance’, ‘*E*′-phase’ and ‘*V*′-instance’ to signify with respect to *C* what ‘*E*-instance’, ‘*E*-phase’ and ‘*V*-instance’ signify with respect to *M*:

(1) For each human mind *m*, there is a way of 1-1 correlating streamal extents with *T*′-extents whereby it is nomologically ensured that any stream-phase *A* in *m* is causally generated by an *E*′-phase *X* such that (a) the streamal order of the sensation-slices in *A* matches the *D*-order of

their causes in X, and (b) the streamal extent of A is correlated with the T'-extent of X.

(2) For each human mind m, there is a way of 1-1 correlating streamal extents with T'-distances (the same, in effect, as the correlation in (1)) such that, for any m-streams A and B, respectively generated by E'-phases X_1 and X_2, A subjectively precedes B by extent e iff X_1 is D-before X_2 and the T'-distance between X_1 and X_2 is correlated with e.

(3) Given two human minds m_1 and m_2 and given a causal line from a volition at $x[m_1]$ to a sensation-slice at $y[m_2]$, x is IS-earlier than y and the IS-distance between x and y is fixed by and in effect proportional to the T'-distance covered by that portion of the line (i.e. from the direct effect of the volition to the direct cause of the sensation) which passes through C. (To achieve exact proportionality we only have to subtract from the IS-distance that constant IS-amount which represents, as it were, the time taken for a volition to directly cause a V'-instance plus the time taken for an E'-instance to directly cause a sensation-slice.)

Putting (1), (2) and (3) together, there is a way of correlating subjective moments with T'-points (the correlation is 1-1 with respect to each mind) such that it is nomologically ensured that any sensation-slice at moment x is directly caused by an E'-instance at the T'-correlate of x and such that the IS time-arrangement of moments exactly matches, in order and relative distance, the T'-arrangement of their correlates.

If we were physical realists and accepted θ', we would obviously identify T' with physical time and identify the other three dimensions in C with the dimensions of physical space. Moreover, although the intrinsic nature of T' is unspecified, we would regard θ' as the complete physical theory. For, given the topic-neutrality thesis, we could not expect the intrinsic nature of physical time to be specifiable in physical terms, any more than we could expect this in the case of physical space and matter. T' would qualify as physical time solely in virtue of its formal and functional properties, and its intrinsic nature would lie outside the scope of physical theory. Now, of course, our position is *not* that of the physical realist. Our position is that of the reductive phenomenalist, who takes the physical world to be the logical creation of the constraints on human experience. None the less, the same point, suitably adapted, applies. For given that the constraints incorporate the framework of IS-time, θ' presumably provides, in the relevant sense, the simplest topic-neutral explanation of them. And if it does, then, by the already established principle of phenomenalistic creation, θ', whether true or false as a theory of ultimate reality, determines the character of the physical world. That is to say, the C-structure and organization specified in θ' are *physically* (thus non-ultimately) realized in virtue of the fact that their *ultimate* realization would constitute the simplest (in particular, the most nomologically uniform) explanation of the IS-pattern of constraints. And then the existence of physical time will simply be the physical realization of the relevant dimension in the C-structure – that dimension to which θ' accords, in the way explained, a distinctively temporal role.

If θ' is the correct theory of ultimate reality, then physical reality is isomorphic with the external reality which ultimately underlies it. We have already seen, in some detail, that such isomorphism is not essential to the creation of a physical world. For there are various ways of altering the structure and laws of the ultimate reality without disturbing the IS-pattern of constraints, and it is this pattern alone which determines the character of the physical world. We have focused, in particular, on examples in which the isomorphism breaks down in the case of physical space – in which the geometry of physical space differs from the intrinsic geometry of that which underlies it. But it is also possible for the breakdown to occur in the case of physical time. Thus suppose, altering θ, we postulate an ultimate external reality containing two streams of experience M_1 and M_2, with, respectively, streamal time-dimensions T_1 and T_2, such that, for a certain period P_1 in T_1 and a certain period P_2 in T_2, (1) everything is nomologically organized as if, by the standard of uniformity, P_1 and P_2 were interchanged, (2) the portion of this external reality which is nomologically linked with human sensation and human volition is the non-P_1 portion of M_1 plus the P_2-portion of M_2, and (3) if P_2 were substituted for P_1, M_1 would be qualitatively identical to M, as characterized by θ, and the laws controlling processes in M_1 and controlling the causal links between M_1 and human minds would coincide with α, β and γ. An ultimate reality of this sort would generate the same IS-pattern of constraints as that generated by the θ-reality and, consequently, create a qualitatively identical physical world – one whose character conforms to that topic-neutral theory (θ') by which the constraint-pattern is most simply explained. In such a case the geometry of physical time would differ from the intrinsic geometry of the external item which underlies it, since the external item would be composed of portions of different streamal dimensions (the non-P_1-portion of T_1 and the P_2-portion of T_2) which do not stand to each other in any intrinsic temporal relations. Obviously, this example is one among many in which there is a lack of isomorphism in respect of physical time.

We might expect to get the greatest disparity between the physical world and what ultimately underlies if it, like Berkeley, we took the ultimate reality to consist solely of God and human minds (perhaps angels too), human experience being directly controlled by divine volition (though, of course, we would have to show that such a reality could yield an IS-pattern of constraints adequate for the creation of a physical world). However, the most obvious and most authentically Berkeleian way of developing such a position conforms, in effect, to θ'. Taking θ as our starting-point, the first step is to replace M by a divine image (DI) (or perhaps some other form of divine conception) of a 4-dimensional phenomenal pattern, comprising a 1-dimensional time-field T^* and, at each point in T^*, a 3-dimensional arrangement of Q_1 and Q_2 – an arrangement which matches the arrangement at the corresponding T-point in M. It might be thought that this replacement is unnecessary and that we could manage just as well by taking M itself to be a stream of divine sensations, so long as the sensations were the effects of divine volition. But my preference, on theological grounds, is to keep the mental life of God wholly timeless and not subject even to self-induced change . The second step is to suppose that all human sensations and all aspects of DI are directly caused by divine volition, divine volition itself being uncaused (though not unmotivated) except in the sense of being the action of God himself. This means that there are no genuinely causal relations between different aspects of DI and no genuinely causal relations between DI-aspects and human sensations or between human volitions and DI-aspects. At best, there is only room for quasi-causal relations of an 'occasionalistic' kind: i.e. God may take one DI-aspect as an occasion for volitionally causing another or for causing a human sensation, and he may take a human volition as an occasion for causing an aspect of *DI*. Although it lacks genuine causal efficacy, we may assume that the human will is free and that human volitions are not causally determined by divine volition or by anything else. The third step is to suppose that divine volitions are not arbitrary, but the implementation of certain fixed policies – policies sufficiently comprehensive to cover all the contingencies of human free will. These volitional policies are the occasionalistic counterparts of the laws α, β and γ in θ: they order conditions occasionalistically in human minds and *DI* in exactly the way that the laws order conditions causally in human minds and *M*. For example, if we let 'E^*-state' signify with respect to *DI* what 'E-state' signifies with respect to *M*, then where it is a β-law that any instance of a certain E-state directly causes a certain type of human sensation, it is God's fixed policy to take any instance of the corresponding E^*-state as an occasion for volitionally causing the same type of sensation. Thus these volitional policies serve as a framework of law for *DI*, human minds and the quasi-causal links within and between them – a framework isomorphic, *modulo* occasionalism, with the laws in θ. Consequently, given a slight adjustment to our definition of V-priority (so as to allow V-priority to be occasionalistic), they also yield the potentialities required for a framework of inter-subjective time and, within that framework, the constraints on human experience required for the creation of a physical world.

Such a theory comes as close as we can get, without embracing mentalistic realism, to Berkeley's final position – the position he endorses in the *Three Dialogues*. It is, in effect, what this position would become if the phenomenalism of the *Principles* were retained and the physical world not identified with God's archetypal image. Whether it has any advantages over θ is another question and one which, despite its interest, I shall not attempt to answer here. Certainly, in one respect, it is a more natural theory. For if we suppose the ultimate reality to be mental, it is more natural to suppose that it functions in what is, by our standards, a characteristically mental way. In that respect, to postulate an external rational agent who controls human experience by volition, in accordance with certain policies designed to achieve some purpose (e.g. the spiritual refinement of human nature), is, however speculative, closer to our ordinary conception of the mind and its place in nature than to postulate an external stream of experience

293

which operates on us in a blindly mechanistic way. But it would be foolish of me to put much weight on this point in a book which is, in so many ways, at variance with our ordinary modes of thought.

Of course, I have not even established that ultimate reality is wholly mental (and my arguments for anti-realism and phenomenalism do not presuppose that it is). The reason I have confined myself exclusively to mentalistic examples is that there are no others available: we cannot form any transparent conception of what a non-mental reality might be like. But I have not established that the ultimate reality has to be transparently conceivable. Nor, indeed, would I want to, if 'transparently conceivable' means 'transparently conceivable by *us*'. For there may well be more things in heaven and earth (especially in heaven) than can be dreamt of in *our* philosophy. In the case of a *non-mental* reality, I believe the problem goes deeper than this. My intuition is that a non-mental reality would not be transparently conceivable at all, even by a being with supreme intelligence. And my intuition is that what is not transparently conceivable at all is not logically possible. I hope one day to replace these intuitions by arguments and make the case for mentalism irresistible. But until then, I must be content with a defence of idealism in its anti-realist and phenomenalist forms.

NOTES

1 THE OPTIONS

1 It is *possible* to construe numbers as contingent. E.g. if, *à la* Russell, we construe each natural number *n* as the class of *all n*-membered classes, each number is contingent since it has contingent constituents.

2 Here, I am more or less following S. Kripke, *Naming and Necessity*, Blackwell, Oxford, 1980, pp. 100-5. The only difference is that, while, like Kripke, I take 'Hesperus' and 'Phosphorus' to be rigid designators (hence the logical necessity that Hesperus = Phosphorus), I also, unlike Kripke, take them to differ in Fregean sense (hence the impossibility of knowing *a priori* that Hesperus = Phosphorus). Thus on my view, if '*A*' is used as a rigid designator of the actual world, we can take 'Hesperus' to mean, roughly, 'the heavenly body which in *A* shines in the evening' and 'Phosphorus' to mean, roughly, 'the heavenly body which in *A* shines in the morning'. This is why I speak of a difference in the concepts *Hesperus* and *Phosphorus*.

2 BERKELEY'S SYSTEM

1 A. Luce and T. E. Jessop (eds), *The Works of George Berkeley*, Nelson, London, 1949, Vol. 2, p. 262. All subsequent page-references to the *Dialogues* will be to this edition.

2 Thus see his discussion of the Mosaic account of creation in the *Third Dialogue*, pp. 250-6.

3 THE NATURE OF ANTI-REALISM

1 At least it seems so at this stage. Much later (chapter 11) we will consider (though only to reject) a form of realism of this sort.

2 See e.g. Dummett's 'The Reality of the Past' in *Proceedings of the Aristotelian Society* 1968-9, pp. 239-58 and his 'Common Sense and Physics' section II, in G. F. Macdonald (ed.), *Perception and Identity*, Macmillan, London, 1979. Incidentally, in characterizing Dummett's distinction in terms of bivalence, I am assuming that there are only two truth-values. For I think that Dummett would say, more generally, that, given n truth values, the distinction turns on the acceptance or rejection of the law of n-valence.

3 'The Reality of the Past', p. 239.

4 Ibid., pp. 239-40.

5 See e.g. his 'On Referring' in *Mind*, 1950.

6 'Common Sense and Physics', p. 5.

4   THE INSCRUTABILITY OF MATTER

1 Hume, *A Treatise of Human Nature,* in the edition of L. A. Selby-Bigge, Clarendon Press, Oxford, 1896, p. 167.

2 Locke, *Essay Concerning Human Understanding,* in the edition of A. C. Fraser, Dover, New York, 1959, Book II, Chapter iv.

3 Ibid., p. 152.

4 Ibid., p. 153.

5 Ibid., Book II, Chapter xxvii, sections 1-2.

6 See S. Kripke, *Naming and Necessity,* Blackwell, Oxford, 1980, p. 48 and *passim.* Kripke's distinction, of course, is between rigid and non-rigid *designators.* But there is a parallel distinction for type-signifiers. Thus taking 'envelopoid' as a rigid signifier, we have, with E as the particular envelope:

$\forall T$ (If E contains a figure of type T, then
$\square$ $\forall x$ [x is an envelopoid iff x is of type T])

while taking 'envelopoid' as a non-rigid signifier, we have:

$\square$ $\forall T$ (if E contains a figure of type T, then
$\forall x$ [x is an envelopoid iff x is of type T]).

7 Locke, op. cit., pp. 156-7.

8 He allowed material objects to have colour only in the sense of having the power to produce colour-experience in us.

APPENDIX TO CHAPTER 4: THE POWERS-THESIS

1 They include Leibniz, Boscovich, Kant, Priestley and Faraday. On the historical development of the thesis, see Harré and Madden, *Causal Powers,* Blackwell, Oxford, 1975, chapter 9.

2 It will concern us later, in chapter 10.

5 MATTER IN SPACE

1 Following the normal conventions, I am using '∼' to mean 'It is not the case that' and '□' to mean 'it is logically necessary that'. Notice, however that '□ $\phi(x_1 \ldots x_n)$' is equivalent to 'For each possible world *w in which* $x_1 \ldots x_n$ *exist*, ϕ-in-*w* $(x_1 \ldots x_n)$'. Diamond brackets '⟨...⟩' are used to signify an ordered set.

2 The contingency of an *S*-member does not, of course, entail that there is a possible world in which all the other *S*-members exist and it does not.

3 Notice that although on this interpretation *S*-members are properties, they are still *contingent* entities and so satisfy clause (2). For, given any *x*, the property of being identical with *x* only exists in virtue of the existence of *x*.

4 I shall explore the second strategy in chapter 11, after any physical realism based on the primitiveness of space has been refuted.

5 Incidentally, this strategy does not conflict with the claim (whether or not the claim is true) that we can only identify and re-identify the points of space by selecting some material object as a frame of reference. Nor, of course, does it exclude the possibility that different and non-equivalent frames of reference are equally serviceable for the purposes of scientific theory.

6 Strictly speaking, of course, since the series is *continuous*, a region-moment does not have a successor.

7 Re-expressed in spatial terms, *L* ensures that (a), at any time, the total distribution of *M* over *S*-members exhaustively divides into non-overlapping spherical regions of radius *n*, and (b) any change over time in the momentary distribution of *M* is spatially continuous.

8 Compare the case of T_1 and T_2 discussed in the previous chapter, pp. 65-6.

6 THE CONFINEMENT OF QUALIA

1 Chapter 4, p. 58.

2 Hume, *A Treatise of Human Nature* Book I, part I, section I, in the edition of L. A. Selby-Bigge, Clarendon Press, Oxford, 1896 and *An Enquiry Concerning Human Understanding*, section II, in the third edition of L. A. Selby-Bigge, Oxford, 1975.

3 I say 'without the *capacity* to combine with colour' because any non-sensory realization of visual extension would have to be *essentially* non-sensory.

7 MENTALISTIC REALISM

1 Hume, *A Treatise of Human Nature,* in the edition of L. A. Selby-Bigge, Clarendon Press, Oxford, 1896, p. 27.

297

2 However, there is one phenomenon which I find it hard to explain without abandoning the assumption that visual space is continuous. The phenomenon in question is that of the apparent increase in the indeterminacy of spatial arrangement as one moves from the centre of the visual field to its periphery. On my view, the appearance of indeterminacy must be illusory, since (1) the sensing of a colour-pattern equals its ultimate realization and (2) ultimate reality must be determinate. At the moment, I can see no way of accounting for the phenomenon except by supposing that what we are tempted to construe as an increase in indeterminacy is really an increase in the crudity of the spatial grain. And this supposition would involve abandoning the assumption of continuity. I have yet to reach some definite conclusion on this matter.

8 NOMOLOGICAL DEVIANCE

1 See chapter 4, pp. 60-2.
2 With respect to the psychophysical laws, the crucial case is that in which someone is just entering one of the two regions, with part of his brain in Oxford and part in Westminster.

9 A DEFENCE OF THE NOMOLOGICAL THESIS

1 Thus see chapter 7.
2 'Characterized' has here, of course, its ordinary sense. It has no connection with the homonymous predicate introduced in the previous chapter in the specification of Σ.

10 SPATIAL ANTI-REALISM

1 There is an interesting (if only partial) analogy here with the different ways in which we might construe the properties signified by such dispositional terms as 'brittle' and 'inflammable'. Thus should we equate the brittleness of glass with its law-governed disposition to break, when struck, so that, in a possible world, something with all the intrinsic properties of glass may fail to be brittle, because, governed by different laws, it lacks the relevant disposition? Or should we, rather, equate the brittleness of glass with that intrinsic property on which, in the actual world, this disposition is nomologically grounded, and, in consequence, hold that, in a possible world, something which lacks the disposition still qualifies as brittle if it has that property? Adopting the first alternative is rather like asserting the A-thesis with respect to physical geometrical properties. Adopting the second is rather like asserting the B-thesis.
2 Specified in chapter 7.
3 p. 74.

11   FULL ANTI-REALISM

1   In this version, we postulate an uncountable set D of 2-place relations, each relation being symmetric, irreflexive and non-transitive, a 1-1 function f'' from D to the set of all real numbers greater than 0, a set $\alpha *$ of physical laws and a set $\beta *$ of psychophysical laws, such that, for some number n greater than 0 (a number representing the atomic radius):

(a)   Ultimate reality is composed of time, human minds, atoms, the obtaining of D-relations between atoms at times, and $\alpha *$ and $\beta *$.

(b) $\alpha *$ ensures that, for any atoms x and y and any time t, there is one and only one D-relation between x and y at t.

(c)   If we say that d is the D-*distance between* atoms x and y at time t iff, for some R, R is the unique D-relation between x and y at t and $f''(R) = d$, then

(1) $\alpha *$ ensures that, at any time, the D-distance between any two atoms is no less than 2n.

(2) $\alpha *$ ensures that, for any time t, there is a 1-1 function g from atoms to certain S-points (indeed, infinitely many such functions) such that, for any two atoms x and y, the D-distance between x and y at t = the distance between $g(x)$ and $g(y)$ in S (as computed by the Euclidean metric).

(3) $\alpha *$ ensures that any change in the D-distance between two atoms is numerically continuous. Indeed, more strongly.

(4) $\alpha *$ imposes exactly the same constraints on changes of D-relations as α imposes on changes of physical distance.

(5) $\beta *$ assigns the same experiential effects to D-distance configurations as β assigns to the corresponding configurations of physical distance.

(d)   Physical space is the logical creation of this quasi-spatial organization of the atoms.

We could call this version of matter-selective realism the *relations-version* (RV). The crucial difference between SV and RV is that SV yields a physical space with *absolute* positions, while RV yields one with only *relative* positions. Given any atom x and two times t_1 and t_2, where t_1 is earlier than t_2, it makes sense in SV to ask, independently of a frame of reference, whether x is stationary or moving between t_1 and t_2, and, if moving, what distance it covers and, at each moment, with what velocity. These questions are significant and have objective answers because, according to SV, the physical position of an atom at a time is determined by its intrinsic state at that time, independently of its relations to other atoms, and the relative positions of the atoms are determined by these absolute, intrinsic positions. But these questions are not significant in RV. For according to RV, the physical

299

position of an atom at a time is simply its position in the pattern of distance-relations, so that it is only within a chosen frame of reference that it makes sense to ask whether, between t_1 and t_2, x is stationary or moving. Of course, this distinction between the absolutism of SV and the relativism of RV is metaphysical rather than scientific. The absolute character of the SV-space does not preclude there being alternative and non-equivalent frames of reference which are equally serviceable for science. Nor does the relativistic character of the RV-space preclude the possibility of some frames of reference being more serviceable than others.

2 Chapter 5, pp. 83-4.
3 We could underline this point by supposing (altering our original assumptions) that there are two physical types of atom (e.g. the large, heavy and the small, light) and that, underlying these types, there are two non-auditory sensory states (N-states) such that the physical type of an atom depends on the N-state of the K-mind with which it is associated. Then whenever two minds in different N-states exchange their A^*-positions (and, with them, their velocities and directions), they would also (in exchanging all their physically relevant properties) exchange their N-states and thus exchange the atom-types with which they are associated. In such a case, the spatiotemporal continuity of the atom-types would serve to reinforce the point that the exchanges leave the paths of the atoms unaffected.

12 THE REJECTION OF THE ISOMORPHISM-REQUIREMENT

1 In chapter 1, pp. 12-14.
2 pp. 15-16.
3 Arguably, it would have been more plausible to take the experiential effects as immediately subsequent to, rather than simultaneous with, their causes. (Indeed, it may be incoherent to suppose a cause and its effect to be simultaneous.) I have taken them as simultaneous simply to make the example easier to state and easier for the reader to follow.
4 I say *'almost* in full' because, as I mentioned earlier, I shall slightly modify the phenomenalist's account at the end of the next chapter.

13 THE PRINCIPLES OF CREATION

1 Such theorizing is, of course, a cumulative process, in which new pieces of experiential evidence are evaluated in the framework of an already (supposedly) established theory. Indeed, at any time, we do not possess much information about the previous course of human experience independently of the current explanatory theory which such experience has led us to adopt. This point will be given more prominence in the next chapter.
2 In the case of E_5 this characterization was not made explicit. But,

obviously, it is that in which we treat pairs of corresponding places in the two fields as points of a single space, a point being Q_1-characterized (Q_2-characterized) at a time t iff both its elements are Q_1-characterized (Q_2-characterized) at t.

3 Here, we must remember our assumption that α' is deterministic, so that, although R-T is wholly Q_2-pervaded in E_6 the R-T distribution of Q_1-association in E_6 matches the R-T distribution of Q_1 in E.

14 THE CHALLENGE OF NIHILISM

1 Chapter 7, p. 119-20.
2 Chapter 1, p. 5.
3 See chapter 1, p. 5.
4 For a fuller defence of this claim, see H. Putnam, 'The meaning of "meaning"' in K. Gunderson (ed.), *Language, Mind and Knowledge,* Minnesota Studies in the Philosophy of Science, VII, University of Minnesota Press, 1975, and republished as chapter 12 of H. Putnam, *Mind, Language and Reality,* Cambridge University Press, 1975.
5 Chapter 12, p. 192.
6 Hume, *A Treatise of Human Nature,* in the edition of L. A. Selby-Bigge, Clarendon Press, Oxford, 1896, p. 187.
7 This is the position of J. L. Mackie. Thus see his *Ethics: Inventing Right and Wrong,* Penguin, Harmondsworth, 1977, chapter 1.
8 See chapter 7.

15 THE TWO FRAMEWORKS

1 The use of 'E' to signify a certain type of set of link-laws must not be confused with its use, in chapters 12 and 13, to signify a certain external reality.
2 I am also, of course, using '∃' as an existential quantifier (= 'For some ...') and '∼' as a negation-operator (= 'It is not the case that ...').

16 THE CONSTRUCTION OF INTER-SUBJECTIVE TIME

1 More precisely, a sensation is *complete* iff there could be a qualitatively identical sensation which is not part of any larger sensation.
2 When I speak here of a *colour-pervaded region,* I do not insist that the pervasion be homogeneous. I allow for the possibility that the pervasion varies continuously, in shade, from point to point (varying in hue along one spatial axis and in brightness along the other). Likewise, in speaking of a sound-filled period, I allow for the possibility of a continuous variation in pitch or loudness from moment to moment.
3 The Σ_1-sensations omitted from Σ_2 would realize more complex

time-patterns. E.g. between S_2 and S_3 there is $S_{2.5}$ with the pattern: $\frac{1}{2}\phi$-unit of silence before 1 ϕ-unit of C_1 before 1 ϕ-unit of silence before $\frac{1}{2}\phi$-unit of D. If Σ_1 is continuous in mental time, there are infinitely many such sensations between successive Σ_2-sensations.

4 The point of the additional requirements in (3) and (4) ('is the realization of it *qua* ...') is to ensure that the relation of O-precedence is asymmetric and can form the basis of temporal order in the stream. After all, there may be a case in which, apart from these additional requirements, all the specified conditions are satisfied, but in which the temporal pattern realized by *z* is, being twice realized in *x*, both the last *and the first* portion of the *x*-pattern and also, being twice realized in *y*, both the first *and the last* portion of the *y*-pattern. Without the additional requirements, we would have to say, in such a case, not only that *x* O-precedes *y*, but also that *y* O-precedes *x*.

5 Of course, the concept of *series* here is purely formal, not temporal. There is no circularity.

6 However, I have discussed it elsewhere, namely in 'In *Self*-Defence' in G.F.Macdonald (ed.), *Perception and Identity,* Macmillan, London, 1979.

7 Since the ultimate laws of IS-causation will not be directly concerned with IS-time (IS-time being what we have to construct partly out of IS-causation), I might have said, more precisely: 'If α is the uncountable set of relations underlying IS-temporal distances (so that, for each temporal distance *d*, there is an α-relation *R* such that, for any subjective moments *x* and *y*, if *x* and *y* are *d*-related, they are so in virtue of the conjunction of (i) their *R*-relatedness and (ii) the ultimate laws of nature), there may be an IS-temporal distance *d* such that, if β is that subset of α whose members underlie temporal distances less than *d*, then (i) the ultimate laws ensure that, for any $x[m]$ and $y[m']$, if $m \neq m'$ and *x* and *y* stand in a β-relation, then there is no causal line from a volition at *x* to a sensation at *y*, and (ii) *a* and *b* stand in a β-relation.

8 Remember that subjective time-dimensions are infinitely extended in both directions.

9 That we can envisage an ultimate reality which yields relationships of RPV-priority is shown in the next chapter.

17 THE UNDERLYING REALITY

1 In chapter 14.

2 In G.F.Macdonald (ed.), *Perception and Identity,* Macmillan, London, 1979, pp.168-70. The example that follows is also taken from there.

3 Following the normal practice, I am using 'V' as a universal quantifier to mean 'For every ...' and '⊃' as a binary sentential operator to mean (construed as a material conditional) 'If ... , then ...'.

4 This ties in with what was said in the previous chapter, p.269.

5 General, that is, apart from their references to M and H. If it was thought desirable, even these references could be eliminated. Thus we could suppose that there are two mind-kinds K_1 and K_2, such that (1) there is a mind of kind K_1, (2) it is either logically or nomologically impossible for there to be more than one K_1-mind, and (3) all and only H-minds are of kind K_2. We could then reformulate the example in such a way that what are nomologically relevant are not the identities of M and H, but the general properties of being a stream in a K_1-mind and of being a K_2-mind.

INDEX

305

mind-independence, of physical world, *see* non-mental-requirement; with respect to human minds, *see* externality

natural necessity, 4-5, 15, 192, 240; *see also* laws of nature

nihilism, 12-14, 20-1, 24, 33, 35, 39-40, 42-3, 45-6, 191-2, 226-7, 233-9

NMR, *see* non-mental-requirement

nomological deviance: definition of, in respect of geometry, 130, 137-8; dimensional, 155-60, 167-8, 173-4; qualitative, 202-4, 217-23; reciprocal topological (RT), 131-43, 149, 153-5, 157-60, 167, 171, 201-2, 211, 215, 291-2; *see also* nomological thesis; nomological uniformity

nomological irrelevance, 204-7, 209, 211-12, 215-16; *see also* nomological relevance

nomological organization, *see* laws of nature

nomological relevance 133-8, 143, 204-7; principle of, 209-13, 222

nomological thesis, 143-60; realist and anti-realist versions of, 160-77

nomological uniformity: and geometry, 130-75; and reductive phenomenalism, 195-23; principle of, 209-13, 222; *see also* nomological deviance; nomological thesis

non-mental-requirement (NMR), 117-22, 152, 238

occasionalism, 292-3

occupancy, of physical space, 56-7, 59-62, 72, 73-4, 77-87, 109-10, 161, 176-88; by human subjects, 70-1, 118

ontological realism/anti-realism, as distinct from factual, 33-7

ontological status: together with factual status, 5-14, 37-40, 43-6; of matter, 81-6, 94, 110, 161, 176-88; of physical space, 81-4, 157-75

ontologically primitive, definition of, 7; versus ontologically derivative, *see*

ontological status

opaque specification: distinguished from transparent specification, 62; of intrinsic nature of matter, 62-7, 89; of intrinsic nature of physical space, 78; *see also* transparent specification

overlapping, of sensations, 257-61

particles, physical, 64-72, 82-6, 177-88, 193-4

perception, 18-32 *passim*, 44-6, 91, 117-18; *see also* sensations

phenomenal time, 254-9; *see also* mental time

phenomenalism, *see* analytical phenomenalism; reductive phenomenalism

physical anti-realism, 7-9; argument for, 127-88; in Berkeley's philosophy, 26-7; compared with mentalism, 8-11; and Dummett, 40-3; in respect of matter, 176-88; ontological versus factual 33-7; options left open by, 12-14, 191-2, 226; in respect of physical space, 162-75; and selective physical realism, 43-6; sense in which anti-realist, 37-40; *see also* nihilism; reductivism

physical geometry, *see* geometry

physical realism, 14; matter-selective, 82-4, 176-88; mentalistic, *q.v.*; ontological versus factual, 33-7; refutation of, 127-88; selective, 43-8, 81-2; space-selective, 82-6, 94, 110; standard, 11-15, 20, 122-3; supposed commitment of our physical beliefs to, 236-8

physical space, 56-9, 73-88, 127-88, 191-225 *passim*, 247-8; *see also under* geometry; logical creation; occupancy; ontological status; physical anti-realism

physical time, 253-4, 288-92, *see also* mental time

physicalism, 12, 52

physicalistic (mental) realism, 52-5

possible worlds, 4-5, 164-75, 181, 185-7,

International Library of Philosophy

Editor: Ted Honderich

(Demy 8vo)

Allen, R.E. (Ed.), **Studies in Plato's Metaphysics** *464 pp. 1965.*
Plato's 'Euthyphro' and the Earlier Theory of Forms *184 pp. 1970.*
Allen, R.E. and Furley, David J.(Eds.), **Studies in Presocratic Philosophy**
Vol.1: The Beginnings of Philosophy *326 pp. 1970.*
Vol. 11: Eleatics and Pluralists *448 pp. 1975.*
Armstrong, D.M., **Perception and the Physical World** *208 pp. 1961.*
A Materialist Theory of the Mind *376 pp. 1967.*
Bambrough, Renford (Ed.), **New Essays on Plato and Aristotle**
184 pp. 1965.
Barry, Brian, **Political Argument** *382 pp. 1965.*
Becker, Lawrence C., ⸂**On Justifying Moral Judgments⸃** *212 pp. 1973.*
†Blum, Lawrence, **Friendship, Altruism and Morality** *256 pp. 1980.*
Bogen, James, **Wittgenstein's Philosophy of Language** *256 pp. 1972.*
Brentano, Franz, **The Foundation and Construction of Ethics** *398 pp. 1973*
The Origin of our Knowledge of Right and Wrong *184 pp. 1969.*
Psychology from an Empirical Standpoint *436 pp. 1973.*
Sensory and Noetic Consciousness *168 pp. 1981.*
Broad, C.D., **Lectures on Psychical Research** *462 pp. 1962.*
Crombie, I.M., **An Examination of Plato's Doctrine**
*Vol.1:*Plato on Man and Society *408 pp. 1962.*
Vol. 11: Plato on Knowledge and Reality *584 pp. 1963.*
Dennett, D.C., **Content and Conciousness** *202 pp. 1969.*
Dretske, Fred I., **Seeing and Knowing** *270 pp. 1969.*
Ducasse, C.J., **Truth, Knowledge and Causation** *264 pp. 1969.*
Fann. K.T. (Ed.), **Symposium on J.L. Austin** *512 pp. 1969.*
Findlay, J.N., **Plato: The Written and Unwritten Doctrines** *498 pp. 1974.*
Flew, Anthony, **Hume's Philosophy of Belief** *296 pp. 1961.*
Glover, Jonathan, **Responsibility** *212 pp. 1970.*
Goldman, Lucien, **The Hidden God** *424 pp. 1964.*
Hamlyn, D.W., **Sensation and Perception** *222 pp. 1961.*
†*Hornsby, Jennifer, **Actions** *152 pp. 1980.*
Husserl, Edmund, **Logical Investigations** *Vol.1: 456 pp. Vol.11: 464 pp.1970.*
Körner, Stephan, **Experience and Theory** *272 pp. 1966.*
*Linsky, Leonard, **Referring** *152 pp. 1967.*
Mackenzie, Brian D., **Behaviourism and the Limits of Scientific Method**
208 pp. 1977.
†*Mackie, J.L., **Hume's Moral Theory** *176 pp. 1980.*
Merleau-Ponty, M., **Phenomenology of Perception** *488 pp. 1962.*
Naess, Arne, **Scepticism**, *176 pp. 1969.*
† Nelson, William, **On Justifying Democracy** *192 pp. 1980.*
† Newton-Smith, W.H., **The Structure of Time** *276 pp. 1980.*
Perelman, Chaim, **The Idea of Justice and the Problem of Argument**
224 pp. 1963.
†*Putnam, Hilary, **Meaning and the Moral Sciences** *156 pp.1978.(Paperback
1980).*
Sayre, Kenneth M., **Cybernetics and the Philosophy of Mind** *280 pp. 1976.*